# Inspired *to* Write

Readings and tasks to develop writing skills

JEAN WITHROW
GAY BROOKES
MARTHA CLARK CUMMINGS

CAMBRIDGE
UNIVERSITY PRESS

# CAMBRIDGE
### UNIVERSITY PRESS

32 Avenue of the Americas, New York, NY 10013–2473, USA

Cambridge University Press is part of the University of Cambridge.

It furthers the University's mission by disseminating knowledge in the pursuit of education, learning and research at the highest international levels of excellence.

www.cambridge.org
Information on this title: www.cambridge.org/9780521537117

First published 2004
10th printing 2013

Printed in the United States of America

A catalog record for this publication is available from the British Library.

ISBN 978-0-521-53711-7 paperback

*Art direction, book design, and layout services:* Adventure House, NYC

# Table *of* Contents

# UNIT 3 A CHANGING WORLD . . . . . . . . . . . . . . . . . . . . . . . **151**

# TO THE INSTRUCTOR

## The approach

The goal of **Inspired *to* Write** is to expose students to well-written, provocative texts that encourage them to think and inspire them to write. **Inspired *to* Write** adopts a collaborative and student-based approach, and gives students tools to develop their reading and writing skills. The book is intended for adults and young adults. It may be used by ESL students at the post intermediate level, by high school students preparing to write at college level, or by anyone who wants to develop from a basic writer and become a more accomplished writer.

## The content

**Inspired *to* Write** offers a choice of forty-five readings with related activities. The readings vary in genre, voice, moods, and cultural origin, and therefore appeal to a wide range of interests. Texts include stories, poems, essays, letters, folktales, articles, and excerpts from non-fiction books and textbooks. The authors of the pieces, too, represent a variety of backgrounds. All readings are original, not adapted, though some have been shortened. Readings vary in length and level of difficulty.

All the readings in the book relate in some way to the question of how individuals react to the challenges of change in their personal lives and change in the world around them. The readings have been grouped into three units: Becoming, New Vistas and Ventures, and A Changing World. And the units themselves have been further divided into four thematically related subsections, each containing three to five readings.

## Level and progression

**Inspired *to* Write** can be used with learners in all kinds of settings, although it may be especially beneficial to students in academic settings. The kind of writing students produce varies from personal and private to public and expository, depending on what they read and what they choose to write about. In general, readings and writing topics tend to be more personal at the beginning of the book and more expository toward the end of the book.

The activities in **Inspired *to* Write** build upon one another. Often references are made to previous readings or activities to encourage students to make connections between ideas or to use strategies already introduced. However, since doing one reading with all its related activities may take from two to four hours, you may wish to pick and choose readings and activities, shaping your choices to suit your students' needs. You should also feel free to change the order of the readings and activities as you see fit.

## Writing and reading skills

In **Inspired** *to* **Write**, reading is a prelude to writing. We believe that when students interact with texts, it leads not only to improved reading comprehension, language, and thinking skills, but also to better writing skills.

Activities take students through major aspects of the writing process: gathering ideas, drafting, sharing and getting feedback, and revising. Students are exposed to a variety of viewpoints when they see what others have written about a topic; they explore how they think and feel about the topic by responding in several ways; they share their explorations with others; they exchange feedback about their written texts; and they revise their writing when appropriate.

## The activities

Each reading is accompanied by five types of activities: *Before Reading, After Reading, How It's Written, Topics for Writing,* and *After Writing.* The *Before Reading* and *After Reading* activities support students' understanding of a written text and provide a basis for the early stages of the writing process: gathering ideas and getting started. The *How It's Written* section helps students look at written text as writers, focusing on the form rather than the content. In *Topics for Writing,* students choose one of three topics related to the reading. Finally, the *After Writing* activities help students get feedback on their writing. The *Revision* activities that follow each section of a unit help students focus on an aspect of revising a piece. More details about each section follow.

### Before Reading

Pre-reading activities help students bring what they know about a topic to the surface of their minds and prepare for the text that follows. Activities vary from associating words and ideas about the topic to asking questions or making guesses about the content of the reading selection.

### After Reading

By responding to what is read, readers come to understand what the text says, how they feel about it, and how they interpret it. Responding to the texts helps create meaning and deepens understanding.

The types of *After Reading* responses vary: freewrite, answer questions, write a "double entry" response, annotate the text, retell the story or restate parts of the text, find the main point, acquire new vocabulary, and so on. All of the activities are designed to help students increase understanding and make personal connections.

### How It's Written

Many professional writers say they learned to write by noticing what good writers do. *How It's Written* activities call students' attention to a specific writing technique a writer used, for example, details appealing to the senses, or an example supporting an idea, or the use of active verbs. The activities are designed to encourage students to read as writers.

### Topics for Writing

A major goal of this book is to help students develop as writers. Writing topics are derived from the reading selection and the prior activities. In each case, students choose from a list of three topics, with the types of writing called for varying from personal essay to expository writing based on research. Students and teachers should, of course, feel free to develop their own topics or use a different focus if they wish.

### After Writing

Students now have an opportunity to read and respond to one another's writing. Readers' comments or feedback may lead writers to see things in a new way and may give them ideas for how to revise their writing, should they choose to do so. Several different feedback techniques are suggested. Feedback is sometimes given orally, sometimes in writing.

### Revision

After working through thematically-related groups of three to five readings in a subsection of a unit, and writing on topics related to those readings, students then choose one piece of writing they wish to revise. If students were to work through all sections of all three units, they would end up with twelve revised pieces.

Each revision section focuses on a different revising strategy. Strategies include working on titles, trying different beginnings or endings, finding ways to keep readers interested, adding information, clarifying language, and so on. By the last revision section, students will have acquired a repertoire of revision techniques.

## Toolboxes and Writer's Tips

*Toolboxes* contain writing techniques, like freewriting or using your senses. Based on techniques used by experienced writers, these strategies provide students with instruction in important how-to's of writing. Once students have gone through the book and learned all the strategies that appear in the toolboxes, they should have the tools needed to become accomplished, independent writers.

The first time a particular technique is introduced, it appears in a toolbox. When the same technique occurs later in the book, students are referred back to the toolbox in case they need to be reminded of how it works. An index of all the toolboxes appears at the end of the book on page 217 for easy reference.

*Writer's Tips* are quotes from writers that give advice about writing in general or about a particular writing strategy. Such quotes help students feel connected to professional writers and teachers. *Writer's Tips* appear on the side of a page and often supplement information in toolboxes.

### Reading/Writing logs

Students will, in a sense, be writing their own "book" while reading **Inspired** *to* **Write** by responding in a journal or log to what they read. The purpose of the log is to give students an opportunity to interact with texts and to develop their thinking. Their logs become a resource for ideas for compositions.

### Student collaboration

Small groups can be a powerful learning resource. Talking with others gives students chances to consider the perspectives of other people, and the conversations they have in class continue in their minds when they are writing alone. When peers read and respond to each other's writing, students can further develop and clarify their written pieces. Finally, working in groups gives all students more talk-time than they would have if just giving occasional answers to questions posed by an instructor.

### The instructor's role

In this student-centered text, the role of the instructor is often implied. Some of your tasks will include the following: setting up groups or pairs; answering questions about activities, readings, and instructions for writing; and structuring and facilitating class discussion, to help make sense out of sometimes conflicting interpretations.

One thing to remember is that we think there are many acceptable ways to respond to or interpret a reading and many ways to write in response to them. We see your role as facilitator and coach. To this end, you may prod and encourage, suggest and question. But primarily we hope you will provide a student-centered classroom where students feel free to express themselves honestly, ask questions, make tentative propositions, and respond openly to what they read and to each other.

## TO THE STUDENT

In **Inspired *to* Write** you will do a lot of reading, and you will write a lot about what you have read. We ask you to do a lot of writing because writing is a skill that needs practice, just like swimming or playing the guitar. The more you practice, the better you become.

**Inspired *to* Write** is a book designed to help you make connections between your ideas and the ideas of other writers. You will be asked to read, to pay attention to what you feel and think as you are reading, and to write about your thoughts and feelings. Your responses and your classmates' responses to the readings will become the basis of your own writing.

As you read this book, you will be writing your own "book," your reading/writing log. You will find an explanation of the log in the toolbox below.

### Reading/Writing Log

Professional writers spend a great deal of time reading, thinking, and writing down their ideas before they start writing a story, an essay, or a poem. Student writers can benefit from this practice as well by using a Reading/Writing log.

Your *log* can be a spiral notebook or a section of a loose-leaf notebook. In it, you will use a variety of responding techniques to record your thoughts and reactions to what you read. Keep everything you write so that when you look back at your log, you will find many ideas for writing.

As you read the various instructions in this book, you will often find a box such as the one above. We call this kind of box a "toolbox" because it contains a tool or technique that can be useful to reading or writing. This kind of box always has the symbol of a toolbox next to it.

You will find another kind of box in **Inspired *to* Write** – a *Writer's Tip* box, which contains hints or suggestions from well-known authors and writing teachers. Their experiences are helpful to people who wish to improve their writing and want ideas about how to do it.

One set of activities – *Before Reading*, *After Reading*, and *Topics for Writing* – asks you to write as a way of making connections. *Before Reading* activities help you bring to mind what you already know about a topic. Once you have read the story or essay or poem, the *After Reading* activities invite you to respond to what you've read – to consider the text and to explore your feelings, thoughts, and interpretations. The activities in *Topics for*

### Writer's Tip

*Think about your notebook. It is important. This is your equipment, like hammer and nails to a carpenter... Give yourself a lot of space in which to explore writing. A cheap spiral notebook lets you feel that you can fill it quickly and afford another. Also, it is easy to carry.*

**Natalie Goldberg**

*Writing* offer you a choice of topics on which to write a piece of your own. A final activity, *After Writing*, gives you a chance to share your ideas with a group and get feedback on your writing.

The *How It's Written* section contains a different kind of activity. Since one way to learn how to write is to study how other writers do it, these activities direct you to look carefully at the author's writing techniques or style. Here you will be encouraged to look at *how* a piece is written rather than *what* the piece says. By "reading as a writer," you will learn ways to improve your own writing.

Many activities in this book suggest that you work with a group or a partner. You can learn a great deal by working with others. As you share ideas, compare reactions, solve problems, and look at each other's writing, you will have the opportunity to talk; and good talk leads to good thinking. Furthermore, as you collaborate, your own thinking changes, and you become enriched.

We hope that **Inspired *to* Write** will make you a better reader, a better thinker and a better writer. We hope that you find the readings, the activities, and the topics to be challenging and of interest. And finally, we hope that when your instructor gives you a writing assignment, you won't just feel that you are required to write, but you will in fact be inspired to write.

## AUTHORS' ACKNOWLEDGEMENTS

**Inspired *to* Write** is a product of collaboration. We would like to thank those who have collaborated with us, knowingly or unknowingly. First, our teachers whose ideas shine through *Inspired to Write* and instruct us how to teach writing. Second, the many authors whose works and words of advice appear in the book and who implicitly teach how to write. Third, our colleagues who share their thoughts and experiences with us. And, fourth, our students who teach us how to teach. We thank our reviewers: Ellen Clarkson, American Language Institute, New York University; Matthew Holsten, San Francisco State University; Catherine Salin, Columbus Torah Academy; and Beth Udoma, University of Connecticut at Stamford. We thank the Cambridge University Press editors and staff for their assistance and support, especially Mary Sandre for her help with the permissions process and our project editor, Anne Garrett. And finally, we are ever thankful to our editor, Bernard Seal, for his keen eye and guiding hand in helping bring this project to completion. We are grateful to all of you.

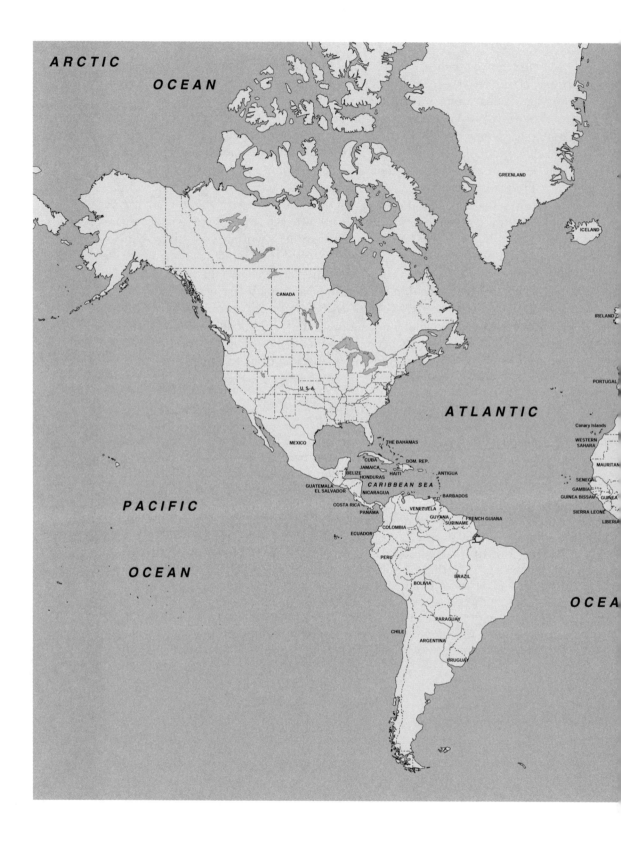

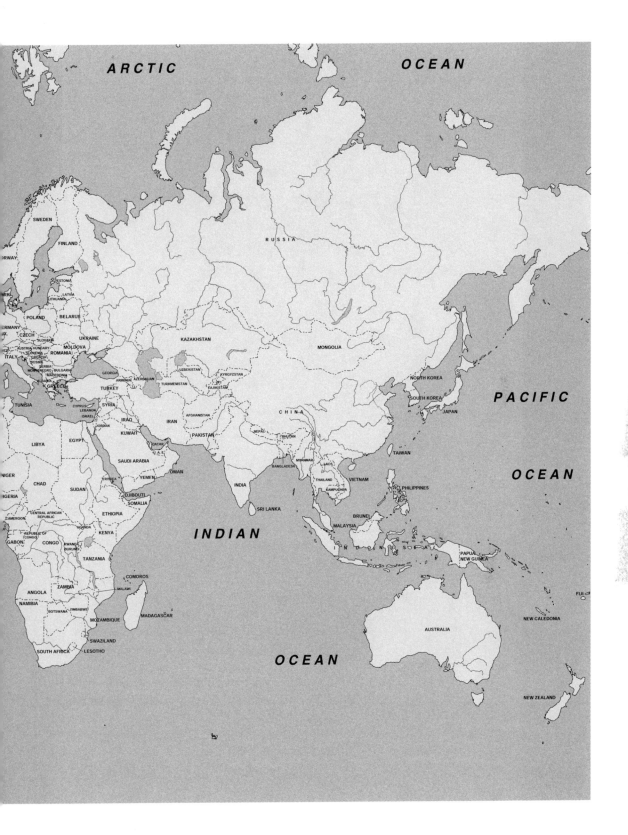

# UNIT 1

# Becoming

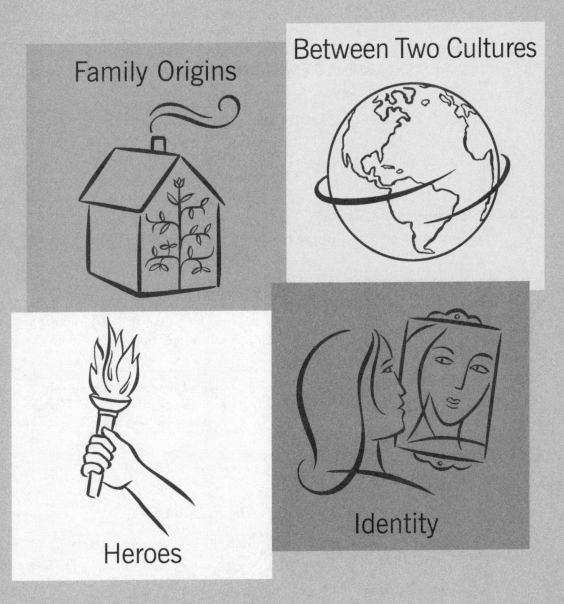

Family Origins

Between Two Cultures

Heroes

Identity

UNIT 1

# Becoming

*All of your history is written on the walls inside you – your parents, family, upbringing, and education, the homes you lived in, the places you visited, every book you ever read, every song you ever sang, every person you ever loved and who loved you. They are all present inside you. So is every person you ever disliked or ignored, and who hated you. Each of them is also present within you.*

Joan Sauro

## A Make connections

1 Read about a technique that can be used to gather ideas about a topic before reading or writing.

### *Freewriting*

Freewriting involves writing without stopping for a short period of time, usually five to ten minutes. Although it is called freewriting, it has some very strict rules.

■ Don't stop writing until the time is up. That's the most important rule. If you can't think of anything to say, write, "I have nothing to say. I have nothing to say. I have nothing to say. . . . " until you have something to say again.

■ Don't go back as you write. Don't cross out or erase anything. Just keep writing.

■ Don't worry about grammar, spelling, or punctuation.

■ If you can't think of a word in English, write it in your native language. Then continue in English.

■ Don't worry if your ideas seem out of order or unrelated.

2 Read the title of the unit and the quote by Joan Sauro. Freewrite for ten minutes in your log about any connections you see between the unit title and the quote.

3 Share your freewriting with a partner. Talk about the similarities and differences in what you each wrote.

## B Make a map of your life

1 On a blank sheet of paper, draw a map of your life. Represent the significant times in your life, such as the turning points, the high and the low points. Start at your birth and move to the present. Draw pictures or use graphic representations. Add words and color if you wish.

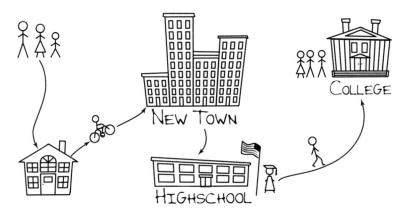

2 Show your map to a group of classmates. Tell them about one or two points on the map. Answer their questions.

3 Choose one point on your map and freewrite about it for five minutes.

4 Read about kernel sentences and then write a kernel sentence for your freewriting.

### Kernel Sentences

After freewriting, write one sentence that summarizes the most important thing you said in your writing. This important idea is called the **kernel** – the nucleus or core of what you are saying.

## C Preview Unit 1

1 Read the section headings for the readings in this unit. Look for connections between the title of this unit, the section headings, and your freewriting.

2 Discuss the connections with your group.

## Family Origins

# BEFORE READING

## Think about the title

1 Read the title of the reading. Think about these questions: Do you have a brother or sister? If not, did you have a close childhood friend? What memories do you have of conflicts between you and a brother or sister, or between you and a childhood friend? Choose one incident or event that reveals something about your relationship with the other child.

2 Tell the story of this incident to a partner.

 # Brothers
### Bret Lott

*Bret Lott writes novels, short stories, memoirs, and essays. He teaches creative writing at the College of Charleston, where he lives with his wife and two sons. This excerpt comes from his memoir* Fathers, Sons, and Brothers: The Men in My Family.

This much is fact: There is a home movie of the two of us sitting on the edge of the swimming pool at our grandma and grandpa's old apartment building in Culver City. The movie, taken sometime in early 1960, is in color, though the color had faded, leaving my brother Brad and me white and harmless children, me a year and a half old, Brad almost four. . . . Our mother, impossibly young, sits next to me on the right of the screen. . . . Next to me on the left of the screen is Brad, in his white swimming trunks. I am in the center, my fat arms up, . . . fingers curled into fists, my legs kicking away at the water, splashing and splashing. I am smiling, the baby of the family, the center of the world at that very instant. . . . The pool water before us is only a thin sky blue, the bushes behind us a dull and lifeless light green. There is no sound.

My mother speaks to me, points at the water, then looks up. She lifts a hand to block the sun, says something to the camera. . . . I am still kicking. Brad is looking to his right, . . . his feet in the water, too, but moving slowly. His hands are on the edge of the pool, and he leans forward a little, looks down into the water. My mother still speaks to the camera, and I give an extra-hard kick, splash up shards of white water.

Brad flinches at the water, squints his eyes, while my mother laughs, puts a hand to her face. She looks back to the camera, keeps talking, a hand low to the water to keep more from hitting her. I still kick hard . . . and I am laughing a baby's laugh, mouth open . . . arms still up, fingers still curled into fists.

More water splashes at Brad, who leans over to me, says something. Nothing about me changes: I only kick, laugh. He says something again, his face leans a little closer to mine. Still I kick.

This is when he lifts his left hand from the edge of the pool, places it on my right thigh, and pinches hard. It's not a simple pinch, not two fingers on a fraction of skin, but his whole hand, all his fingers grabbing the flesh just above my knee and squeezing down hard. He grimaces, his eyes on his hand, on my leg.

My expression changes, of course: In an instant I go from a laughing baby to a shocked one, my mouth a perfect O, my body shivering so that my legs kick even harder. . . . They stop, and I cry, my mouth open even more. . . . My hands are still in fists.

Then Brad's hand is away, and my mother turns from speaking to the camera to me. She leans in close, asking, I am certain, what's wrong. The movie cuts then to my grandma, white skin and silver hair, seated on a patio chair by the pool, above her a green-and-white-striped umbrella. She has a cigarette in one hand, waves off the camera with the other . . . annoyed, at my grandpa and his camera, the moment my brother pinched hell out of me already gone.

## AFTER READING

### A  Retell the story

1  Reread the story and underline or mark the main actions of the mother and the two boys.

2  Using what you marked to guide you, retell the story to a partner.

3  Freewrite about what happened in the story and how you felt about it.

4  Share your freewriting with your group.

### B  Make a picture quiz

1  Draw a simple picture of the situation Lott describes. Include the mother and the two boys and the setting (the pool, etc.).

2  Below the picture, list at least three words or phrases from the text that describe some of the facial expressions and actions of the characters in your picture.

3  Show the picture to your partner and ask your partner to indicate which words and phrases on your list go with which details in your picture.

## HOW IT'S WRITTEN

### Notice verbs

1 With a partner, choose a paragraph in the reading and underline all the verbs. Different pairs should take different paragraphs.

2 Report to the class the verb tense used in each paragraph. What effect does that tense have? Why did the author choose that tense?

3 Most of the verbs in the first paragraph could be called "static." Most of the verbs in the next three paragraphs are "active." With the class look at verbs in the first two paragraphs and put each one into a category, either "static" or "active."

4 Discuss the effect these two types of verbs have on the story.

## TOPICS FOR WRITING

### Choose one topic to write about

1 Find a photo of yourself as a young child with your family or some family members. Describe the photo, including how the people looked and their relationship to you and to each other. Include an interesting detail about each person.

2 Write a story of an incident or event that showed conflict between you and a sibling (either a brother or a sister) or a close childhood friend. Choose an incident or event that tells a lot about your childhood relationship with the other child.

3 Where are you in the birth order of children in your family – are you the oldest, the middle child or the youngest, or are you an only child? Write about yourself and your position in the family. Tell what effect, if any, you think your place in the birth order has had on your personality, behavior, and attitude toward your family.

## AFTER WRITING

### Share your writing

1 Read your writing aloud to your group. As a group, tell what you like about each piece.

2 Choose one person's writing to read to the class.

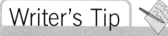

## Writer's Tip

*Where do we get our ideas for writing? . . . You get your ideas from assignments teachers give you, from books and movies and television, from things you observe on the street or at the beach or at home or at the mall. You use your memory too – experiences you've had as recently as this morning, as long ago as when you were a baby.*

**Meredith Sue Willis**

. . . . . . . . . . . . . . . . . . . . . . . . . . . . . . . . . . . . . . . . . . . . . . . . . . . . . . . . . . . . . . .

# BEFORE READING

### Make a list

1 Read about one way to gather ideas before reading or writing about a topic.

## Brainstorming a List

Making a list helps you collect ideas. Start by writing the name of the topic. Underneath it, list whatever words, phrases, or ideas come to you. Just let your mind flow. Don't be critical or reject any ideas.

You can also brainstorm a list with a small group or the whole class. Group brainstorming can generate a lot of ideas because listening to someone else's ideas can prompt a new idea of your own.

2 Think of some times in your childhood when you disobeyed an authority figure or when you were punished for something you did. Brainstorm a list of the incidents you recall.

3 Share your list with a partner.

# The Brown Hen
## Esmeralda Santiago

*This excerpt from* When I Was Puerto Rican *tells of one of the author's memories of her early childhood in Puerto Rico. Later, Esmeralda Santiago and her family moved to New York City.*

The day he was to put in the new floor, Papi dragged our belongings out to the yard. Mami's sewing machine, the bed, her rocking chair, the small dresser where Papi kept his special things, baked in the sun, their worn surfaces scarred, their joints loose and creaky. A stack of new floorboards was suspended between cinder blocks near the door. Mami asked me and Delsa to find small stones to plug the holes in the dirt inside the house, so that snakes and scorpions wouldn't get out and bite us.

"Let's go see if the hen laid more eggs!" Delsa whispered.

We sneaked around the house to the path behind the latrine. On the way we picked up a few pebbles, just in case Mami asked what we were doing. A brown hen sat on the nest, her wings fluffed around the eggs. As we came near, she clucked softly.

"We'd better not come too close, or she'll beak us," I whispered.

The hen watched us, cackling nervously, and when we walked around the bush, her beady eyes followed us.

"If we keep walking around her," Delsa said, "we'll make her dizzy."

We circled the bush. The hen turned her head all the way around, as if her neck were not attached to her body. Delsa looked at me with a wicked grin, and without a word, we looped around the bush again then switched and went in the opposite direction. Possessive of her eggs, the hen kept her eyes fixed on us, no matter how fast we moved. We broke into a run. Her scared twitterings rose in pitch and had a human quality, like Mami's words when she swore we were driving her crazy. The hen's reproachful eyes followed us as we ran around the bush, her body aflutter, her head whirling on her body until it seemed that she would screw herself into the ground.

"Negi! Delsa! What are you doing back there?" Mami stood in the clearing, hands on hips.

"We were looking at the hen," I said in a small voice. Delsa giggled. I giggled. Mami didn't. The hen buried her head into her feathers the way a turtle crawls into a shell. I wanted to slide under her wings and get away from Mami.

"Get back to the front yard and let that poor animal be."

"We just wanted to see the eggs."

"You've frightened her. Now she won't give us any more eggs."

We had to go by Mami to get to the front yard. Her eyebrows were scrunched together, the eyes under them as round and black and reproving as the hen's, her lips stretched across her face so tight that all I could see was a dark line under her nose. "What are you waiting for? Didn't you hear me?" Her voice quivered with fury, her whole body enlarging with each breath.

Delsa hid behind me. I shuffled forward, and Mami stepped back to let me by. Delsa whimpered. Mami stared at me, immobile, hands on hips. I was very small. I took a deep breath, closed my eyes, and walked past her. As I did, she knuckled me hard on the head. I ran home, rubbing the bump that was forming under my hair. Behind me, Delsa screeched and ran past, covering her ear.

Papi raked the dirt in the house. He looked up when we came to the door, holding our heads and crying.

"Don't come bawling to me," he said. "You both know better than to cross your mother." He turned his back and pushed more dirt against the zinc walls.

Delsa sat on a stump and sobbed. I stared at his back, willing him to scold Mami, even though we'd done something wrong. He heaped piles of dirt into the corners of the house and hummed a song under his breath. Mami stood at the mouth of the path, her fingers laced under her belly. She looked small against the thick green behind her. She too seemed to be waiting for Papi to do or say something, and when he didn't, she walked to the kitchen shed, rubbing her stomach, a pained expression on her face.

A bubble of rage built inside my chest and forced out a scream meant for Mami's harshness and Papi's indifference but directed at Delsa who was smaller. I pushed her off the stump, sending her small body sprawling on the dirt. For a moment she looked dazed, as she tried to figure out what she had done, but when she realized she'd done nothing, she fell on me, her tiny fists as sharp as stones. We tussled in the dusty yard, pulled each other's hair, kicked and scratched and bit until our parents had to separate us and drive us away from one another, Mami with a switch, Papi with his leather belt. I ran to the bittersweet shade of the oregano bushes and wept until my chest hurt, each sob tearing off a layer of the comfort built from my parents' love, until I was totally alone, defended only by the green, the scent of cooking spices, and the dry, brushed dirt under my feet.

## AFTER READING

### A Respond to the reading

1 Read about how to use questions for writing a response to a text.

> ### Response Questions
>
> One way to respond to a reading is to write answers to these questions in this order:
>
> ■ What do you understand the reading to say?
>
> ■ How does the reading make you feel?
>
> ■ What does the reading make you think about?

2 In your log, write answers about "The Brown Hen" to the three response questions.

3 Share your answers with your group.

### B Analyze the story

1 List the characters and identify their relationship to each other.

2 List the major events in "The Brown Hen" in the order they occurred.

3 Compare your lists with your group.

4 With a partner, on a separate piece of paper, create a chart like the one on the next page with the main events and the characters in each event. In the last column, put what you perceive the characters to be feeling during the event.

| Events | Characters | Feelings |
|---|---|---|
| • found stones | Delsa, Negi | bored, restless |
| | | |

5 Compare your charts with the class.

## HOW IT'S WRITTEN

### A Practice a sensory awareness exercise

1 Good writers appeal to the senses in their writing. Read about a way to
exercise your senses.

> ## Using Your Senses
>
> Writers need to develop their sensory awareness. One way is to do these
> exercises, many of which require you to close your eyes so that you can
> focus on senses other than sight.
>
> - **Notice what you hear.** Close your eyes. Are some sounds louder than
>   others? What sound is the softest? Sit quietly until you notice at least
>   five different sounds. List these sounds.
>
> - **Notice what you smell.** Close your eyes. What smells are strongest? Sit
>   quietly until you notice three different smells. List these smells.
>
> - **Notice your sense of touch.** Close your eyes. What is the weather like?
>   Are you hot or cold? Is your seat hard or soft? What textures can you
>   touch with your hands? How does your clothing feel against your skin?
>   List these details of touch.
>
> - **Notice your sense of taste.** Close your eyes. Recall your last meal. What
>   did you eat? How did it taste? List the tastes you recall.
>
> - **Notice your surroundings.** Look around you. Pay attention to colors,
>   shapes, and sizes. What color dominates? What is the tiniest thing you
>   see? What is hanging on the walls? What is above you and below you?
>   List visual details.
>
> Repeating these exercises will help you develop your sensory awareness.

2 Follow the instructions in the toolbox to practice using your senses.

**B** **Find examples of sensory details**

1 Write down these headings: "sound," "taste," "smell," "touch," and "sight." With a partner, list details Santiago used in "The Brown Hen" that appeal to each sense.

2 Talk about how sensory details help Santiago's story come alive for readers.

3 Share your findings with the class.

## TOPICS FOR WRITING

### Choose one topic to write about

Whichever topic you choose, before you start writing, refer back to the toolbox *Using Your Senses* on page 10 and make lists of sights, sounds, smells, tastes, and feelings you associate with the topic you have chosen. Then, include as many sensory details as you can in your writing to help readers picture the incident or the place that you have chosen to describe.

❶ Choose one event from the list you created in **Make a list** on page 7 and describe in detail what happened.

❷ Describe a house or apartment you lived in while growing up.

❸ Write a description of a place. Go to somewhere you can observe and take notes for a few minutes, for example, the school cafeteria, a park, or the steps of a museum. Choose a place that is new to you, one you have never been to before.

## AFTER WRITING

### Share your writing

1 Read your writing aloud to a partner. After listening to your partner's writing, tell the person what you understood and what you liked about the piece.

2 Together, decide which piece of writing to read to the class.

## BEFORE READING

### Gather ideas about the topic

1 Read about one way to gather ideas about a topic.

### Clustering

Clustering can be done before you read, after you read, or before you write. It's one way to gather ideas about a topic.

When you do clustering, you start by writing the name of the topic in the middle of a piece of paper. Then you let your mind move off from the central topic in different directions. You quickly write down any word or idea that comes to you, sometimes connecting it to the previous idea with a line. When a different idea comes to your mind, one unrelated to a previous word, you begin a new branch off the main topic.

Clustering allows your mind to bring forth ideas and thought patterns you might not see if you were simply writing. You can also do clustering with a group or the whole class. When you do this, you will find that your group will think of associations you might not think of on your own.

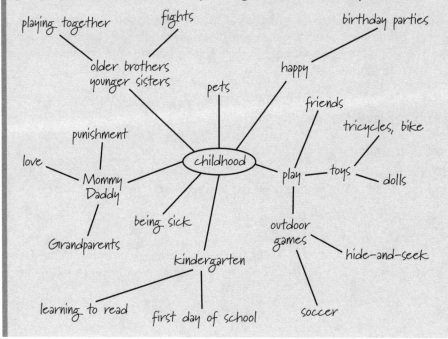

2 Make a cluster of words and phrases you associate with the topic "My Mother."

# Memory: My Mother
Amy Tan

*Amy Tan has written several novels about California's immigrant Chinese population. This memoir appeared in* The New Yorker *magazine.*

The most hateful words I have ever said to another human being were to my mother. I was sixteen at the time. They rose from the storm in my chest and I let them fall in a fury of hailstones: "I hate you. I wish I were dead." I waited for her to collapse, stricken by my cruel words, but she was still standing upright, her chin raised, her lips stretched in a crazy smile. "O.K., maybe I die," she said. "Then I no longer be your mother!"

We had many similar exchanges. Sometimes she actually tried to kill herself, by running into the street, holding a knife to her throat. She, too, had storms in her chest. And what she aimed at me was as fast and deadly as lightning bolts.

For days after our arguments, she would not speak to me. She tormented me, acted as if she had no feelings for me whatsoever. I was lost to her. And, because of that, I lost battle after battle, all of them: the times she criticized me, humiliated me in front of others, forbade me to do this or that without even listening to one good reason that it should be the other way. I swore to myself I would never forget these injustices. I would store them, harden my heart, make myself as impenetrable as she was.

I remember this now, because I am also remembering another time, just a couple of years ago. I was forty-seven, had become a different person by then, had gone on to be a fiction writer, someone who uses memory and imagination. In fact, I was writing a story about a girl and her mother when the phone rang.

It was my mother, and this surprised me. Had someone helped her make the call? For three years, she had been losing her mind to Alzheimer's disease. Early on, she forgot to lock her door. Then she forgot where she lived. She forgot who people were and what they had meant to her. Lately, she had been unable to remember many of her worries and sorrows.

"Amy," she said, and she began to speak quickly in Chinese. "Something is wrong with my mind. I think I'm going crazy."

I caught my breath. Usually she could barely speak more than two words at a time. "Don't worry," I started to say.

"It's true," she went on. "I feel like I can't remember many things. I can't remember what I did yesterday. I can't remember what happened a long time ago, what I did to you . . . " She spoke as a person might if she were drowning and had bobbed to the surface with the force of the will to live, only to see how far she had already drifted, how impossibly far she was from the shore.

She spoke frantically: "I know I did something to hurt you."

"You didn't," I said. "Really, don't worry."

"I did terrible things. But now I can't remember what. And I just want to tell you . . . I hope you can forget just as I've forgotten."

I tried to laugh, so that she wouldn't notice the cracks in my voice. "Really, don't worry."

"O.K., I just wanted you to know."

After we hung up, I cried, both happy and sad. I was again a sixteen-year-old, but the storm in my chest was gone.

My mother died six months later. But she had bequeathed to me her most healing words, those which are as open and eternal as a clear blue sky. Together, we knew in our hearts what we should remember, what we can forget.

## AFTER READING

### A Respond to the reading

1 In your log, write answers to the three questions in the toolbox *Response Questions* on page 9.

2 Share your answers with your group.

### B Understand the time periods

1 Amy Tan writes about three different times in her life – when she was 16, when she was 47, and the present. With a partner, find the sections where she talks about each time period. Bracket them [ ] and label them "16," "47," and "Now."

2 Share your findings with your group.

3 Why does the author write about different time periods? Discuss with your group.

4 Have one member of your group summarize your discussion for the class.

### C Think about a quote

1 Reread the last two sentences: "But she had bequeathed to me her most healing words, those which are as open and eternal as a clear blue sky. Together, we knew in our hearts what we should remember, what we can forget." With your group, discuss what Tan meant.

2 Write in your log for a few minutes about the kinds of things people should remember and the kinds of things people should forget.

3 Discuss what you wrote with a partner.

## HOW IT'S WRITTEN

### Think about describing people

1 Reread the memoir and underline some words and phrases that help you know what the mother was like.

2 Talk with the class about how a writer can help readers understand a person by describing their words and actions.

3 In your log, write something you learned about writing from this activity.

## TOPICS FOR WRITING

### Choose one topic to write about

Whichever topic you choose, before you start writing, use the technique of clustering to help you recall details.

❶ Write a reminiscence (memory) of someone who was close to you and has died. Recall some words and events you associate with the person.

❷ In "Memory: My Mother," the author recalls several conversations between herself and her mother. Can you recall something your parent or grandparent told you many years ago? Write a story about this memory.

❸ Choose a sentence or several sentences from the story that relate to your own experience. Begin a piece of writing with the quote and explain its significance in Tan's essay. Continue writing, explaining how the quote relates to you.

## AFTER WRITING

### Give feedback

1 Read about one way to help your classmates revise their writing.

### Reader's Response Feedback

After you have read or listened to your classmates' writing, your main role is to give appreciative and encouraging responses. One way to do this is to use these guidelines:

■ Say what you understand about the writing.

■ Say what you like. Be specific.

■ Tell one sensory detail that stands out for you.

■ Say one or more things you would like to know more about.

2 Exchange papers with a classmate. On a separate sheet of paper, write a response to your classmate's piece of writing using the guidelines above.

3 Read your classmate's comments and save them.

## BEFORE READING

### Make a personal connection

1 Your parents may be of the same nationality or race, but their backgrounds are different, for example, social class or education or religion and so on. These differences contribute to the person you are. What differences do your parents represent? Freewrite an answer to the question.

2 Share your freewriting with your group.

# There Was Rice at Every Meal

Eric Koji Stowe

*Eric Koji Stowe's mother is Japanese-American and his father is African-American. He was 26 years old and living in Sacramento, California, when he wrote this essay for the book* What Are You? Voices of Mixed Race Young People *edited by Pearl Gaskins.*

Among my friends' parents, my parents are one of the few couples who have lasted. My father is six foot six, 270 pounds, whereas my mom is five foot two and a little Asian woman. They've been married for thirty-four years. Yet they still go out to eat. They still laugh and they still hold hands. They still enjoy their time together. They're very cute.

When I was growing up, they were a great example of a relationship and a monogamous marriage. They provided for my brother and myself – we never had to struggle for anything because they made many sacrifices for us. I think my brother and I realize what they've done for us and what we have to do to pay them back, which is to be good sons.

Looking at my friends' households, I would say our household has more of an Asian influence. My father chose to learn the Japanese language and culture in order to get to know my mother and her family. That helped him get accepted in their society. So the Asian perspective, or the Asian philosophy, had more influence in our house. Although my dad made the rules, he was really soft-spoken and never had to yell at us, never hit us. That whole Asian "respect" thing was there.

A lot of the showing of love and affection in our household is done through actions. I think that's an example of the Asian influence. I look at some of my African-American friends and they give big hugs and say "I love you" to their parents. And some of them didn't understand the fact that I've only told my parents that I love them once. I respect them, and I do what they say, and that's how I show my love for them. It's just unspoken. We're definitely a lot tighter than some of my friends' families.

I chose to accept a lot of the Japanese philosophy and religion. I chose to cling to it and learn it. When I was growing up, we went to a Buddhist temple. But it wasn't until I got to college that I started reading a lot of the literature and philosophy. I learned Japanese, I kept that as a minor. I noticed how people are so quick to judge and lash out at other people. I try to keep an open mind and an open heart. Being raised a Buddhist and adhering to some of the philosophy, I think it was easier for me to accept other people.

There are also little things I learned – like, if you stick your chopsticks straight down into your rice, the Japanese superstition is that someone's going to die. I'd always do that as a kid, playing around, and my mom would get mad at me. And taking your shoes off in your house – all my shoes were at the door. And the furniture in the house – the paintings, dolls, and stuff that my parents bought in Japan – there was definitely a Japanese influence in that respect.

On holidays, like New Year's, we'd eat *mochi* [rice dumplings or patties] and sukiyaki [a Japanese dish]. And there was rice at every meal. My mother still cooks Japanese food daily. She'd cook another meal for my father – he grew up back east and prefers steak and potatoes. And so I'd eat both. I guess the dinner table was a kind of a mixture of the cultures – Japanese culture and American, as well as African-American, the good old ribs and chicken and all that stereotypical stuff.

My dad loves music so I grew up with R&B and Motown and hip-hop and country and folk music. Don't limit yourself to just one style – that was a definite theme throughout my childhood. My parents obviously tried to steer us in the direction of being open-minded and accepting of other people and having a broad worldview.

I'm going to Japan. I'll be teaching English in this town between Osaka and Kyoto. I don't know how I'll be accepted there as a foreigner and being biracial. I'm sure in some circles I'll be looked down upon because of it. My mother feels the same way – that she would be discriminated against there because she married an African-American person.

I'm going to go there with an open mind. I'll travel as much as I can and enjoy the experience. I'm excited, I can't wait. My parents are more excited than I am. They know it's always been a dream of mine. And my family in Japan is just stoked about it.

**EDITOR'S NOTE**

*I heard from Eric one year later. He was enjoying his life in Japan so much that he decided to extend his stay another year. Here's what he said:*

> "I haven't had any problems living in Japan. I am obviously a foreigner, but I think being half Japanese has been a great advantage. The cultural transition was very easy. And many Japanese have pointed out that I act very Japanese and not like the typical *gaijin* [foreigner]. I take that as a compliment."

## AFTER READING

### A Look for topics in the reading

1 With another person, make a list of some of the topics Stowe talked about.

2 Share your list with the class.

3 Add topics mentioned by your classmates to your list.

### B Write a discussion letter

1 Read the toolbox about writing a discussion letter as a way of responding to a reading.

### Discussion Letter to Classmates

Another way of responding to a reading is to write a discussion letter. The purpose of the letter is to explore a reading and provoke discussion with classmates. It is not meant to be a finished piece of writing but rather it is intended to be more like a journal or freewriting. It should pose and consider questions, not necessarily answer them.

Here is how to write your discussion letter:

■ Reread the selection and mark places that interest or puzzle you.

■ Start the letter with "Dear Class."

■ Write about connections you see between what you read and your own experience. Do some exploratory thinking about issues in the reading, or ask some questions the reading raised for you.

■ Sign your name at the end.

2 Write a discussion letter to the class about "There Was Rice at Every Meal." Finish the letter at home and bring four copies of it to the next class.

3 Share and discuss your letter with your group.

## HOW IT'S WRITTEN

### Learn about the essay

1 Read the toolbox to learn about two types of essays.

## The Essay

An essay is a piece of writing that presents the personal views of the writer. Essays can be of two types, both of which you will be writing as you work through this book.

TYPE 1: In the classical definition, an essay is like taking a trip through the writer's mind. This type of essay may be inconclusive and incomplete, showing that the writer has not finished thinking about the topic or has not chosen a side. It does not necessarily try to convince the reader of a certain point of view. It may wander or seem to ramble as the writer tries to find out what he or she really means. The writer uses facts, observations, associations, or examples to consider various aspects of the subject, not to support a thesis.

TYPE 2: The kind of essay you may be more familiar with is one that makes a point and supports it. It might be called a "thesis/support" essay. A thesis is a statement that you want to defend – an opinion or a point of view that not everyone believes or agrees with. In thesis/support writing, you know what your point is before you write your final draft. This kind of writing is important in school, although this is not the only type of writing that you should be able to do.

*Adapted from* The Essay *by P. Heilker.*

2 Reread "There Was Rice at Every Meal" and see how it fits the definition of an essay. Does it seem like the first type or the second type of essay? Discuss this with the class.

## TOPICS FOR WRITING

### Choose one topic to write about

❶ Write an essay about yourself and your background in the same manner as Stowe did. Talk about your parents, life in your home, your cultural background as it influenced you, and your family. You might compare your family to others. Have you developed a particular philosophy of life or set of values like Stowe?

❷ Have you ever felt discriminated against because of your background or because you were a foreigner? Have you ever been treated badly because of someone's stereotype of you? Write an essay about discrimination or stereotypes. Use your own experience to illustrate how you feel. If you wish, suggest some ways to reduce discrimination or stereotyping.

❸ Choose a topic from your discussion letter or the discussion you had with your group. (See **Write a discussion letter** on the opposite page.) Develop the topic into a Type 1 essay (see the toolbox *The Essay* on this page).

# AFTER WRITING

## Share your writing

1 Read about one way to share writing.

### Writing Circle

When other people tell you what they observe in your writing, it can help you to reflect on what you said or how you said it. One way to hear people's observations of your writing is to form a writing circle. In this activity, a group of three to five people form a circle and read or listen to each other's writing. Each person then tells one thing that he or she noticed. The observations should not be judgments, suggestions, or criticisms, but rather they should sound something like this:

*"You wrote a lot about . . . "*

*"You talked about . . . "*

*"You described . . . "*

*"I didn't know this word you used: . . . "*

It is not easy to make nonevaluative observations, to stand back and simply observe. It takes practice.

2 Form a writing circle with two to four classmates and read your papers to each other.

3 As your listeners make comments about your writing, take notes.

4 Look over your notes and think about what people said. How do your classmates' comments make you see your writing differently? What did you learn? Write a few ideas in your log.

## A Revise one piece of writing

1 Read about drafts and revising.

> ### Drafting
>
> All professional writers know a first draft is never the final draft. A first draft is a chance to get your thoughts and impressions down on paper. This preliminary writing may be disorganized and incomplete. This is normal.
>
> After you have a first draft, you can think of changes you need to make. You may need to develop your ideas. You can see where you need to add details or where your writing is confusing. You can try to clarify your thoughts. Most writers do several revisions before they are satisfied with their work.
>
>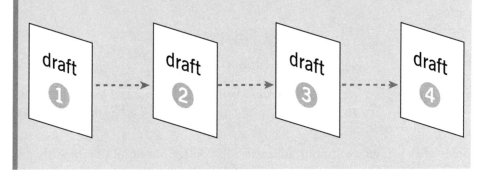

2 Reread the pieces you wrote for the **Topics for Writing** sections of FAMILY ORIGINS. Also read any notes you made after sharing your writing with classmates.

3 Choose one piece to revise. Think about what you could add and what you could clarify.

4 Write a second draft.

## B Share your writing

1 Read your second draft to your group.

2 With your group, choose one person's writing to read to the class.

### Writer's Tip

*Most writers share the feeling that the first draft, and all those that follow, are opportunities to discover what they have to say and how best they can say it.*

**Donald Murray**

## Between Two Cultures

## BEFORE READING

### Think about the topic

1 Make a list of situations in which you feel unsafe. Next to each item on your list, write what you do or could do to protect yourself.

2 Explain your list to a partner. Discuss similarities or differences between your and your partner's lists.

## Safe

Cherylene Lee

*Cherylene Lee is a prizewinning fiction writer, playwright, and poet. The story "Safe" appeared in an anthology of contemporary Asian-American fiction. This is an excerpt from it.*

Safe. That is the most important consideration for our family. Perhaps there is a Chinese gene encoded with a protein for caution. Or perhaps it's because my family's tailor shop is not doing so well or because of my mother's blindness. Perhaps it's because my mother and father married late in life and weren't sure how to protect their children.

We try to take precautions. My mother won't go out at night for fear of what the darkness holds. She doesn't like me to take a shower after dinner for fear I might get a cramp and somehow drown in the shower's spray. She doesn't like me to walk home from school alone, nor does she like me to walk home with boys. She'd rather I walked home with girls, at least three for maximum protection so one can always run for help. I've tried to explain to her, I like walking alone, it's not always possible to walk in female threes, I don't even have that many girl-friends. "You have to watch out at your age, you can't be too safe," she warns, "but don't hang around with the fast ones."

My father is just as bad. He's so afraid someone will dent his car, he won't park in a lot that doesn't have two spaces side by side for his ten-year-old station wagon. He refuses to go into a grocery story if he could be the first or last customer – "That's when robbers are most likely to come." He won't eat in restaurants without first wiping the chopsticks, rice bowl, tea cup, or plate, silverware, and glass – "So many germs everywhere." He has more locks and alarms on his tailor shop door than the bank that's two doors down. It takes him ten minutes to open them up each day, turn off the alarms, before calling my mother to let her know that he has arrived safely.

We live in San Francisco – a city with its share of dangers, though my parents have done their best to shield my brother and me from having to face most of them. More than from just physical harm, they've tried to protect us from loss – loss of face, loss of happiness, loss of innocence. So far we have been protected by their constant vigilance. Not that I have been sheltered so much I can't go places on my own or do things without my parents' consent, but their warnings, cautions, and dire predictions have had an effect.

## AFTER READING

### A  Understand the reading

1  Reread the story. With a partner, complete the chart below.

| Who | Fears | Precautions |
| --- | --- | --- |
| Mother | | |
| Father | | |

2  Share your chart with your group.

3  With your group choose two or three precautions from the chart. Discuss the effectiveness of these precautions.

### B  Make a personal connection

1  Lee lists several ways her character's mother and father try to protect themselves and their children from harm. Reread the story and mark with a plus (+) ways that you or your parents have tried to protect yourselves. Mark with a minus (-) ones you have not employed.

2  Discuss what you marked with a partner.

3  Freewrite for a few minutes about your own fears and what you do to protect yourself.

## C Think about a quote

1 Reread the last sentence of the reading. What effect do you think the parents' "warnings, cautions, and dire predictions" had on the narrator?

2 Discuss this question with your group.


## HOW IT'S WRITTEN

### Look for details

1 Reread the passage and underline every word that relates in some way to the idea of safety. With a partner discuss why the author uses so many of these words. What effect does it have on the reader?

2 With your partner, reread the passage and look for places where the author tells us how her character feels about her parents' efforts to protect her. Write the name of each feeling in the margin. Discuss one or two clues the author gives to help readers understand the feelings of the narrator.

3 Discuss your findings with the class.


## TOPICS FOR WRITING

### Choose one topic to write about

The techniques that you have used to gather ideas before you read can also be used to gather ideas before you write. (See the following toolboxes: *Freewriting* on page 2, *Brainstorming a List* on page 7 and *Clustering* on page 12.) Whichever topic you choose to write about, make sure you use one of these pre-writing techniques to gather ideas.

1 Tell the true story of a time you did something you were warned not to do because it wasn't safe. What happened? Why did you ignore the warning? Were you in danger? Did the person who warned you find out what you did? What did you learn from this experience?

2 The narrator of "Safe" talks about her parents' desire to protect and shelter her and her brother. Do you think this attitude is especially true of parents who have recently brought their families to a new place or culture? Write an account of a person, either yourself or someone you know about, who has been in this situation and experienced this type of protectiveness.

3 Nowadays, people in both cities and small towns worry about crime. What precautions do you think people should take to protect themselves from becoming the victims of crime? Write an essay in which you tell at least three things people can do for protection. Be sure to give examples and explain why you think such precautions are necessary.

## AFTER WRITING

### Share your writing

1 Exchange papers with a partner. Write responses to your partner's paper, following the suggestions in the toolbox *Reader's Response Feedback* on page 15.

2 Save your partner's comments.

. . . . . . . . . . . . . . . . . . . . . . . . . . . . . . . . . . . . . . . . . . . . . . . . . . . . . . . . . . . . . . . . . . . . . . . . . . . . . . .

## BEFORE READING

### Think about the title and the author

1 Read the title and introductory information.

2 With the class discuss what the phrase "paper daughter" might mean.

 # I Answer to "Elaine"
M. Elaine Mar

*M. Elaine Mar immigrated to the United States from Hong Kong in 1972 as a five-year-old. Her memoir,* Paper Daughter, *tells of her struggles growing up in a new culture. "I Answer to 'Elaine'" is an excerpt from this memoir.*

I was proud of how American I'd become: I answered to "Elaine" first and only spoke Chinese when absolutely necessary, with my adult relatives. Even this was embarrassing, and publicly, I sometimes tried to talk to my parents in English. I genuinely believed that they could understand if they only tried harder. After all, I had done it.

More than anything, I wanted to obscure my foreignness, that combination of ethnicity and poverty. I would have given anything to slip into the ordinary. But my parents foiled all attempts. They turned me into an object of ridicule. Mother chose my clothes for me, cotton dresses and skirts sewn out of restaurant flour sacks, acrylic sweaters from Kmart,[1] and – the best of the lot – hand-me-downs donated by Diana, a waitress's daughter. During the fall and winter chill, Mother sent me to school in taupe nylon stockings and knee socks beneath my skirts. I cringed when classmates touched my gauzy, discolored legs curiously. *If only I could be normal and wear Levi's,* I wished. I wanted stiff, new jeans badly, but never bothered to ask. I already knew the answer – *too expensive.* . . .

1 A popular department store in the US that carries low cost items.

My mother had stopped styling her hair. She dressed in the same clothes every day; they were years old and sometimes didn't match. After my brother's birth, she developed a low, poofy belly, as if the baby had never left her body at all. Admiring [my friend's mother] Mrs. Harper's slenderness, I asked Mother why she was so fat. Repeatedly, Mother said that she kept the weight for my sake. "If I weren't fat, how would you know you were thin?" she retorted.

The dialogue epitomized our relationship. We were entering a long period of mutual struggle over our identities. I believed that she reflected poorly on me, and vice versa. I thought she should become more stylish – a code for "American." She dreamed of a dutiful Chinese daughter with my face, inhabiting my body.

I had a dreadful power over my mother, one that grew with each word in my American vocabulary. As I gained fluency in English, I took on greater responsibility for my family, and parent and child roles became murky. Mother spoke and read virtually no English. She needed my help to buy groceries, interpret the news, and complete all manner of forms. I filled out our "alien registration" cards. I wrote out bank deposit slips. I showed Mother where to sign my report cards.

She continued to sign Father's name. I threatened legal action: "That's forgery! It's not your name."

Mother explained again, "You always sign the man's name. It's the only one with meaning."

A deep frustration set in. I was sickened by her statement's implication for my future. I hated her helplessness, believing it unique to her alone. I knew it couldn't be ingrained to my gender, because I fulfilled such essential tasks already. I was the American voice of the family, the connection between our basement room and the outside world. I'd accepted a hollow name, an empty construct, and created an identity with it in four short years. "Elaine" was adored by teachers, got A's in everything except penmanship, and watched *The Brady Bunch*[2] faithfully every day after school. I didn't ask for these challenges, yet I responded and excelled. How dare Mother tell me that I would eventually amount to nothing? I had trouble respecting her. I grew increasingly willful, violating the most sacred of cultural tenets: absolute fealty to family and elders.

2 A popular TV series in the early 1970s that featured a very well-mannered, polite, happy family.

## AFTER READING

### A Respond to the reading

1 Read about another way to respond to a reading.

### Double Entry Response

A double entry allows you to note places in a reading that interest you and to react to them. Here is how it works.

Draw a line down the middle of one page of your notebook. On the left-hand side of the page, jot down interesting or important words, phrases, sentences, ideas, points, details, and the like that caught your attention as you read the passage. You can write down the exact words as they appear in the text (*quote*), you can say some of the ideas in your own words (*paraphrase*), or you can retell the most important ideas or main events from the passage (*summarize*).

Then, on the right-hand side of your notebook page, write your own comments about the material you jotted down on the left-hand side. You can question the reading, react to it, relate it to other readings or your own experience, or express your thoughts and feelings about it.

| Title: _____ | |
| (Put the name of the reading, the author, and the page number here.) | |
| What it says | My response |
| (In this column, write a sentence, a phrase, a word, an idea, an event, etc. from the reading that you find interesting or important.) | (In this column, write your response to what you wrote in the column opposite. Respond with questions, connections, thoughts, feelings, confusions etc.) |

2 Reread "I Answer to 'Elaine'." As you read, stop at least three times and write a double entry response in your log.

3 Discuss your double entry responses with a partner. How are they similar or different?

## B Check your understanding

1 With a partner, find one or two sentences in the reading you had trouble understanding. Figure out their meaning, using a dictionary if necessary.

2 Explain one of these sentences to your group.

## C List the conflicts

1 With your group, make a list of ways in which Elaine felt in conflict with her mother. (See the toolbox *Brainstorming a List* on page 7.)

2 Share your list and other groups' lists by making a class list on the chalkboard.

3 Discuss which of these conflicts might be typical only of families who move into a new culture and which might occur between parents and children in all families.

# HOW IT'S WRITTEN

## Look for details

1 In paragraph two, Mar said she felt like "an object of ridicule." With your partner, underline the details in this paragraph that show why she felt that way.

2 With the class, discuss how using such specific details helps readers understand a point.

# TOPICS FOR WRITING

## Choose one topic to write about

Whichever topic you choose, make sure you use specific details in your writing that create images.

**1** It is typical of children growing up to struggle with their parents over their identity. Write a personal essay about a period in your life when you were in conflict with your parents because of your struggle for your identity.

**2** The writer had mixed feelings about her name. How do you feel about your name? Do you use different names with different people? Write an essay about your name. Tell who gave you your name and why, what it means, what importance it has played in your life, and how you feel about it.

**3** Pick an issue or sentence from the reading that jumps out at you, that relates to you in some way. Write an essay about it. State the sentence or describe the issue and tell why it's meaningful to you. You may compare or contrast yourself with Elaine.

> ## Writer's Tip
>
> *Be specific . . . It is much better to say "the geranium in the window" than "the flower in the window." "Geranium" – that one word gives us a much more specific picture. It penetrates more deeply into the beingness of that flower. It immediately gives us the scene by the window – red petals, green circular leaves, all straining toward sunlight.*
>
> **Natalie Goldberg**

# AFTER WRITING

## Share your writing

1 Read aloud what you wrote to your group.

2 Ask your listeners to restate orally what they think your important points are and to tell what details stand out for them.

3 Take notes on what your listeners say.

## BEFORE READING

### A  Ask questions before reading

1  Read the title and introductory information. Write down several questions you think the article will answer.

2  With your partner, read and discuss each other's questions. Pool your questions into one list.

### B  Think about the topic

1  With a group, suggest activities that come to mind when you think of the role of parents and the role of children. List the activities below.

| Role of Parents | Role of Children |
|---|---|
|  |  |
|  |  |
|  |  |
|  |  |

2  Share your lists with the class.

 # Translating for Parents Means Growing Up Fast
Misha Kratochvil

*The article discusses the feelings – some positive, like strengthening self-esteem, some negative, like guilt and stress – that arise when parents' and a child's roles are reversed. This article appeared in the* New York Times.

Diana Belozovsky was 13 when she and her parents set out on a complicated getaway from the Soviet Union. At the American Embassy in Rome, the girl's elementary-school English proved indispensable to her parents for the first time.

"This was very crucial," said Ms. Belozovsky, who is now 24. "They were deciding whether we get to America or not." Ms. Belozovsky's parents were not only deaf but also understood no English. The daughter answered some of the official's questions directly and translated others for her parents, using Russian sign language. The official's last question to the girl was whether she would help her parents in America.

"In fact, I've been helping them ever since," said Ms. Belozovsky, a resident of Sheepshead Bay, Brooklyn, who now works as a sign-language interpreter at Coney Island Hospital. Before her parents learned English sign language, she said, "I went with them everywhere, from a hospital to a garage or post office."

Ever since America has had immigrants, children have been translating for their parents. But there is a downside to this custom. Psychologists say that in the long run, the practice may buttress children's self-esteem, but it can also cause short-term stress, embarrassment and psychological and practical difficulties.

Given New York's yeasty ethnic mix . . . the need for interpreters is great. Although a state law requires that translators be provided to those seeking welfare or other public services, they are often in short supply. And in dealing with doctors or shopkeepers or others in the private sphere, non-English speakers are left on their own.

As a result, many immigrants come to depend on their children. But when children are their parents' interpreters, sociologists say, the dynamics of the typical family become inverted.

"The children are forced to act much older than they are," said Sarah Martin, a social worker at Mount Sinai Hospital who works with immigrants in East Harlem.

The duties can bring great strain. Brian Palmer, associate executive director of Coney Island Hospital, which offers ambitious translation services because its patients speak many languages, recalled an Italian-American teenager who translated for his ill grandmother. The diagnosis was cancer, but the boy systematically omitted the word cancer in speaking to her. "He did not and could not deal emotionally with his grandmother's diagnosis," Mr. Palmer said.

Stress can arise in other high-stakes settings, from the immigration office to the social services department. "As the child feels increasingly responsible for not being able to solve a problem for the parent – for example, get food stamps – he might suffer from anxiety or even depression," Ms Martin said. . . .

These burdens add to the children's natural desire to see their parents independent and deep-seated in their new society. Shaleena Khalique, a 17-year-old immigrant from Bangladesh, was shocked when she found out that her mother was being treated unfairly at work because she was too shy to use her rudimentary English. Shaleena urged her to stand up for herself, saying, "Mum, you know some English."

Social workers say the stress of translating can make some children nervous and tired at school and neglectful of homework, and when children become indispensable to the functioning of the household, the parents often find it harder to discipline them.

Ms. Martin recalled an 8-year-old Mexican boy who told his mother he had joined a gang. The only thing the mother dared to do was caution the child to be careful. "There is a feeling among immigrant parents they can't stop their child from doing anything," Ms. Martin said. . . .

Child translating can prompt several smaller problems – including that bane of teenagers, embarrassment. . . .

Consider Anna Gekker, a 15-year-old Russian immigrant whose family lives in Bensonhurst. "At a P.T.A. meeting, my teacher said I should tell my mother I spoke too much during classes," Anna said. An honest girl, she translated the teacher's complaints word for word. But of course, she said, "I was getting myself in trouble."

Despite the drawbacks, child translating carries a few unexpected benefits.

"I took advantage of it many times," said Paul Bolotovsky, 16, a Russian immigrant from Midwood. A favorite trick was to write notes to excuse his absence from school and have his parents sign them, not disclosing the real contents.

But there are also more noble satisfactions. At age 8, Polina Rozen, now 17, accompanied her Russian-speaking grandfather to a voting booth. She not only read him the candidates' names but also showed him how to pull the lever.

"It was a great day," said Polina, whose family lives in Staten Island. "I was the only kid running around. I voted."

## AFTER READING

### A Answer your prereading questions

1 With your partner, mark and number places in the text that provide a satisfactory answer to the questions on your list from **Before Reading** on page 29. Put the numbers next to the questions.

2 Tell the class which questions were answered by the text. See if your classmates can answer them.

### B Freewrite a response

1 Freewrite a response to "Translating for Parents Means Growing Up Fast" in your log. Begin with your thoughts and feelings about the ideas in the article.

2 Share your freewriting with a partner.

## C Restate general statements

1 With a partner, explain and restate the following statements in your own words:

① "Ever since America has had immigrants, children have been translating for their parents. But there is a downside to this custom."

② "Psychologists say that in the long run, the practice may buttress children's self-esteem, but it can also cause short-term stress, embarrassment and psychological and practical difficulties."

③ "But when children are their parents' interpreters, sociologists say, the dynamics of the typical family become inverted."

④ "Child translating can prompt several smaller problems – including that bane of teenagers: embarrassment. . . ."

2 With your group, come up with an example from your experiences or observations of others to support one of the statements above. Share the example with the class.

# HOW IT'S WRITTEN

### Find supporting examples

1 With your partner, look through the article and underline two general statements about what happens to immigrant children or family relationships – either positively or negatively – when children have to translate for parents.

2 Look in the text for a specific example that *supports* the general statement – that is, explains or illustrates it.

3 Share one of your statements and examples with your group and explain to the group how the example supports the statement.

4 Discuss with the class how well you think the examples in the article support the statements.

5 In your log, write something you want to remember about using examples.

# TOPICS FOR WRITING

### Choose one topic to write about

❶ Write about a similar, or contrasting, experience you've had to one of the people mentioned in the article. Discuss what makes your experience similar or different from the one(s) in the article. Tell what conclusions or general statements your experience leads to.

**2** Pick one or two of the general statements in the article that you agree or disagree with. Use quotes from the article. With examples from your own experience or your observations of others, support each statement you agree or disagree with.

**3** Overall, do you think the effects on children of translating for parents are negative or positive? Why? Do you think that institutions or businesses should not allow children to translate? Do the benefits to children and families outweigh the negative effects? Write an essay giving your opinion. Support your answer with examples from your experience or observations. You may begin with this sentence:

> *In the long run, the effect of children translating for their parents is positive/negative.*

## AFTER WRITING

### Share your writing

1 Join a group of three or four people who wrote about the same topic as you did. Read your writing aloud to the group. Listen to your group members read their writings. As a group, tell each writer what you like and what you would like to read more about to make his or her piece clearer.

2 Join a second group of people who wrote about different topics. Follow the same procedures as Step 1 above.

3 Write in your log about what you learned from listening to the different pieces.

## BEFORE READING

### Think about the topic

1 Read the title and introductory information. With your group, discuss these questions: Are there immigrants in your community? If so, do they tend to learn the language of your country? Do you think they should? How many become bilingual?

2 With your group, discuss the best ways to learn a new language.

3 Summarize your group's discussion for the class.

**No Comprendo**
Barbara Mujica

*This essay appeared as an op-ed piece (guest editorial) in the* New York Times *on January 3, 1995, with a caption that read "Students need English more than bilingualism." Barbara Mujica is a professor of Spanish at Georgetown University in Washington, D.C.*

Last spring, my niece phoned me in tears. She was graduating from high school and had to make a decision. An outstanding soccer player, she was offered athletic scholarships by several colleges. So why was she crying?

My niece came to the United States from South America as a child. Although she had received good grades in her schools in Miami, she spoke English with a heavy accent and her comprehension and writing skills were deficient. She was afraid that once she left the Miami environment she would feel uncomfortable and, worse still, have difficulty keeping up with class work.

Programs that keep foreign-born children in Spanish-language classrooms for years are only part of the problem. During a visit to my niece's former school, I observed that all business, not just teaching, was conducted in Spanish. In the office, secretaries spoke to the administrators and the children in Spanish. Announcements over the public-address system were made in an English so fractured that it was almost incomprehensible.

I asked my niece's mother why, after years in public school, her daughter had poor English skills. "It's the whole environment," she replied. "All kinds of services are available in Spanish or Spanglish. Sports and after-school activities are conducted in Spanglish. That's what the kids hear on the radio and in the street."

Until recently, immigrants made learning English a priority. But even when they didn't learn English themselves, their children grew up speaking it. Thousands of first-generation Americans still strive to learn English, but others face reduced educational and career opportunities because they have not mastered the basic skills they need to get ahead.

According to the 1990 census, 40 percent of the Hispanics born in the U.S. do not graduate from high school, and the Department of Education says that a lack of proficiency in English is an important factor in the dropout rate.

People and agencies that favor providing services only in foreign languages want to help people who do not speak English, but they may be doing them a disservice by condemning them to a linguistic ghetto from which they can not easily escape.

And my niece? She turned down all of her scholarship opportunities, deciding instead to attend a small college in Miami, where she will never have to put her English to the test.

# AFTER READING

## A Find the main idea

1 Read about finding the main idea in a reading and about how important it is for the writer to have a main idea and to support it.

> ### Main Idea
>
> The main idea of a piece of writing is the central idea or focus. It's the main point the writer wants to make. The reader can usually find a sentence or two that best expresses it. Sometimes, though, it's implied, and you have to read between the lines to find it.
>
> Writers may start a piece of writing not knowing what the main idea is going to be and may only discover it in the process of writing. However, once they establish their main idea, the rest of the text will develop that idea by giving examples, giving reasons, making comparisons and contrasts, providing information or data, referring to other texts, or adding other support. Thus, when you look at a finished piece of writing, like "No Comprendo," you can find the writer's main idea and see that everything in the text – the examples and reasons – all relate to and support it.

2 In "No Comprendo," what is the author's main idea? Work by yourself to find the sentence that best states the main idea. Then work with your small group to agree on one sentence.

3 Decide with your group if the example of Mujica's niece supports this sentence. Can you connect that sentence to all aspects of the example?

## B Respond to the reading

1 What are your thoughts and feelings about this editorial? Write for a few minutes in your log.

2 Share your writing with a partner.

# HOW IT'S WRITTEN

## Analyze the essay

1 Read about one way to analyze a piece of writing.

> ### Descriptive Outlining
>
> A descriptive outline can help you see a piece of writing clearly. You can use it to help you understand something you read or as a tool for revising your own writing.
>
> Set up your descriptive outline by first writing the main idea of the whole text, using your own words. Then underneath in columns, write

a one-sentence summary of what each paragraph "says" and a description of what each paragraph "does," that is, the purpose or function of the paragraph. For example, the paragraph might introduce an idea, develop a reason, give examples, tell a story, describe something or someone, explain something, analyze a problem, synthesize ideas, argue a point, or provide a conclusion. When you tell what a paragraph does, you are telling how it develops or supports the main idea or main point.

Main idea _____

What each paragraph SAYS    What each paragraph DOES
Par. 1 _____    _____

Par. 2 _____    _____

Par. 3 _____    _____

2 Work with a partner. After numbering the paragraphs, make a descriptive outline of "No Comprendo."

3 Compare your outlines with the class and from the outline answer these questions:

① Which paragraphs are about the author's niece?

② Which paragraph starts with a general statement and then talks about the niece?

③ What are the other paragraphs about? What purpose do they have?

## TOPICS FOR WRITING

### Choose one topic to write about

❶ Do you know someone you consider to be a model bilingual? Prepare questions you could use to interview that person. Here are some possible questions:

■ What is it like to be bilingual?

■ What activities do you conduct in English?
In your other language? Why?

■ What are the benefits of being bilingual? The pitfalls?

Interview the person. Take notes and tape-record the interview if possible.

Think about what main point you can make in your piece of writing. Then write a profile of the person.

❷ Do you agree or disagree with Mujica? Write an essay explaining why you agree or disagree. Begin with a summary of what Mujica says. Then, pick an idea that you agree or disagree with. Tell how you feel and what you think about this idea, why you agree or disagree.

❸ Do you have a "no comprendo" story of your own? Have you had a personal experience in which you didn't understand what was happening because of your language ability or a cross-cultural misunderstanding? Write about this experience. Begin by telling the story. Think about what the story means and make a point at the end. Try to surprise yourself with your ending.

## AFTER WRITING

### Share your writing

1 Exchange papers with another person. Analyze your partner's piece of writing using the following questions as a guide:

① What is the main idea?

② Do the other paragraphs relate to the main idea? Explain.

2 Discuss your analysis with your partner.

3 Write a note to yourself – in your log or on the bottom of your draft – about some changes you might make to improve your piece.

# BETWEEN TWO CULTURES: REVISION

## A Choose one piece of writing

1 Reread the pieces you wrote for the **Topics for Writing** sections of BETWEEN TWO CULTURES. Also read any notes you made about your pieces or comments from classmates.

2 Choose one piece to revise.

## B Think about titles

1 With your group, discuss what titles can tell you about a piece of writing before you read it. What kinds of titles appeal to you? Why?

2 Look at the table of contents of this book and find three titles of texts that you haven't yet read that appeal to you. Then explain to a partner why you like these titles.

3 Choose one of the titles and write down what you expect to read about in the text.

4 Turn to that selection and quickly read it. Were your predictions about the title accurate? Why or why not?

5 Tell your partner how the title prepared you for what you read.

> ## Titles
>
> Finding the right title is important. But you don't need to find one before you start writing. In fact, many writers use a "working title" while they're drafting and revising; this may just be the name of the topic itself, for example, "Cell Phones."
>
> Once you have finished your piece, you'll want to come up with the "perfect" title, one that does at least one of the following:
>
> ■ **Attracts the reader's attention.** One technique for doing this is to find a phrase or a quote in the piece itself to use as a title: "Turn Off That Cell Phone!"
>
> ■ **Gives the reader an idea of what the piece is about.** If you do this, you don't have to reveal your opinion in the title: "The Use and Misuse of Cell Phones."
>
> ■ **Connects to the main idea of the piece of writing.** One technique is to think of a short phrase that expresses your point of view on the topic and use that as the title: "I Hate Cell Phones!"

> If you have trouble finding the right title, show a list of three or four possible titles to friends and classmates and ask them which one they prefer and why. Talk about the titles and then choose the one that seems right.

## C Revise

1 Make a list of several titles you could use for your piece, trying to see how each different title helps you find a focus for the piece. Choose one.

2 Think about what needs to be added to your writing and what needs to be clarified. What changes do you need to make because of your choice of title?

3 Write a second draft.

## D Share your writing

1 Read your second draft to your group.

2 Choose one person's writing from your group to read to the class.

### Writer's Tip

*Almost reluctantly I begin to write titles – as many as a hundred – at odd moments. Each helps me focus on the subject, limit it, take a point of view towards it, for each title is a quick draft which helps eliminate what doesn't belong.*

**Donald Murray**

## Heroes

## BEFORE READING

### Think about the topic

1 Read the title and introductory information for this reading. Freewrite about connections you see between the theme of Ying's essay and the title of this section, HEROES.

2 Share your freewriting with a partner.

## Five New Words at a Time
### Yu-Lan (Mary) Ying

*Yu-Lan (Mary) Ying was a junior in an American high school when she wrote this essay and entered it in a contest sponsored by a college. She won a prize for her essay, and it was published in a major newspaper. The theme of the competition was "A Woman I Admire."*

My family came to America in 1985. No one spoke a word of English. In school, I was in an English as a Second Language class with other foreign-born children. My class was so over-crowded that it was impossible for the teacher to teach English properly. I dreaded going to school each morning because of the fear of not understanding what people were saying and the fear of being laughed at.

At that time, my mother, Tai-Chih, worked part time in a Chinese restaurant from late afternoon till late in the night. It was her unfamiliarity with the English language that forced her to work in a Chinese-speaking environment. Although her job exhausted her, my mother still woke up early in the morning to cook breakfast for my brother and me. Like a hen guarding her chicks, she never neglected us because of her fatigue.

So it was not surprising that very soon my mother noticed something was troubling me. When I said nothing was wrong, my mother answered: "You are my daughter. When something is bothering you, I feel it too." The pain and care I saw in her moon-shaped eyes made me burst into the tears I had held back for so long. I explained to her the fear I had of going to school. "Learning English is not impossible," my mother said. She cheerfully suggested that the two of us work together to learn the language at home with books. The confidence and determination my mother had were admirable because English was as new to her as it was to me.

That afternoon I saw my mother in a different light as she waited for me by the school fence. Although she was the shortest of all the mothers there, her face with her welcoming smile and big, black eyes was the most promising. The afternoon sun shone brightly on her long, black hair creating an aura that distinguished her from others.

My mother and I immediately began reading together and memorizing five new words a day. My mother with her encouraging attitude made the routine fun and interesting. The fact that she was sacrificing her resting time before going to work so that I could learn English made me see the strength she possessed. It made me admire my mother even more.

Very soon, I began to comprehend what everyone was saying and people could understand me. The person solely responsible for my accomplishment and happiness was my mother. The reading also helped my mother learn English so that she was able to pass the postal entrance exam.

It has been seven years since that reading experience with my mother. She is now 43 and in her second year at college. My brother and I have a strong sense of who we are because of the strong values my mother established for herself and her children. My admiration and gratitude for her are endless. That is why my mother is truly the guiding light of my life.

## AFTER READING

### A  Respond to the reading

1  Read the toolbox *Response Questions* on page 9. Then reread the essay and write answers to the three questions from the toolbox in your log.

2  Read your responses to a partner.

### B  Make a visual representation

1  With your group, draw a series of four or five pictures that recreate Ying's story on a sheet of poster paper.

2 Post the group's drawing on the wall or board.

3 Explain your group drawing to the class.

**C Look for the main idea**

1 Pick a sentence that you think best expresses the main idea of "Five New Words at a Time."

2 Share the sentence you picked with the whole class and explain why you chose it.

# HOW IT'S WRITTEN

### Examine the ending

1 Read some guidelines on writing endings.

## *Writing Endings*

The ending is as important as the beginning of an essay. Some writers put a lot of energy into writing the beginning and middle of their essay; but when they come to the ending, they seem to have run out of steam.

Here are some guidelines to help you write your ending:

- Instead of writing the ending of your essay right after you have finished writing the middle, take some time off to rest, think, and gather your ideas. Then write the ending with as much energy and as much purpose as you wrote the rest of the essay.

- Restate your main idea at the end of your essay, but make sure you use different words from what you used before so the reader doesn't say, "You already said this."

- Finish your essay by giving your readers something interesting or entertaining to think about, but make sure it is something that naturally flows from the rest of the paper.

> ■ Writing an ending should be like landing a plane. You let your reader down gently and with satisfaction.
>
> *Adapted from* Writing: Brief Edition *by Elizabeth Cowan.*

2 Reread the ending of "Five New Words at a Time." With your group, discuss how Ying's ending does or does not fulfill the guidelines for writing endings, as explained in the toolbox.

3 Share your thoughts with the class.

## TOPICS FOR WRITING

**Choose one topic to write about**

1 Make a list of women in your life; then pick one you admire. List some specific moments (times, places, events) when you were with this woman and were affected by her. Use your list as the basis of an essay called "A Woman I Admire."

2 Ying tells how her mother taught her a valuable strategy to improve her language learning. Interview someone you know who has learned a second language well. Ask the person how he or she learned the language, what strategies he or she used, what was most effective, and what he or she recommends to someone learning a second language. Using ideas from the person you interviewed and your own experience, write an essay about the best way(s) to learn a new language.

3 The author says she "dreaded going to school each morning" because of her fear of not understanding English. Have you ever experienced fear or dread of something you had to do every day? Make a list of experiences you have feared or dreaded. Choose one experience to write about. Begin your piece, "I dreaded _____ each day" and tell what happened.

## AFTER WRITING

**Share your writing**

1 Exchange papers with a partner.

2 Respond to your partner's writing by answering these questions:
   ① Does the ending provide a summary? Show where.
   ② Does the ending give the reader a new thing to think about? If so, what is it?
   ③ Does the ending complete the piece or leave the reader hanging? Explain.

3 Read your partner's response to your paper. Write down one thing you could do to make the ending stronger.

············································································

## BEFORE READING

### Pool your knowledge

1 What do you know about World War II? With the class, make a cluster on the board of words and phrases you associate with World War II. (See the toolbox *Clustering* on page 12.)

2 Look at the map of Eastern Europe. Locate these countries on the map: Poland, Germany, Russia (including Siberia), and Belarus. If you need to check your answers, look at the Map of the World on page xii.

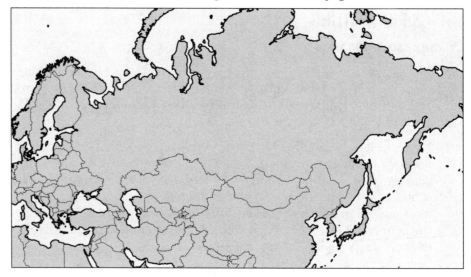

3 If you know what happened in these countries during World War II, share that information with the class.

 My Family Hero
Katarzyna McCarthy

*Katarzyna McCarthy, a Polish immigrant to the United States, was a student at Borough of Manhattan Community College in New York City when she wrote this essay about her grandmother.*

My grandmother Elizabeth was born and raised in Poland, in the city of Bialystock, in a rather wealthy family. Her mother died when she was very little, so she was brought up by her father, a nanny and her four older brothers. She was well-educated, which was still pretty uncommon for women during this period of time (it was before World War II). She was delicate, rather petite, pretty, and very elegant. She had a boyfriend, who lived in Warsaw, and they were planning on getting married.

In 1939, when she was twenty-six, there were major changes for the millions of people in Poland and all over Europe. World War II had begun. My country was under occupation from Germany from the west and Russia from the east, splitting Poland in half. Now the new border was separating my grandmother and her fiancé. She decided to cross it illegally and be reunited with her future husband. Elizabeth and seven other people paid a person who was supposed to take them safely to the other, now German, side. However, they were captured by Russian soldiers, and in the last second Elizabeth gave them a fake name so her family would not get in trouble. She was put in prison back in Bialystok and sentenced for three years in a concentration camp in Belorussia, Russia. Before all the prisoners were taken to the camp, they were put on a cattle train and kept there for two weeks and treated like animals, without any sanitary conditions. Her father and brothers were looking for her, but because of her false name, they could not find her on the prisoners' list. Elizabeth wanted to leave them a message. She found in her pocket a picture of her little white longhaired husky dog. Somebody gave her a pen, and on the back of the picture she wrote a few words to her father:

> Dear Dad,
> I don't know where they are taking me.
> Don't worry, I will see you again.
> Love, Elizabeth

She pushed the picture outside, through a hole in the wall. One of her brothers, who heard about the prisoners locked up on the train, was wandering around the station. He recognized their dog from the picture and his sister's handwriting. It was too late to help her, but at least they knew that she was still alive.

I don't know too much about the years in Belorussia. My grandmother never really wanted to talk about it, and I was only fourteen when she died. What I do know is that she met a young man, Joseph, who was in the Polish Armed Forces and he was also captured and became a prisoner of war. They fell in love and were married. In 1942, my mother was born. During her delivery, Elizabeth could hear air raids outside of the camp coming from the German occupation of Stalingrad. Around this time Joseph was taken away by Russian soldiers, and two weeks later Elizabeth received a letter informing her of his death. In that cruel world she lived in, she had found the love of her life and had it taken away so quickly. As if that wasn't enough suffering, she was taken to war camp hundreds of miles away from her home, deep in Siberia. This part of Russia is very large, made up of forests, with a very cold climate, where winters last up to six months and the temperatures go way below zero. Elizabeth had to work among other women prisoners cutting the trees. The conditions they lived in were unbearable. They slept in little houses dug in the cold ground, with no heat or water. They were given only a certain amount of food daily, which was generally a small piece of black bread, a cup of coffee, and raw beets or potatoes. Elizabeth thought that God had no mercy on her. She even thought about suicide, but did not want to leave her two-year-old daughter alone.

In the spring of 1945, there was a train going by very slowly next to the place where she was working. The workers on the train were Polish, and my grandmother recognized their language. After she found out what their destination was, she did not think for a moment. She always carried my mother wrapped in a blanket over her shoulder. She did not look back but ran and jumped on the train. It took her about six weeks to get back to Poland, hiding on various trains. All those six years her family hadn't heard a word from her. They thought she was dead. You could only imagine their happiness when she got back home. Her brother Anthony picked up my mother and gave her to his father saying, "Catch your little granddaughter," while Elizabeth was still waiting outside the door. They all said that my great grandfather would have had a heart attack if he had seen Elizabeth first. She weighed only eighty-seven pounds; she looked like a ghost. It took years for her to recover. My grandmother was afflicted with asthma and tuberculosis for the rest of her life, but she survived and she kept my mother alive. She remarried after a few years, but she never had more children.

This story is always very close to me. We still have the picture of the white dog with my grandmother's letter on the back. She was a brave and strong woman, and that helped her to survive. Her success as a mother and her courage through everything made her my hero.

## AFTER READING

### A Create a time line

1 Read about a technique that can help readers recreate the events of a story in the order they happened.

### Time Lines

A time line is a graphic representation of the chronological events of a story. Making a time line can help a reader understand what happened first, second, third, and so on. It is a tool often used in studying history, but it is equally useful when reading stories. This is especially true when the author goes back and forth in time – for example, from one time in the past to an earlier time in the past.

To make a time line, draw a straight line across your paper. Place the earliest event with its date at the left end of the line and the last date and event at the right end of the line. Then put all the events between the first and last at appropriate places on the line with their dates, if you know them. This will help you "see" the story in a linear way, in the order it actually happened.

Here is an example of a time line showing the events in the reading "Five New Words at a Time" on page 40.

| 1985 | | | | 1993 |
|---|---|---|---|---|
| family immigrated to U.S.A. | Mary in school; mother helps Mary study | Mary's English improves | mother passes postal exam | mother is 43, in college; Mary is junior in high school |

2 With a partner, make a time line for Elizabeth's life, marking on it the critical events and dates as reported in "My Family Hero."

3 As a class, make a time line of the story on the board.

## B Respond to the reading

1 In your log, write about the event(s) in Elizabeth's life that made the strongest impression on you and why.

2 Share what you wrote with your group.

## C Think about the topic

1 List the qualities in Elizabeth that show her to be a hero.

2 Share your list with your group.

3 With the class, make a list of qualities of heroes in general.

# HOW IT'S WRITTEN

### Think about historical references

1 The events of World War II are an essential part of this essay. The writer wrote about World War II events, places, and actions and reminded us that the war affected many people who were in a situation similar to the grandmother's. Look over the essay and see how the writer weaves history and the story together. With your group, find two sentences that combine both history and the story.

2 Talk with your group about whether the author told enough history to make the grandmother's story clear.

3 With the class, discuss the effect of the author's use of history and historical details.

4 Make a note in your log about what you might apply to your own writing.

# TOPICS FOR WRITING

### Choose one topic to write about

Whichever topic you choose, do some pre-writing activities such as freewriting, making a list, or clustering, before you begin writing.

❶ Write an essay about a hero – someone in your family or someone you know personally. The person may be just an ordinary person to the world, but extraordinary to you. Describe the person's experiences in detail and tell what makes the person a hero in your eyes.

❷ Write an essay describing the experience of someone who lived through a hardship, for example, a natural disaster, a serious health problem, or a war. Interview this person, who could be a neighbor, a friend, a family member, or a teacher. Before the interview, prepare some questions that will encourage the person to tell about his or her experience and give details. Here are some possible questions:

  ■ What was the event or hardship and how were you involved?

  ■ Is there one particular story or incident you want to talk about?

  ■ What effect did this event have on you?

❸ Choose a person from your culture who is considered a hero, for example, a historical or political figure, or a famous artist or athlete. Research the person's heroic actions. Write an essay describing the person's experiences in as much detail as necessary. Give enough historical information for the reader to understand the context.

# AFTER WRITING

## Share your writing

1 Exchange papers with a classmate. After reading your partner's paper, give feedback following the suggestions in the toolbox below.

> ### Sentence Starter Feedback
>
> One way to make comments and suggestions about a piece of writing is to complete some sentence starters. Here is a set of sentence beginnings:
>
> - *I especially liked . . .*
> - *I was most surprised by or interested in . . .*
> - *I would like more information on . . .*
> - *I was confused by one thing: . . .*

2 Save your classmate's comments about your writing.

. . . . . . . . . . . . . . . . . . . . . . . . . . . . . . . . . . . . . . . . . . . . . . . . . . . .

# BEFORE READING

## A Pool your knowledge

1 What do you know about Native Americans in North America today? With your group, share what you know, writing down words and phrases to represent your group's pooled knowledge. Use the following categories to help you:
  - social and political systems
  - cultural traditions
  - history
  - locations of major tribes

2 Share your findings with the class. If you find you have very little information, assign each group a category to research.

## B Write as you read

Look through the reading. Note the breaks marked by [pause]. When you get to a break, stop and write in your log about what you are thinking at that point. If you have questions the author hasn't answered, write them down and write what you think the answer will be.

# An Act of Courage
Ian Frazier

*From childhood, the author was fascinated by Native Americans of the West, calling them "the original free." He particularly admired the Oglala Sioux and their heroes: Red Cloud, a great chief and statesman; Crazy Horse, a legendary warrior who fought for his people; and Black Elk, a holy man. When he went to Pine Ridge, South Dakota, to write the book,* On The Rez, *from which this excerpt is taken, he learned of another Oglala hero, a fourteen-year old girl named SuAnne Big Crow. He calls her "one of the great Oglala of all time."*

SuAnne Marie Big Crow was born on March 15, 1974, at Pine Ridge Hospital – the brick building, now no longer a hospital, just uphill from the four-way intersection in town. Her mother, Leatrice Big Crow, known as Chick, was twenty-five years old.

SuAnne's birth came at a dark time on the reservation.[1] The ongoing battle between supporters and opponents of the tribal president Dick Wilson's government showed no signs of letup, with violence so pervasive and unpredictable that many people were afraid to leave their home. Wilson's people . . . were on one side, and supporters of the American Indian Movement on the other . . .[2]

In those days if you were on the Pine Ridge Reservation, you picked a side, and Chick Big Crow was for Dick Wilson all the way . . . Before SuAnne's sixteenth birthday she would have a lot to do with helping those divisions to heal.

As a Big Crow, SuAnne belonged to a *tiospaye* – the Lakota word for an extended family group – that's one of the largest on Pine Ridge. Chick says that her branch of the family descends from Big Crows of the Sans Arc Lakota, a tribe much smaller than the Oglala, who lived on the plains to the north and west.

[pause]

SuAnne grew up with her sisters in her mother's three-bedroom house in Pine Ridge. Even today people talk about what a strict mother Chick Big Crow was. Her daughters always had to be in the house or the yard by the time the streetlights came on. The only after-school activities she let them take part in were the structured and chaperoned kind; unsupervised wanderings and (later) cruising around in cars were out. In an interview when she was a teenager, SuAnne said that she and her sisters had to come up with their own fun, because their mother wouldn't let them socialize outside of school.

As strongly as Chick forbade certain activities, she encouraged the girls in sports. At one time or another they did them all – cross-country running and track, volleyball, cheerleading, softball, basketball. . . . SuAnne had big posters of Magic Johnson on her bedroom walls.

1 The Pine Ridge Reservation, where SuAnne was born, is described by Frazier as "one of America's poorest places." It is a piece of land in South Dakota assigned by the government to the Oglala Sioux.

2 In the mid-1970s, the supporters of the American Indian Movement (AIM), a politically active group who promoted a strong, separate Indian identity and independence, battled the supporters of tribal government, who worked with the U.S. government and tended toward assimilation.

She spent endless hours practicing basketball. When she was in the fifth grade, she heard somewhere that to improve your dribbling you should bounce a basketball a thousand times a day with each hand. She performed this daily exercise faithfully on the cement floor of the patio; her mother and sisters got tired of the sound. For variety she would shoot lay-ups against the gutter and the drainpipe, until they came loose from the house and had to be repaired.

By the time SuAnne was in eighth grade, she had grown to five feet five inches ("But she played six foot," [Coach] Zimiga says); she was long-limbed, well-muscled, and quick.

Some people who live in the cities and towns near reservations treat their Indian neighbors decently; some don't. In Denver and Minneapolis and Rapid City police have been known to harass Indian teenagers and rough up Indian drunks and needlessly stop and search Indian cars. . . . In a big discount store in a reservation-border town a white clerk observes a lot of Indians waiting at the checkout and remarks, "Oh, they're Indians – they're used to standing in line." Some people in South Dakota hate Indians, unapologetically, and will tell you why; in their voices you can hear a particular American meanness that is centuries old.

When [basketball] teams from Pine Ridge play non-Indian teams, the question of race is always there. When Pine Ridge is the visiting team, usually the hosts are courteous and the players and fans have a good time. But Pine Ridge coaches know that occasionally at away games their kids will be insulted, their fans will feel unwelcome, the host gym will be dense with hostility, and the referees will call fouls on Indian players every chance they get.

[pause]

One place where Pine Ridge teams used to get harassed regularly was the high school gymnasium in Lead, South Dakota.

In the fall of 1987 the Pine Ridge Lady Thorpes went to Lead to play a basketball game. SuAnne was a full member of the team by then. She was a freshman, fourteen years old. Getting ready in the locker room, the Pine Ridge girls could hear the din from some of the fans. They were yelling fake Indian war cries, a "woo-woo-woo" sound. The usual plan for the pre-game warm-up was for the visiting team to run onto the court in a line, take a lap or two around the floor, shoot some baskets, and then go to their bench at the courtside. After that, the home team would come out and do the same, and then the game would begin. Usually the Thorpes lined up for their entry more or less according to height, which meant that senior Doni De Cory, one of the tallest, went first. As the team waited in the hallway leading from the locker room, the heckling got louder. Doni De Cory looked out the door and told her teammates, "I can't handle this." SuAnne quickly offered to go first in her place. She was so eager that Doni became suspicious. "Don't embarrass us," Doni told her. SuAnne said, "I won't. I won't embarrass you." Doni gave her the ball, and SuAnne stood first in line.

She came running onto the court dribbling the basketball, with her teammates running behind. On the court the noise was deafening. SuAnne went right down the middle and suddenly stopped when she got to center court. Her teammates were taken by surprise, and some bumped into each other. Coach Zimiga, at the rear of the line, did not know why they had stopped. SuAnne turned to Doni De Cory and tossed her the ball. Then she stepped into the jump-ball circle at center court, facing the Lead fans. She unbuttoned her warm-up jacket, took it off, draped it over her shoulders, and began to do the Lakota shawl dance. SuAnne knew all the traditional dances (she had competed in many powwows as a little girl), and the dance she chose is a young woman's dance, graceful and modest and show-offy all at the same time. "I couldn't believe it – she was pow-wowin', like, 'Get down!'" Doni Ce Cory recalls. "And then she started to sing." SuAnne began to sing in Lakota, swaying back and forth in the jump-ball circle, doing the shawl dance, using her warm-up jacket for a shawl. The crowd went completely silent. "All the stuff the Lead fans were yelling – it was like she *reversed* it somehow," a teammate says. In the sudden quiet, all they could hear was her Lakota song. SuAnne dropped her jacket, took the ball from Doni De Cory, and ran a lap around the court dribbling expertly and fast. The audience began to cheer and applaud. She sprinted to the basket, went up in the air, and laid the ball through the hoop, with the fans cheering loudly now.

This was one of the coolest and bravest deeds I ever heard of.

[pause]

For the Oglala, what SuAnne did that day almost immediately took on the status of myth. People from Pine Ridge who witnessed it still describe it in terms of awe and disbelief. Amazement swept through the younger kids when they heard. "I was like, '*What* did she do?'" recalls her cousin Angie Big Crow, an eighth grader at the time. All over the reservation people told and retold the story of SuAnne at Lead. Any time the subject of SuAnne came up when I was talking to people on Pine Ridge, I would always ask if they had heard about what she did at Lead, and always the answer was a smile and a nod – "Yeah, I was there," or "Yeah, I heard about that." To the unnumbered big and small slights of local racism that the Oglala have known all their lives SuAnne's exploit made an emphatic reply.

There's a magic in what she did, along with the promise that public acts of courage are still alive out there somewhere. Mostly I would run the film of SuAnne again and again for my own braveheart song. I refer to her, as I do to the deeds of Crazy Horse, for proof that it's a public service to be brave.

### EPILOGUE

*SuAnne Marie Big Crow died in 1992 at the age of 18 in a car accident, but her memory lives on, and she is still regarded as a hero. In addition to performing this act of courage, SuAnne was opposed to drugs and alcohol and, even as a teenager, gave talks to school and youth groups and made a video urging her message against the use of these substances. People who knew her think she saved a lot of kids' lives.*

# AFTER READING

## A  Respond to the reading

1 Share your written responses and questions with a partner.

2 Together, write down some questions you still have about the story.

3 With your group, discuss at least one question posed by each pair.

4 By yourself, write your reactions to the story.

## B  Look for more information

1 With your group, look over the story for any words and phrases to add to information about Native Americans developed in **Pool your knowledge** on page 49.

2 Share your findings with the class.

## C  Write a summary of the reading

1 Read about what to include when writing a summary.

### Writing a Summary

A summary is a short version of a story, essay, or article. When you summarize a story, retell only the most important events in the order they happened. When you summarize an essay or an article, tell the writer's main points. It helps to make a list of the events or main points before you start writing. When writing the summary, use your own words, not the words of the writer. Do not include unimportant details. Do not add your own opinions or interpretations. Only tell what happened or what the important points are.

2 Write a summary of "An Act of Courage." Include SuAnne's story and Frazier's thoughts about it.

3 Exchange summaries with a classmate. Read each other's summaries and see how they are similar and different.

# HOW IT'S WRITTEN

### Appreciate action words

1 This piece describes a lot of action – SuAnne and her team practicing and playing basketball and SuAnne dancing. To convey action, the writer uses vivid verbs and nouns. With your partner, look over one of the paragraphs about the game or the dance and underline all the nouns or verbs and verb phrases that show action.

2 While your partner reads a sentence from the paragraph, close your eyes and let an image of the action come to your mind.

3 Talk with the class about the images that came to you, the words that gave you the clearest images, and the value of using such words in writing.

4 In your log, write down one thing you want to remember about conveying actions in words.

## TOPICS FOR WRITING

**Choose one topic to write about**

1 The author says that SuAnne's dance was "one of the coolest and bravest deeds" he'd ever heard of. He thinks "it's a public service to be brave." Do you agree? How did you feel about SuAnne's dance? Write an essay that describes SuAnne's act of courage and your thoughts, feelings, and reactions.

2 Do some research in the library or on the Internet and prepare a written report on one of the following: a Native American tribe, or a historical character mentioned in the story, or how Native Americans, like SuAnne, live today.

3 Write a true story of an act of courage. It may be about someone you know personally or someone you know about and admire, perhaps from your culture or your family. Tell about the person's background, what the person did, and how people remember the person.

## AFTER WRITING

**Share your writing**

1 Join three or four other people who wrote on the same topic you did. Pass your papers around the group until you have read everyone's writing.

2 After you read each piece, write down something you want to remember. Save your notes.

3 With the group, discuss what each person said. Notice similarities and differences.

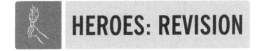 **HEROES: REVISION**

## A Choose one piece of writing

1 Reread the pieces you wrote for the **Topics for Writing** sections of HEROES. Also read any notes you made about your writings or comments from classmates.

2 Choose one piece to revise, and explain to your partner why you have chosen this piece.

## B Revise your writing

1 Make notes on what to add, for example, specific details or vivid verbs and nouns.

2 Rewrite parts that need to be clearer.

3 If you haven't chosen a title, do so now.

4 Does the title change the focus of the piece? If so, make any necessary changes.

5 Rewrite and revise.

> ### Writer's Tip
>
> *I still read everything aloud. Good writing requires good rhythms and good words. You cannot know whether the rhythms and the words are good unless you read them aloud.*
>
> **Richard Marius**

## C Read your writing aloud

1 Read about a technique that may help you judge the quality of your writing.

> ### Reading Aloud
>
> Writers often read their writing aloud in order to hear how it sounds. Sometimes the ear is a better judge of writing than the eye. As you read to yourself, listen to your sentences. Do they flow smoothly? Do they say exactly what you want to say? Are there places where a different word would express your idea more clearly? Do the ideas run smoothly from sentence to sentence, from idea to idea, and from section to section? Reading your writing aloud is a good technique to use both while you're writing and while you're rereading what you have written.

2 Read your writing aloud to find out what could be improved.

3 Change what you think should be changed to make the writing smoother and clearer.

> ### Writer's Tip
>
> *Always write (and read) with the ear, not the eye. You should hear every sentence you write as if it was being read or spoken aloud.*
>
> **Archibald MacLeish**

## D Share your writing

1 Form a writing circle and read your papers to each other. (See the toolbox *Writing Circle* on page 20.)

2 Choose one piece to read to the class.

## Identity

## BEFORE READING

### Make a personal connection

1 The title of this section of the unit is IDENTITY. If someone said to you, "Tell me about yourself," how would you identify yourself? What would you say? Tell your partner.

2 Telling someone about your identity may not be the same as talking about "your true self" – what you are really like and how you think and feel. Make a list of the characteristics of your true self in your log.

3 What connections or conflicts do you see between your true self and your identity? Freewrite for a few minutes about this question.

 **Believing in the True Self**
Gloria Steinem

*Gloria Steinem has been a campaigner for women's rights since the 1960s. In 1972, she founded* Ms., *a magazine focused on women's issues. In her book,* Revolution from Within: A Book of Self-Esteem, *she discusses how and why we develop, or don't develop, self-esteem.* "Believing in the True Self" *is an excerpt from her book.*

> *If you bring forth what is within you, what you bring forth will save you. If you do not bring forth what is within you, what you do not bring forth will destroy you.*

> *Jesus*, The Gnostic Gospels [1]

Why does one baby reach for certain toys, while another doesn't? Why does one respond more to touch and another to sound? Or one thrive on company and another on calm? No one knows – but we do know that frequent frustration of these preferences will make an infant irritable and angry, then uncertain, passive, and finally unlikely to initiate anything at all.

---

1 The Gnostic Gospels were written about two centuries after the death of Jesus, rediscovered only in 1945, and not fully translated until the 1970s. They are the record of a Jesus who represented himself as a teacher, not the son of God, and taught that God is within each of us. For background and major quotations, see Elaine Pagels, *The Gnostic Gospels*, New York: Random House, 1979; Vintage, 1981.

Why does one child choose to color with paints while another builds with blocks? Why does one create adventures in the imagination while another seeks them in the outside world? No one knows – but we do know that children who are encouraged to follow their own interests actually learn more, internalize and retain that learning better, become more creative, and have healthier and more durable self-esteem than those who are motivated by reward, punishment, or competition with other children.

Why do some adults absorb information better by hearing it than seeing it? Why does one sibling remember stories and ideas while another remembers names and numbers? Why are some people gifted at languages, and still others drawn to anything mechanical? Why do some have perfect pitch and others have "green thumbs"? Why are some of us alert in the morning and others hopeless until noon; some gregarious and others shy; some sexually attracted to the same gender, some to the opposite gender, and some to the individual regardless of gender? No one knows. But we do know that, like children, adults whose inner-most feelings and preferences are ignored, ridiculed, punished, or repressed come to believe that there is something profoundly, innately "wrong" with them. And conversely, those who are able to honor these inner promptings know what it is to feel at home with themselves.

## AFTER READING

### A Understand the reading

1 With a partner, find one sentence you both had trouble understanding. Restate it in your own words.

2 Now, with the same partner, write a one-sentence summary that captures the author's main point.

3 Share your one-sentence summary with the class.

### B Find deeper meanings

1 Look at the passage and number the "Why" questions that the author poses. Choose one of the questions and freewrite about it in your log for a few minutes.

2 With your partner, discuss what you wrote. Then look at how Steinem answered the question. Is her answer similar to or different from yours?

## HOW IT'S WRITTEN

### Appreciate the structure

1 Quickly reread "Believing in the True Self." Notice that the sentences are arranged the same way in each paragraph. This is called *parallel structure*. Describe the structure to your group.

2 With the class, discuss the effect of using parallel structure.

## TOPICS FOR WRITING

**Choose one topic to write about**

1. Think of a family member or close friend who is different from you in one or more of the ways mentioned by Steinem. Write about the difference(s) and include an incident that shows the difference(s) clearly.

2. Interview an older person who has known you all your life. Find out what you were like as a child. Write an essay telling what the person said and what you learned about yourself.

3. Reread the quotation from the Gnostic Gospels at the beginning of this reading. Write an essay explaining what the quotation means to you. Use personal examples to illustrate its meaning.

## AFTER WRITING

**Share your writing**

1 Exchange your paper with two other people. Read each paper several times. Think about what each person is saying or trying to say. If you wish, mark some of the key sentences. Then write a three- or four-sentence summary of what you think each person is saying.

2 Read your readers' summaries of your own paper. Think about how you could make your ideas clearer.

3 Write your thoughts or insights in your log.

. . . . . . . . . . . . . . . . . . . . . . . . . . . . . . . . . . . . . . . . . . . . . . . . . . . . . . . .

## BEFORE READING

**Think about the topic**

1 Read the title and introductory information. Freewrite for five minutes about what might make someone decide to become a writer.

2 Share one idea with a partner.

# Becoming a Writer
### Russell Baker

*Growing Up, Russell Baker's autobiographical account of his youth, includes this story of his early decision to become a writer.*

The notion of becoming a writer had flickered off and on in my head . . . but it wasn't until my third year in high school that the possibility took hold. Until then I'd been bored by everything associated with English courses. I found English grammar dull and baffling. I hated the assignments to turn out "compositions," and went at them like heavy labor, turning out leaden, lackluster paragraphs that were agonies for teachers to read and for me to write. The classics thrust on me to read seemed as deadening as chloroform.

When our class was assigned to Mr. Fleagle for third-year English, I anticipated another grim year in that dreariest of subjects. Mr. Fleagle was notorious among City students for dullness and inability to inspire. He was said to be stuffy, dull, and hopelessly out of date. To me he looked to be sixty or seventy and prim to a fault. He wore primly severe eyeglasses, his wavy hair was primly cut and primly combed. He wore prim vested suits with neckties blocked primly against the collar buttons of his primly starched white shirts. He had a primly pointed jaw, a primly straight nose, and prim manner of speaking that was so correct, so gentlemanly, that he seemed a comic antique.

I anticipated a listless, unfruitful year with Mr. Fleagle and for a long time was not disappointed. We read *Macbeth*. Mr. Fleagle loved *Macbeth* and wanted us to love it too, but he lacked the gift of infecting others with his own passion. He tried to convey the murderous ferocity of Lady Macbeth one day by reading aloud the passage that concludes

> . . . I have given suck, and know
> How tender 'tis to love the babe that milks me.
> I would, while it was smiling in my face,
> Have plucked my nipple from his boneless gums. . . .

The idea of prim Mr. Fleagle plucking his nipple from boneless gums was too much for the class. We burst into gasps of irrepressible snickering. Mr. Fleagle stopped.

"There is nothing funny, boys, about giving suck to a babe. It is the – the very essence of motherhood, don't you see."

He constantly sprinkled his sentences with "don't you see." It wasn't a question but an exclamation of mild surprise at our ignorance. "Your pronoun needs an antecedent, don't you see," he would say, very primly. "The purpose of the Porter's scene, boys, is to provide comic relief from the horror, don't you see."

Late in the year we tackled the informal essay. "The essay, don't you see, is the . . . " My mind went numb. Of all forms of writing, none seemed as boring as the essay. Naturally we would have to write informal essays. Mr. Fleagle distributed a homework sheet offering us a choice of topics. None was quite so simpleminded as "What I Did on My Summer Vacation," but most seemed to be almost as dull. I took the list home and dawdled until the night before the essay was due. Sprawled on the sofa, I finally faced up to the grim task, took the list out of my notebook, and scanned it. The topic on which my eye stopped was "The Art of Eating Spaghetti."

This title produced an extraordinary sequence of mental images. Surging up to the depths of memory came a vivid recollection of a night in Belleville when all of us were seated around the supper table – Uncle Allen, my mother, Uncle Charlie, Doris, Uncle Hal – and Aunt Pat served spaghetti for supper. Spaghetti was an exotic treat in those days. Neither Doris nor I had ever eaten spaghetti, and none of the adults had enough experience to be good at it. All the good humor of Uncle Allen's house reawoke in my mind as I recalled the laughing arguments we had that night about the socially respectable method for moving spaghetti from plate to mouth.

Suddenly I wanted to write about that, about the warmth and good feeling of it, but I wanted to put it down simply for my own joy, not for Mr. Fleagle. It was a moment I wanted to recapture and hold for myself. I wanted to relive the pleasure of an evening at New Street. To write it as I wanted, however, would violate all the rules of formal composition I'd learned in school, and Mr. Fleagle would surely give it a failing grade. Never mind. I would write something else for Mr. Fleagle after I had written this thing for myself.

When I finished it, the night was half gone and there was no time left to compose a proper, respectable essay for Mr. Fleagle. There was no choice the next morning but to turn in my private reminiscence of Belleville. Two days passed before Mr. Fleagle returned the graded papers, and he returned everyone's but mine. I was bracing myself for a command to report to Mr. Fleagle immediately after school for discipline when I saw him lift my paper from his desk and rap for the class's attention.

"Now, boys," he said, "I want to read you an essay. This is titled 'The Art of Eating Spaghetti.'"

And he started to read. My words! He was reading my words, out loud to the entire class. What's more, the entire class was listening. Listening attentively. Then someone laughed, then the entire class was laughing, and not in contempt and ridicule, but with openhearted enjoyment. Even Mr. Fleagle stopped two or three times to repress a small prim smile.

I did my best to avoid showing pleasure, but what I was feeling was pure ecstasy at this startling demonstration that my words had the power to make people laugh. In the eleventh grade, at the eleventh hour as it were, I had discovered a calling. It was the happiest moment of my entire school career. When Mr. Fleagle finished he put the final seal on my happiness by saying, "Now that, boys, is an essay, don't you see. It's – don't you see – it's of the very essence of the essay, don't you see. Congratulations, Mr. Baker."

For the first time, light shone on a possibility. It wasn't a very heartening possibility, to be sure. Writing couldn't lead to a job after high school, and it was hardly honest work, but Mr. Fleagle had opened a door for me. After that I ranked Mr. Fleagle among the finest teachers in the school.

## AFTER READING

### A Respond to the reading

1 Write a response to "Becoming a Writer" by making a double entry response. (See the toolbox *Double Entry Response* on page 26.) Reread the paper as necessary.

2 Share one of your ideas with your group.

### B Expand your vocabulary

1 With a partner, circle five words in the reading that are new to you and that you would like to learn to use. Define each word, using a dictionary if necessary.

2 Teach your words to your group.

## HOW IT'S WRITTEN

### Notice the use of repetition

1 Reread the text. Underline the repeated words: *prim*, *primly*, and *don't you see* each time Baker uses them.

2 Why do you think he repeats these words so many times? What's the effect of the repetition? Discuss this with your group.

3 In your log, make a note of something from this activity that could help you with your own writing.

## TOPICS FOR WRITING

1 Baker describes how he realized what he wanted to do in life: "In the eleventh grade, at the eleventh hour as it were, I had discovered a calling." Write about a moment in your life and the events leading up to it in which you discovered your calling and suddenly knew what you wanted to do in life.

2 Baker describes the moment when Mr. Fleagle read his essay aloud in class as "the happiest moment of my entire school career." Write a short essay about the happiest moment in your school career. Tell the story step-by-step the way Baker did.

3 We have all had people who have influenced us in some way to make a choice about our future. Write an essay in which you tell about how someone has influenced you. Include in your essay a description of this person that helps readers to visualize him or her.

# AFTER WRITING

## Share your writing

1 Give your essay to a classmate to read.

2 Use the guidelines suggested in the toolbox *Sentence Starter Feedback* on page 49 to write comments about your partner's paper.

....................................................................

# BEFORE READING

## A Think about the topic

1 Make a list of features or characteristics of the ideal "beautiful woman" and "handsome man."

2 With your group, discuss differences and similarities in your lists.

## B Think about poetry

1 Read about some ways to appreciate poetry – to hear the sounds and melodies of the words and to see the images that the poet has created.

### Ways To Read Poetry

- Read the poem aloud to yourself.

- Listen to someone else read the poem.

- Read and listen to the poem several times.

- Read one line from the poem, then stop. Close your eyes and let an image develop in your mind to match the words. Then continue, line by line.

2 With your group, discuss the place of poetry in your lives. Do you ever read it? Do you write poetry? Is it popular in your culture?

# homage to my hips
### Lucille Clifton

*Lucille Clifton, an African-American poet, enjoys writing poems to celebrate that she is not what American culture tells her she should be: She is not young, not thin, not white.*

these hips are big hips
they need space to
move around in.
they don't fit into little
petty places. these hips
are free hips.
they don't like to be held back.
these hips have never been enslaved.
they go where they want to go
they do what they want to do.
these hips are mighty hips.
these hips are magic hips.
i have known them
to put a spell on a man and
spin him like a top!

## AFTER READING

### A  Read and respond

1 Listen to your teacher read the poem aloud.

2 With a partner, read the poem aloud to each other.

3 Read it again to yourself and stop briefly at each period to let an image form in your mind. Describe to your partner some of the images you see.

4 Choose one image and freewrite about it for a few minutes.

### B  Find deeper meanings

1 Is this poem really about hips? With a partner, write down one line of Clifton's poem and discuss what else this poem could be about.

2 Summarize your discussion for the class.

## HOW IT'S WRITTEN

### Analyze the use of small letters

1 Note the use of small letters throughout the poem. Go through the poem and put a capital letter wherever you might normally expect to see one.

2 Compare what you did with your group.

3 With the class, discuss why Clifton might have chosen to write this poem completely in small letters. What effect does this "breaking the rules" have on readers?

## TOPICS FOR WRITING

Choose one topic to write about

❶ Clifton says she is not what her culture says she should be, she's "not young, not thin, not white." Write about how you are different from what your culture says you should be.

❷ Think of a part of your own body that you are especially proud of or fond of. Write a poem about it, using Clifton's poem as a model.

❸ Many people today, especially teenagers, worry about their physical appearance. They accept mass media's notion of what it means to be beautiful. Do you judge a person to be beautiful based on his or her physical appearance? Write an essay explaining your point of view.

## AFTER WRITING

### Share your writing

1 Give your paper to another person in your group for feedback. If possible, find someone from a different culture and/or gender to read it. Ask the person to respond to what you wrote from the perspective of his or her culture and/or gender.

2 Write in your log about what you learned from your reader's feedback. Think about the changes you might want to make in your writing.

• • • • • • • • • • • • • • • • • • • • • • • • • • • • • • • • • • • • • • • • • • • • • •

## BEFORE READING

**A Understand key vocabulary**

1 With a partner, define two or three of the words below. Each pair in your group should choose different words.

| | | | |
|---|---|---|---|
| puberty | adolescence | identity crisis | peer |
| teenager | indecision | self-doubt | brooding |
| self-searching | conformity | | |

2 Explain your words to your group.

3 If there are still words that your group can't define, ask another group for help.

## B Make predictions

1 Read the title and the biographical information about the authors.

2 With a partner, discuss what you think the excerpt is going to be about. In your log write two or three predictions you made together.

 # The Search for Identity
Laurence Steinberg & Ann Levine

*In the book from which this reading is taken,* You and Your Adolescent: A Parents' Guide for Ages 10–20, *the authors give advice on how to understand teenage children. Steinberg is a professor of psychology at Temple University. Levine is an expert in child development.*

Identity becomes a central concern in middle adolescence, for a variety of overlapping reasons. Puberty makes adolescents acutely aware of change. Looking in the mirror, the adolescent knows he is no longer the child he used to be – but not what sort of adult he will become. Sexual awakening invites a new type of intimate relationship with members of the opposite sex, unlike any the adolescent has known before. Preparing for adulthood is no longer a game. Decisions about education that will have long-term consequences (especially, whether to go to college and, if so, where) will have to be made in the near future. The array of occupations and lifestyles available to adults in our society is vast. How can a teenager choose? Finally, teenagers have the intellectual capacity to reflect on themselves and their future. They can imagine being someone other than who they are now and living a life that is quite different from that of their parents or the one their parents imagine for them. They are also aware that their parents and peers see them in different lights; that they behave differently in different situations; and that how they appear to others doesn't always reflect how they feel inside.

The challenge for adolescents is to assemble these different pieces of the self into a working whole that serves both the self and society. They must connect the skills and talents they developed in childhood to realistic adult goals; reconcile their private images of themselves with what other people see in them and expect from them. They need to feel unique and special, on the one hand, and to belong or fit in, on the other.

### TRYING ON IDENTITIES

For most adolescents, the development of identity is a gradual, cumulative, and relatively peaceful process that begins in early adolescence and continues into young adulthood. Most adolescents are able to "find themselves" without losing the values and standards they acquired in childhood; to "get it together" without getting into trouble. Only a minority of adolescents experience a full-blown identity crisis. Nevertheless, many go through spells of brooding, indecision, and self-doubt. Although sometimes painful, this self-searching is normal, healthy, and desirable.

In early adolescence the search for identity often leads to over-identification with peers, clannishness, and conformity. The youth culture provides a ready-made identity that sets the new adolescent apart from his former identity as a child and from his identification with his parents. For a time, the adolescent may become a stereotypical teenager.

Middle adolescence is a time for distinguishing oneself from the crowd. The quest for identity now takes the form of exploration and experimentation. The teenager tries on a variety of different political attitudes, religious persuasions, occupational commitments, and romantic involvements. At the time, these tentative identities have an all-or-nothing, do-or-die quality. . . .

In late adolescence and young adulthood the search becomes more introspective ("Who am I really?" "What do I believe?" "What do I want in life?") and also more pragmatic ("How can I achieve my goals?" "Where am I willing to compromise?"). Typically this is a period of "de-illusionment" (though not necessarily disillusionment). The young person must give up the childlike faith that he can be or do anything he wants for a more realistic assessment of his capabilities and opportunities. He must also face the fact that settling on one direction means abandoning others, at least temporarily.

## AFTER READING

### A Check your predictions

1 How accurate were your predictions? Discuss this with your partner.

2 Share one accurate prediction with the class.

### B Reread and respond

1 Reread the selection. As you read, stop at least three times to make a double entry response in your reading log. (See the toolbox *Double Entry Response* on page 26.)

2 Share your double entry with your group and explain what you wrote.

### C Explain what you read

1 With your group, take one paragraph in the section "Trying on Identities." Each group in the class should take a different paragraph.

2 Reread the paragraph and list the ideas in that paragraph.

3 Form a new group with one member from each of the other groups. In this new group, explain the ideas in the paragraph you studied.

# HOW IT'S WRITTEN

### Notice the use of pronouns

1 Reread the first paragraph and circle the personal pronouns. Draw an arrow to the word each pronoun refers to and compare your answers with a partner.

2 Read the rest of the text and discuss the following questions with the class:
   ① In places where the author used "he," could "she" have been used? What effect would that have had?
   ② How does the author sometimes avoid using gender-specific pronouns when referring to people who could be either male or female?
   ③ Should a writer always try to avoid using gender-specific pronouns for people who could be either male or female? Think of as many different ways as you can for a writer to do this.

3 Reflect on what you can apply from this discussion in your own writing and write a note in your log.

## Nonsexist Use of Language

Because English does not have a third person singular pronoun that can refer to either sex, it may be difficult to write about a nonspecific, generalized person without sounding sexist. However, there are several ways to do so:

- Make the sentence plural.
  *Give each student* his *assignment as soon as* he *is ready.*
  *Give students* their *assignments as soon as* they *are ready.*

- Use "he or she" instead of only "he" or only "she."
  *When a student takes an exam,* he *should always . . .*
  *When a student takes an exam,* he or she *should always . . .*

- See if you can drop unnecessary gender pronouns.
  *The average student likes to work with* his *peers.*
  *The average student likes to work with peers.*

## TOPICS FOR WRITING

### Choose one topic to write about

1. The reading states that "decisions about education that will have long-term consequences (especially, whether to go to college and, if so, where) will have to be made in the near future." Who makes these decisions in your culture? Who do you think should make them? Write an essay in which you express your opinion.

2. Find one statement in the reading – a generalization about teenagers – that interests you. Begin your essay with the statement and tell in your own words what it means. Then explore and explain your thoughts, feelings, and opinions.

3. Choose one of the three periods of adolescence mentioned (early, middle, and late) and describe that time in your life. If one or more of the vocabulary terms in the reading describe you, use them in your essay.

## AFTER WRITING

### Share your writing

1 Exchange papers with a partner. Read your partner's paper and give feedback on the writing using the suggestions in the toolbox *Reader's Response Feedback* on page 15.

2 Save your partner's comments.

. . . . . . . . . . . . . . . . . . . . . . . . . . . . . . . . . . . . . . . . . . . . . . . . . . . . . . . . . . . . . . . .

## BEFORE READING

### A Think about the topic

1 With the class, make a cluster of words and phrases you associate with the phrase "teenage smoking." (See the toolbox *Clustering* on page 12.)

2 Do any of the words and phrases in the cluster suggest what encourages teens to smoke or what might discourage them from smoking? Discuss this.

### B Write as you read

Look through the reading. Note the breaks marked by [pause]. When you get to a break, stop reading and write in your log about what you are thinking.

# Smoking
### Judith Rich Harris

*Judith Rich Harris is the author of a book called* The Nurture Assumption. *This excerpt about teens and smoking appears in a chapter titled "Growing Up."*

The environment influences a teenager to smoke or not to smoke in only one way: she is more likely to smoke if her peers do. The genes exert their influence in two ways. First, via their effects on personality: an impulsive sensation seeker is more likely to end up in a peer group that favors smoking. Second, by making it more or less likely that she will become addicted to nicotine.

Exposure to peers who smoke is what determines whether or not a teenager will experiment with tobacco. Her genes determine whether or not she will get hooked.

Since we can't do anything about their genes, the only way to keep them from getting hooked is to keep them from experimenting with tobacco. Anyone who thinks this can be accomplished by putting "Danger! Poison!" on the cigarette pack needs to sign up for clue renewal. . . .

[pause]

Telling teenagers about the health risks of smoking – It will make you wrinkled! It will make you impotent! It will make you dead! – is useless. This is adult propaganda; these are adult arguments. It is *because* adults don't approve of smoking – *because* there is something dangerous and disreputable about it – that teenagers want to do it.

Telling them that smoking is yucky doesn't work either, as I learned to my displeasure. If adults think something is yucky, that makes it all the more appealing to an anti-adult.

Nor does recruiting a person their own age to lecture them about it. The lecturer is seen as a turncoat – a nerd, a goody-goody. A patsy of the adults.

Even making it harder for teenagers to get cigarettes doesn't do the job. When some towns in Massachusetts cracked down on stores that sold cigarettes to minors, the teenagers went right on smoking. The fact that it was more difficult to get cigarettes just made it more of a challenge.

[pause]

Adults have limited power over adolescents. Teenagers create their own cultures, which vary by peer group, and we can neither guess nor determine which aspects of the adult culture they will keep and which they will chuck, or what new things they will think up on their own.

But our power isn't zero. Adults do control a major source of input to the cultures: the media. Media depictions of smokers as rebels and risk-takers – of smoking as a way of saying "I don't care" – make cigarettes attractive to teens. I see no way around this problem unless the makers of movies and TV shows voluntarily decide to stop filming actors (doesn't matter whether they're the heroes or the villains) using tobacco.

Drastically raising the price of a pack of cigarettes might also help. At least it would cut down on the number who become addicted.

Anti-smoking ads? Very tricky. The best bet would be an ad campaign that gets across the idea that the promotion of smoking is a plot against teenagers by adults – by the fat cats of the tobacco industry. Show a covey of sleazy tobacco executives cackling gleefully each time a teenager buys a pack of cigarettes. Show them dreaming up ads designed to sell their products to the gullible teen – ads depicting smoking as cool and smokers as sexy. Show smoking as something *they* want us to do, not something *we* want to do.

## AFTER READING

### A Share your responses

1 Exchange logs with a partner and read each other's written thoughts.

2 Respond orally to each other's responses.

### B Understand the reading

1 Write two or three questions about the reading you would like to have answered.

2 With your group, try to answer everyone's questions.

3 If there are any you can't answer, ask the class for help.

### C Find the main ideas

1 There are three sections in the reading. With a partner choose one sentence or write a sentence that gives the central idea or main point of each section. (See the toolbox *Main Idea* on page 35.)

2 Share your sentences with the class.

## HOW IT'S WRITTEN

### A Notice the use of pronouns

1 Reread the first two paragraphs. Circle the pronouns. Draw an arrow to the word each pronoun refers to.

2 Read through the rest of the text and see if the author ever uses "he."

3 With the class, compare and discuss the use of pronouns in "Smoking" and "The Search for Identity" (see page 65).

## B Think about the writing style

1 Look through the reading and underline any words and phrases that sound like spoken English or *teen talk* (for example, "yucky").

2 With your group, try to figure out the meanings of these words and phrases.

## TOPICS FOR WRITING

### Choose a topic to write about

Whichever topic you choose, use one of these pre-writing techniques to gather ideas: freewriting (see the toolbox *Freewriting* on page 2), clustering (see the toolbox *Clustering* on page 12), or making a list (see the toolbox *Brainstorming a List* on page 7).

❶ Write an essay giving your reaction to "Smoking." Begin by restating the important points of the reading. Then explain your reaction.

❷ Do you know anyone who has tried to break a bad habit or an addiction? Was the person successful? Write an essay describing the person's experience and the outcome. What lesson(s) can you draw from this person's experience?

❸ In "Smoking," Harris defines a teen problem, explains what causes it, says what solutions have been tried but haven't worked, then offers a solution she believes will work. Using her piece as a model, write an essay about a teen problem that concerns you, for example, drinking, truancy, lack of interest in school, disobeying parents, and so on.

## AFTER WRITING

### Share your writing

1 Get together with three or four others who wrote on the same topic you did.

2 Each person should read his or her paper aloud to the group. As you hear your classmates' essays, take notes on ideas that interest you or that trigger ideas for your own essay.

# IDENTITY: REVISION

**A  Choose one piece of writing**

1  Reread the pieces you wrote for the
   **Topics for Writing** sections of IDENTITY.

2  Choose two that you like and may want to revise.

3  Show your choices to a partner and decide
   which one would be best to revise.

**B  Use the ARMS method to revise**

1  Read about four steps that experienced writers
   carry out when they revise. The first four letters
   of each step spell ARMS, but this acronym has
   no special meaning. It is just a convenient way
   to remember the steps.

> ## Writer's Tip
>
> *I enjoy cutting, reordering,
> developing, shaping, polishing my
> drafts. Never have I failed to make
> a text better by my revising and
> editing. . . . Nonwriters think of
> revision as a matter of tinkering,
> touching up, making presentable,
> but writers know it is central to
> the act of discovering.*
>
> **Donald Murray**

## ARMS

Experienced writers know that there is much more to revising than simply
recopying their writing or just checking spelling and punctuation. For
revision is just that: *re-vision* or *re-seeing*. Here are four steps that will help
you to revise or re-see your own writing. When you carry out these steps,
it may be useful to use a different colored pen or pencil to help you see
your changes.

■ **Add:** Add to what you have written. You may add words, phrases,
  sentences, or paragraphs. You may add them at the beginning, in the
  middle, or at the end, wherever you find an appropriate place.

■ **Remove:** Cross out extra words, phrases, or sentences. Look for words
  that don't carry much meaning, places where you have said the same
  thing twice, and things that don't contribute directly to your point.

■ **Move:** This step is one of the most powerful steps of revision. Using
  arrows or other graphics, show what you want to move and where you
  want to put it. You might move whole sentences or paragraphs from one
  place to a new place. For instance, you might switch the order of the
  middle paragraphs or move your conclusion to the beginning of your
  writing.

■ **Substitute:** Substitute a word, a phrase, or a sentence for another. Look
  for synonyms to replace words you repeated or to be more precise. Look
  for colorful words to replace common words. Look for colloquial ways of
  saying things – words that sound like someone is speaking – to replace
  words or phrases that sound awkward.

2 Follow the four steps of ARMS to make changes to your piece of writing. You may incorporate any feedback you've gotten on this piece from classmates or your teacher.

3 When you finish marking up your draft, start rewriting.

4 If you don't yet have a title, choose one. (See the toolbox *Titles* on page 38.)

5 Repeat the steps of ARMS until you are satisfied with your essay. Take time to read each draft aloud to help you decide on changes. (See the toolbox *Reading Aloud* on page 55.)

## C  Share your writing

1 Attach a blank sheet of paper to your piece of writing.

2 Have three classmates read your writing and write one comment each on the blank sheet of paper. The comment can be an observation (something he or she notices), a response (his or her feelings or thoughts), a compliment (something he or she likes about the writing), or a question.

### Writer's Tip

*Writing well involves two gifts – the art of adding and the art of taking away. Of the two, the first is more important, since without it the second could not exist.*

**John Updike**

# UNIT 2
# New Vistas and Ventures

Opening New Doors

Dating and Marriage

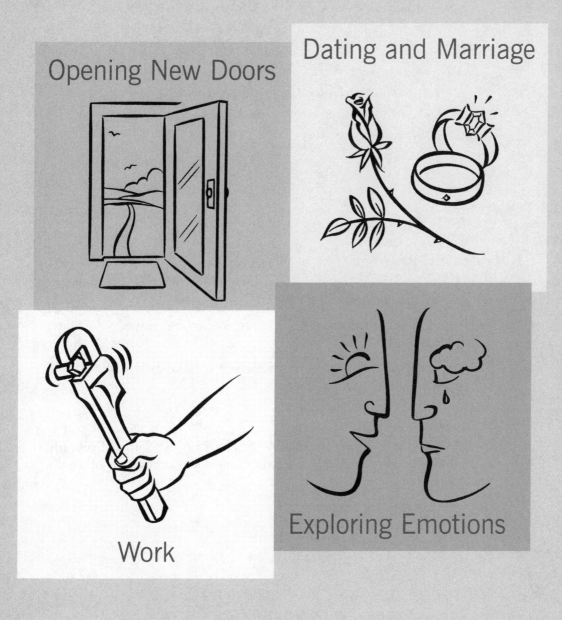

Work

Exploring Emotions

## UNIT 2

# New Vistas and Ventures

> When one door closes, another opens . . . into another room,
> another space, other happenings. There are many doors to
> open and close in our lives. Some doors we leave ajar, where
> we hope and plan to return. Some doors are slammed shut
> decisively – "No more of that!" Some are closed regretfully,
> softly – "It was good, but it is over." Departures entail
> arrivals somewhere else. Closing a door, leaving it behind,
> means opening onto new vistas and ventures, new
> possibilities, new incentives.
>
> *Helen Nearing*

## A Make connections

1 Read the title of this unit and the quote aloud with a partner. Talk about any words you don't understand.

2 Freewrite for five minutes in your log about connections between the title and the quote.

3 Share your writing with your group. Talk about similarities and differences in the connections that you each found.

## B Make a personal connection

1 Look back at the map of your life from the activity **Make a map of your life** in Unit One on page 3. Find a point where one door closed and another one opened.

2 Talk about this with a partner.

## C Respond to quotes

1 Below are some quotations about change. Choose one quotation and think about how it connects to what Nearing said or to your own life. Then freewrite about the quotation for five minutes in your log.

① "One can learn nothing except by going from the known to the unknown." (Claude Bernard)

② "True life is lived when tiny changes occur." (Leo Tolstoy)

③ "Taking a new step, uttering a new word is what people fear most." (Fyodor Dostoyevsky)

④ "In the middle of difficulty lies opportunity." (Albert Einstein)

2 After freewriting, write a kernel sentence. (See the toolbox *Kernel Sentences* on page 3.)

3 Share your kernel sentence with the class.

## D Preview Unit 2

1 Read the section headings for the readings in this unit. Look for connections between the title of this unit, the section headings, and your freewriting.

2 Discuss the connections with your group.

## Opening New Doors

## BEFORE READING

### Gather ideas about the topic

1 Read the title and the information about the author.

2 With the class, make a cluster of words and phrases you associate with the first day at a new school. (See the toolbox *Clustering* on page 12.)

# The First Day

Edward P. Jones

*Edward P. Jones grew up in Washington, D.C. His short story, "The First Day,"*
*tells about a little girl's experience on her first day of school.*

On an otherwise unremarkable September morning, long before I learned to be ashamed of my mother, she takes my hand and we set off down New Jersey Avenue to begin my very first day of school. I am wearing a checker-like blue-and-green cotton dress, and scattered about these colors are bits of yellow and white and brown. My mother has uncharacteristically spent nearly an hour on my hair that morning, plaiting and replaiting so that now my scalp tingles.

Walker-Jones is a larger, newer school and I immediately like it because of that. But it is not across the street from my mother's church, her rock, one of her connections to God, and I sense her doubts as she absently rubs her thumb over the back of her hand. We find our way to the crowded auditorium where gray metal chairs are set up in the middle of the room. Along the wall to the left are tables and other chairs. Every chair seems occupied by a child or adult. Somewhere in the room a child is crying, a cry that rises above the buzz-talk of so many people. Strewn about the floor are dozens and dozens of pieces of white paper, and people are walking over them without any thought of picking them up. And seeing this lack of concern, I am all of a sudden afraid.

"Is this where they register for school?" my mother asks a woman at one of the tables.

The woman look up slowly as if she has heard this question once too often. She nods. She is tiny, almost as small as the girl standing beside her. The woman's hair is set in a mass of curlers and all of those curlers are made of paper money, here a dollar bill, there a five-dollar bill. The girl's hair is arrayed in curls, but some of them are beginning to droop and this makes me happy. On the table beside the woman's pocketbook is a large notebook, worthy of someone in high school, and looking at me looking at the notebook, the girl places her hand possessively on it. In her other hand she holds several pencils with thick crowns of additional erasers.

"These the forms you gotta use?" my mother asks the woman, picking up a few pieces of the paper from the table. "Is this what you have to fill out?"

The woman tells her yes, but that she need fill out only one.

"I see," my mother says, looking about the room. Then: "Would you help me with this form? That is, if you don't mind."

The woman asks my mother what she means.

"This form. Would you mind helping me fill it out?"

The woman still seems not to understand.

"I can't read it. I don't know how to read or write, and I'm askin you to help me." My mother looks at me, then looks away. I know almost all of her looks, but this one is brand new to me. "Would you help me then?"

The woman says Why sure, and suddenly she appears happier, so much more satisfied with everything. She finishes the form for her daughter and my mother and I step aside to wait for her. We find two chairs nearby and sit. My mother is now diseased, according to the girl's eyes, and until the moment her mother takes her and the form to the front of the auditorium, the girl never stops looking at my mother. I stare back at her. "Don't stare," my mother says to me. "You know better than that."

Another woman out of the *Ebony* ads takes the woman's child away. Now, the woman says upon returning, let's see what we can do for you two.

My mother answers the questions the woman reads off the form. They start with my last name, and then on to the first and middle names. This is school, I think. This is going to school. My mother slowly enunciates each word of my name. This is my mother: As the questions go on, she takes from her pocketbook document after document, as if they will support my right to attend school, as if she has been saving them up for just this moment. Indeed, she takes out more papers than I have ever seen her do in other places: my birth certificate, my baptismal record, a doctor's letter concerning my bout with chicken pox, rent receipts, records of immunization, a letter about our public assistance payments, even her marriage license – every single paper that has anything even remotely to do with my five-year-old life. Few of the papers are needed here, but it does not matter and my mother continues to pull out the documents with the purposefulness of a magician pulling out a long string of scarves. She has learned that money is the beginning and end of everything in this world, and when the woman finishes, my mother offers her fifty cents, and the woman accepts it without hesitation. My mother and I are just about the last parent and child in the room.

My mother presents the form to a woman sitting in front of the stage and the woman looks at it and writes something on a white card, which she gives to my mother. Before long, the woman who has taken the girl with the drooping curls appears from behind us, speaks to the sitting woman, and introduces herself to my mother and me. She's to be my teacher, she tells my mother. My mother stares.

We go into the hall, where my mother kneels down to me. Her lips are quivering. "I'll be back to pick you up at twelve o'clock. I don't want you to go nowhere. You just wait right here. And listen to every word she say." I touch her lips and press them together. It is an old, old game between us. She puts my hand down at my side, which is not part of the game. She stands and looks a second at the teacher, then she turns and walks away. I see where she has darned one of her socks the night before. Her shoes make loud sounds in the hall. She passes through the doors and I can still hear the loud sounds of her shoes. And even when the teacher turns me toward the classrooms and I hear what must be the singing and talking of all the children in the world, I can still hear my mother's footsteps above it all.


## AFTER READING

### A Respond to the reading

1 Reread the story. In your log, write answers to the three response questions. (See the toolbox *Response Questions* on page 9.)

   ① What do you understand the reading to say?

   ② How does the reading make you feel?

   ③ What does the reading make you think about?

2 Share your responses with your group.


### B List important events

1 With a partner, reread the story to look for its most important events. List the important events in the order they happened.

2 Share your list with the class.


## HOW IT'S WRITTEN

### A Label emotions

1 Many emotions are evident in this story. With a partner, go through the story, marking words or phrases that show positive emotions with a plus symbol (+) and those that show negative emotions with a minus symbol (-).

2 Name the emotions you marked.

3 Share your work with the class.

## B Learn about showing

1 Read about a technique you can use in your writing.

### Show – Don't Tell

Writers often say it's better to *show* readers a mood or how a character feels than to *tell* readers the name of the mood or emotion. For example, in paragraph 1 of "The First Day," Edward P. Jones says, "My mother has uncharacteristically spent nearly an hour on my hair that morning, plaiting and replaiting so that now my scalp tingles." He doesn't *tell* us that the mother was nervous about taking her daughter to her first day of school, but we can understand that feeling from the fact that the mother spent such a long time fixing her daughter's hair.

2 With a partner, underline at least three details that *show* an emotion or mood rather than *tell* readers what a person was feeling.

3 Share your findings with the class.

4 Discuss why *showing* is a more effective way to communicate a feeling in writing than *telling* or talking about a feeling.

## TOPICS FOR WRITING

### Choose one topic to write about

Whichever topic you choose, include details to *show* how you felt.

### Writer's Tip

*Don't tell us about anger . . . show us what made you angry. We will read it and feel angry. Don't tell readers what to feel. Show them the situation, and that feeling will awaken in them.*

**Natalie Goldberg**

1 Write a personal essay with the title, "The First Day." For example, you could write about the first day of school, the first day on a new job, the first day in a new home, or arriving in a new place. Describe the experience. Be sure to describe the emotions you felt. Were they positive or negative or a mixture of the two? Include one thing someone said, in the person's own words, to show how that person felt.

2 The narrator of "The First Day" was left by her mother in a large, new school. Look back at the paragraph where her mother says goodbye to her. Notice how the writer shows the emotions the child is feeling. Write a personal essay about a time in your life when you were left on your own in a strange place.

3 In "The First Day," the child learns that her mother is illiterate, that is, she can't read or write. Did you ever have the realization that one of your parents wasn't perfect? Write an essay about the experience of this discovery.

# AFTER WRITING

## Share your writing

1 Read about a feedback technique in which you ask your classmates for advice.

## Asking for Feedback

Writers often ask a friend or colleague to read what they have written in order to get a reader's response or to get help with a specific problem. Sometimes specific questions help more than simply asking, "How can I make this piece better?" Here are some typical questions a writer might ask a reader to answer:

■ *Does the beginning make you want to continue reading? Do you have any suggestions for a different, more effective way to start?*

■ *What details stand out for you? Are there any details I could remove?*

■ *Is there any part you don't understand?*

■ *Is anything in the wrong order?*

■ *Is there anything more you'd like me to write?*

■ *Does the ending tie the piece together?*

2 Ask for feedback by writing down one or two questions that you would like a classmate to answer.

3 Give your paper and your questions to one or two classmates for their feedback.

# BEFORE READING

## A Make a list

1 Read the title, the introductory information, and the first two sentences of the reading.

2 Make a list of the places and people you have left. (See the toolbox *Brainstorming a List* on page 7.)

3 Pick one item from your list. Think about how you felt, then write down some words that describe your feelings at that time.

4 Share your writing with a partner.

# A Walk to the Jetty
Jamaica Kincaid

*The novel* Annie John, *by Jamaica Kincaid, tells of one girl's growing into adolescence on the Caribbean island of Antigua. In this excerpt, which comes at the end of the novel, we see Annie at age 17 leaving her parents and her home to study nursing in England (U.K.). "A Walk to the Jetty" is the title of the last chapter of the novel.*

Now . . . I had nothing to take my mind off what was happening to me. My mother and my father – I was leaving them forever. My home on an island – I was leaving it forever. What to make of everything? I felt a familiar hollow space inside. I felt I was being held down against my will. I felt I was burning up from head to toe. I felt that someone was tearing me up into little pieces and soon I would be able to see all the little pieces as they floated out into nothing in the deep blue sea. I didn't know whether to laugh or cry. I could see that it would be better not to think too clearly about any one thing. The launch was being made ready to take me, along with some other passengers, out to the ship that was anchored in the sea. My father paid our fares, and we joined a line of people waiting to board. My mother checked my bag to make sure that I had my passport, the money she had given me, and a sheet of paper placed between some pages in my Bible on which were written the names of the relatives – people I had not known existed – with whom I would live in England. Across from the jetty was a wharf, and some stevedores were loading and unloading barges. I don't know why seeing that struck me so, but suddenly a wave of strong feeling came over me, and my heart swelled with a great gladness as the words "I shall never see this again" spilled out inside me. But then, just as quickly, my heart shriveled up and the words "I shall never see this again" stabbed at me. I don't know what stopped me from falling in a heap at my parents' feet.

When we were all on board, the launch headed out to sea. Away from the jetty, the water became the customary blue, and the launch left a wide path in it that looked like a road. I passed by sounds and smells that were so familiar that I had long ago stopped paying any attention to them. But now here they were, and the ever-present "I shall never see this again" bobbed up and down inside me. There was the sound of the seagull diving down into the water and coming up with something silverish in its mouth. There was the smell of the sea and the sight of small pieces of rubbish floating around in it. There were boats filled with fishermen coming in early. There was the sound of their voices as they shouted greetings to each other. There was the hot sun, there was the blue sea, there was the blue sky. Not very far away, there was the white sand of the shore, with the run-down houses all crowded in next to each other, for in some places only poor people lived near the shore. I was seated in the launch between my parents, and when I realized that I was gripping their hands tightly I glanced quickly to see if they were looking at me with scorn, for I felt sure that they must have known of my never-see-this-again feelings. But instead my father kissed me on the forehead and my mother kissed me on the mouth, and they both gave over their hands to me, so that I could grip them as much as I wanted. I was on the verge of feeling that it had all been a mistake, but I remembered that I wasn't a child any more, and that now when I made up my mind about something I had to see it through. At that moment, we came to the ship, and that was that.

The goodbyes had to be quick, the captain said. My mother introduced herself to him and then introduced me. She told him to keep an eye on me, for I had never gone this far away from home on my own. She gave him a letter to pass on to the captain of the next ship that I would board in Barbados. They walked me to my cabin, a small space that I would share with someone else – a woman I did not know. My father kissed me goodbye and told me to be good and to write home often. After he said this, he looked at me, then looked at the floor and swung his left foot, then looked at me again. I could see that he wanted to say something else, something that he had never said to me before, but then he just turned and walked away. My mother said, "Well," and then she threw her arms around me. Big tears streamed down her face, and it must have been that – for I could not bear to see my mother cry – which started me crying, too. She then tightened her arms around me and held me to her close, so that I felt that I couldn't breathe. With that, my tears dried up and I was suddenly on my guard. "What does she want now?" I said to myself. Still holding me close to her, she said, in a voice that raked across my skin, "It doesn't matter what you do or where you go, I'll always be your mother and this will always be your home."

I dragged myself away from her and backed off a little, and then I shook myself, as if to wake myself out of a stupor. We looked at each other for a long time with smiles on our faces, but I know the opposite of that was in my heart. As if responding to some invisible cue, we both said, at the very same moment, "Well." Then my mother turned around and walked out the cabin door. I stood there for I don't know how long, and then I remembered that it was customary to stand on deck and wave to your relatives who were returning to shore. From the deck, I could not see my father, but I could see my mother facing the ship, her eyes searching to pick me out. I removed from my bag a red cotton handkerchief that she had earlier given me for this purpose, and I waved it wildly in the air. Recognizing me immediately, she waved back just as wildly, and we continued to do this until she became just a dot in the matchbox-size launch swallowed up in the big blue sea.

I went back to my cabin and lay down on my berth. Everything trembled as if it had a spring at its very center. I could hear the small waves lap-lapping around the ship. They made an unexpected sound, as if a vessel filled with liquid had been placed on its side and now was slowly emptying out.

# AFTER READING

## A Read and respond

1 Reread "A Walk to the Jetty." As you read, stop at least four times to write a double entry response in your log. (See the toolbox *Double Entry Response* on page 26.)

2 Read your double entry responses to a partner. How are the responses similar and how are they different from your partner's?

## B Make a visual representation

1 With your group, use a large piece of poster paper to draw a series of pictures that recreate the story. (See **Make a visual representation** in Unit One on page 41.)

2 Post your group's drawing on the board or wall. Explain the pictures to the class.

## C Learn words through context

1 Reread the text and circle five words you don't understand.

2 Read about how you can use the context to guess at the meaning of words that you don't know.

> ### Context Clues
>
> You can often guess the meaning of a word by using the *context* – the words of the sentences around the unknown word. In the same sentence or nearby sentences, writers will sometimes use a word that has a similar meaning (a synonym) or will give an example that helps you understand the meaning of the unknown word.
>
> *. . . she waved back just as wildly, and we continued to do this until she became just a dot in the matchbox-size* **launch** *swallowed up in the big blue sea.*
>
> Since you know that Annie was on a ship waving goodbye to her mother, and that her mother went with her to the ship, you can guess that a "launch" is some kind of boat taking her mother back to shore.

3 As a group, guess the meaning of each person's circled words by using the context.

4 Write a few sentences in your log about what you learned from this activity.

# HOW IT'S WRITTEN

## Appreciate descriptive language

1 Reread the passage, looking for words and phrases Kincaid used to describe colors and sounds. Circle these. (See the toolbox *Using Your Senses* on page 10.)

2 Read about how writers can make their meaning more concrete and vivid by comparing two things.

> ### Metaphors and Similes
>
> A metaphor is the process of describing one thing as if it were another. By doing this, we are suggesting that two things are similar in some way.
>
> *The words 'I shall never see this again' stabbed at me.*
> (This suggests that words are sharp and painful – knives.)
>
> *. . . a voice that raked across my skin . . .*
> (This suggests that a voice can move across our skin in the same way a rake moves across the earth.)
>
> A simile is the process of comparing two unlike things, often using the words "like" or "as." It is similar to a metaphor, except that while a metaphor says that A = B, a simile says that A is *like* B.
>
> *. . . the launch left a wide path in it that looked like a road.*

3 Reread the passage, looking for *metaphors* and *similes* used to describe feelings and events. Underline these. Share your findings with your group.

4 With the class, discuss how Kincaid helped the reader understand the story and Annie's feelings by using colors, sounds, metaphors, and similes.

# TOPICS FOR WRITING

## Choose one topic to write about

Whichever topic you choose, include details of sound and color; also use similes and metaphors.

❶ Annie John left her parents and her country behind. Choose one experience of leaving from the list you made in **Make a list** on page 82. Write a personal essay about what happened, what you observed, how you felt, and why the event was significant. Think about the colors you saw and the sounds you heard during the experience.

❷ Write a personal essay about an experience this story reminds you of. Tell what happened, how you felt, and why the event was significant. Do you remember the color of people's clothes or the colors of any objects in the setting? What sounds do you remember hearing?

③ Choose one sentence from "A Walk to the Jetty" that gives you an idea for a true or fictional story, or an essay. Place the sentence at the beginning, in the middle, or at the end of your story or essay.

## AFTER WRITING

### Share your writing

1 Read your writing to your group. Ask your listeners to tell what details especially stand out for them.

2 With your group, brainstorm possible titles for your writing. Choose the one you like best.

. . . . . . . . . . . . . . . . . . . . . . . . . . . . . . . . . . . . . . . . . . . . . . . . . . . . . . . . . . . . . . . . . . .

## BEFORE READING

### Think about the topic

1 The title of this piece is "On Turning Fifty." The author thought that turning fifty was a milestone or a significant point in her life. Think of an age you consider to be a milestone, either an age in your past or one in your future. Freewrite about it for five minutes.

2 Reread your freewriting and underline the important ideas. Then, unless it is too private, read your freewriting to a partner. Describe any similarities and differences between your writing and your partner's writing.

## On Turning Fifty
### Judy Scales-Trent

*When Scales-Trent was in her mid-forties, she changed her name, changed her profession and moved from Washington, D.C., to Buffalo, New York where she teaches law and writes extensively on issues of gender and race in American life. She thought a great deal about what she had gained and what she had lost during her transition. The week before she turned fifty, she wrote this piece.*

I had thought that I would live my mother's life. I suppose all girls do. Like my mother, I would have a dignified and successful husband, one who would take care of me and our children, who would provide a life of status and comfort. I would be involved in my church. I would take classes and volunteer in my community. I would passionately enjoy my garden and my sewing.

This has not been my life. It has been more the life of my sisters. Like my mother, they are married, each with three children. My eldest sister now has four grandchildren: there will be more. In my eyes, they live a life of comfort – trips to far-off places, a summer house in the country.

This has not been my life. I live alone, with one small dog. A university professor, I do much of my work alone. I am no longer married. My teenage son lives in another state, long miles away. If I am to have any security or status or physical comfort, I must give it to myself.

It is at times like this, reckoning times, that I wonder where I went wrong. For I long for family – a husband, children, grandchildren. And this is not a mild longing. At times like this when I allow myself to feel it, the longing is so fierce that I close my eyes to hold back its power. I started down the path of my mother's life, but somewhere along the way I walked away from it. Where did I go wrong? Or did I go right? For it is at times like these, reckoning times, that I also remind myself that the life I now lead is the right one.

There was a moment, one morning, when I understood its rightness. It took place during the frenzy of my move from Washington, D.C., when I flew to Buffalo to sign closing papers for my new house. Isabel, a new colleague at the law school, picked me up at the airport and made me welcome as an overnight guest in her home. And it was the next morning, as I came downstairs, on my way to go to the attorney's office, that I was struck by something, something not yet clear in my mind. I remember the moment. I can see it clearly. I walked into the living room. The sun was streaming in through a stained-glass piece hung against the window. High ceilings, richly colored rugs on wooden floors, plants spilling over in profusion on a low, wooden bench; mugs and coffee and bread and jam on a coffee table in front of the sofa; stacks of books everywhere. And Isabel, sitting on the sofa, drinking her morning cup of coffee, reading a book. The sun made a golden picture. I stopped and stared, overwhelmed by the beauty and the quiet. "Is this what my life will be like?" I asked. She smiled. "Yes."

I must have longed, without knowing, for this – the sun and books, a quiet room, the generosity of friends. And that is my life now. For the very first time, my life is a seamless piece of fabric. There is no sense of working or not working. For the very first time, I do what I am. There is profound joy in this wholeness. . . .

There is a special poignancy to this fall. I do not want it to come. More than usual, I hold on to summer. This fall feels different. It feels like the announcement of the fall of my life. I accept and deny at the same time. For the first time, I want to plant bulbs. I want to store away the promise of spring, to make sure that its sweetness will return. This fall I will dig in the ground and plant daffodils and jonquils of all different kinds – daffodils and jonquils, and crocuses to announce their coming.

And as I plan this latest addition to my garden, I think that in many ways I am indeed living my mother's life. She is an independent woman who can work alone, contented, joyously, for days and weeks at a time. And she is passionate about her work. She creates her own projects in her garden and in her sewing room. She plans, she designs, she works and reworks until it suits her. . . . [I]n reality that is also how I work. For I too am passionate about my work. And I can work alone – joyously, contented, for days and weeks at a time. . . .

It pleases me to find this similarity between my mother's life and mine. I rejoice in my work. It is a good life.

It is not enough.

That day, my fiftieth birthday, is coming soon now. I am getting ready. Friends in Washington and Buffalo are giving me parties. I am having a dress made – short and red and silky. I am looking for dancing shoes. My parents will fly from Greensboro to the Washington party. I will go to these celebrations, as I go into my fiftieth year, embraced by my family and friends. And I will look at these days the way life teaches me to look – with one eye laughing, one eye weeping.


# AFTER READING

## A  Respond to the reading

1  Read about a variation on double entry responses.

### Triple Entry Response

Instead of talking aloud to someone about your double entry responses, you can have a "conversation in writing" in a triple entry notebook. Here's how it works:

■ Do a double entry response on a left-hand page of your log. (See page 26 for details.)

■ Pass your notebook to another person.

■ This person reads your double entry and, on the right-hand page of your notebook, writes a response to what you wrote.

| "Where did I go wrong? Or did I go right?" | I often am confused, too. I wonder if my life is going in the right direction. It is difficult to know if one has made the right decision. | I try never to regret anything so I don't ask those questions. I say whatever happens is for the best! |
| --- | --- | --- |
| "I thought I would live my mother's life. I suppose all girls do." | When I was a girl, I'm not sure that I thought this way. For example, I couldn't imagine myself even married, and I didn't think I would enjoy doing some of the things my mother did that I really enjoy now — the gardening and baking bread. | Do you enjoy being married too? As for me, I'm more like my father and wanted to be like him. |
| "I too am passionate about my work." | Me too! | I'm not. I'm passionate about what I'd like to do, but not what I do. |

2  Follow the steps in the toolbox.

3  Discuss your entries with your partner. What did you learn about the text from reading your partner's entries?

**B Label emotions**

1 Reread "On Turning Fifty." As you read, mark the places where the author shows emotions. In the margin, write a name for each emotion.

2 Compare what you wrote with your partner or your group. How many different emotions did you name?

## HOW IT'S WRITTEN

### Appreciate the structure

1 In this essay, Scales-Trent compares her life to the lives of several other people. With a partner, answer these questions about the comparisons she makes.

   ① How many people does she compare herself to? Who are they?

   ② In each case, when she compares herself to these people, does she find points of similarity or points of difference between her life and theirs?

   ③ Is there any significance in the order in which she makes these comparisons?

2 In the toolbox *The Essay* on page 19, you read about two different types of essays. In Type 1, you read that sometimes in the act of writing, writers go on a journey of discovery as they write. "On Turning Fifty" is a Type 1 essay. With a partner, mark the beginning and end of each part of the essay where the writer makes a new discovery about herself. Then say what each discovery is.

## TOPICS FOR WRITING

### Choose one topic to write about

❶ Did you ever make a major decision not to stay on the path you were on but to take a completely different one? What happened? Write an essay about your experience and whether you think it was the best thing for you. At the end or beginning of your essay, compare your experience to Scales-Trent's.

❷ Was one of your birthdays momentous? Write an essay (or a poem or song) entitled "On Turning _____." Like Scales-Trent, you might start your piece as a journal entry.

❸ Choose an age in your future. Write an essay with the title "On Being _____." Imagine yourself at that age. Tell what your life has been like so far. You might want to write about how your life has been similar to or different from your parents' lives. Tell about your successes, your major turning points, and so on.

# AFTER WRITING

## A  Read your writing aloud

1  Read your piece aloud to yourself. (See the toolbox *Reading Aloud* on page 55.)

2  After you have finished reading, write down the emotions you felt as you wrote the piece and the emotions you wanted to express.

## B  Share your writing

1  Exchange your paper with one person. Ask that person to read it and mark in the margins the emotions he or she thinks are being expressed.

2  Compare what the person wrote with what you intended.

........................................................................

# BEFORE READING

## A  Gather ideas about the topic

1  With your group, brainstorm a list of four to six major milestones in the average person's life. Compare at what age range people reach each milestone in the cultures represented in your group.

2  Talk with your group about how people in your culture commonly react toward a person who doesn't reach one of the milestones at the expected age. For example, how do they react toward a person who doesn't get married at the typical age for getting married or who has a child at a particularly early or late age.

## B  Write as you read

As you read, stop after each section and write down one thing you learned.

 # The Transitions of Life
Carole Wade & Carol Tavris

*The excerpt is taken from the best-selling college psychology textbook* Psychology, sixth edition. "The Transitions of Life" *is found in a chapter titled* "Development over the Life Span."

Today theories of adult development emphasize the *transitions* and milestones that mark adult life (Baltes, 1983; Schlossberg, 1984). Having a child has strong effects on you and will affect your life in predictable ways, whether you become a parent for the first time at 16 or 46. Entering the workforce affects your self-confidence and ambition regardless of whether you start work at 18 or 48. Some experiences are hallmarks of major life transitions, notably getting a job, getting married or committed to a partner, having children, retiring, and becoming a grandparent. But as we will see, what affects most people psychologically about transitions is not whether they occur, but whether people feel that the transitions are expected or unexpected, and whether most other people of their gender and generation are sharing them.

### STARTING OUT: THE SOCIAL CLOCK

In all societies, people evaluate their transitions according to a *social clock* that determines whether they are "on time" for their age or "off time" (Helson & McCabe, 1993; Neugarten, 1979). Cultures have different social clocks that define the "right" time to marry, start work, and have children. In some societies young men and women are supposed to marry and start having children right after puberty, and work responsibilities come later. In others, a man may not marry until he has shown that he can support a family, which might not be until his 30s. Society's reactions to people who are "off time" vary as well, from amused tolerance ("Oh, when will he grow up?") to pity, scorn, and outright rejection.

Doing the right thing at the right time, compared to your friends and age-mates, is reassuring. When nearly everyone in your group goes through the same experience or enters a new role at the same time – going to school, driving a car, voting, marrying, having a baby, retiring – adjusting to these *anticipated transitions* is relatively easy. . . .

As we have noted, though, traditional social clocks in Western societies are changing. Increasingly, people face *unanticipated transitions*, the events that happen without warning, such as being fired from a job or becoming too ill to finish school. . . .

One of the reasons that young adulthood is often the most stressful time in people's lives is that young adults are often making many rapid transitions at once: leaving home for college or a job, starting a career, finding a serious relationship. These transitions will be more difficult for those who feel they are not keeping up with their peers: "I'm a junior and haven't declared a major," "I'm almost 30 and not even in a serious relationship" (Helson & McCabe, 1993). Being freed of a cultural social clock can be liberating, but people who cannot do things "on time," for reasons out of their control, may feel depressed and anxious.

## THE MIDDLE YEARS

Most people think that the most important issues of the middle years are, for women, the misery of menopause and the "empty nest" (when grown children leave home), and, for men, a corresponding "midlife crisis." But they are wrong.

Actually, according to a large-scale research project that has followed 8,000 Americans for 10 years, for most women and men the midlife years – between 35 and 65 – are the prime of life (MacArthur Foundation, 1999). It is true that these years are often a time of reflection and reassessment, as people look back on what they have accomplished, take stock of what they regret not having done, and think about what they want to do with their remaining years (Steward & Vandewater, 1999). But far from being a time of turmoil, midlife is typically a time of psychological well-being, good health, productivity, and community involvement. American women in their 50s today are more likely than those in any other age group to describe their lives as being "first-rate" and to report having a high quality of life (Mitchell & Helson, 1990). Midlife crises are the exception, and when they occur it is not for reasons related to aging but to specific events, such as the loss of a job or spouse. Another stereotype bites the dust!

## OLD AGE

In Western youth-oriented cultures, old people are typically assumed to be forgetful, somewhat senile, and physically feeble. On television and in the movies, old people are usually portrayed as objects of amusement, sympathy, or scorn. But *gerontologists* – researchers who study aging and the old – have been challenging these stereotypes.

To begin with, when does old age start? Not long ago you would have been considered old in your 60s. Today, the fastest-growing segment of the population in North America consists of people over the age of 85. There were 4 million Americans age 85 or older in 2000, and the Census Bureau projects that there may be as many as 31 million by 2050 (Schneider, 1999). And there will be more than 600,000 Americans over the age of 100. How will these people function?

## FIRST, THE BAD NEWS

Various aspects of intelligence, memory, and other forms of mental functioning decline significantly with age; older adults score lower on tests of reasoning, spatial ability, and complex problem solving than do younger adults (Verhaeghen & Salthouse, 1997). As people age, they lose some of their sense of smell (which is why food doesn't taste as appealing as it once did), hearing, and vision. It takes them longer to retrieve names, dates, and other information; in fact, the speed of cognitive processing in general slows down significantly (Bashore et al., 1997). . . .

Fortunately, gerontologists have made great strides in separating conditions once thought to be an inevitable part of old age from those that are preventable or treatable. For example, osteoporosis (having extremely brittle bones), senility and mental confusion, and lesser insults such as wrinkles and "age spots" are often a result of malnutrition, overmedication, disease, or cellular damage from too much sun. . . .

Gerontologists estimate that only about 30 percent of the physical losses of old age are genetically based; the other 70 percent have to do with behavioral and psychological factors (Rowe & Kahn, 1998). The strongest predictors of a vigorous and healthy old age are remaining intellectually active and mentally stimulated, getting exercise (especially weight-bearing exercise to strengthen bones and muscles and prevent or offset physical deterioration), and cultivating psychological resilience – the ability to bounce back after life's losses and stresses.

## AFTER READING

### A Share your responses

1 Compare what you wrote down about each section with what your partner wrote. If you missed any important points, add them.

2 Find one or two statements in the text that surprised you. Underline these. Share them with your partner and together discuss why they surprised you.

### B Compare cultures

1 With a partner, fill in the middle column of the chart below with information from the text.

2 Complete the right hand column on your own.

| Major Milestone or Transition of Life | The "Right" Time in Western Culture | The "Right" Time in Your Culture |
|---|---|---|
| Moving out of parents' home and living on your own | | |
| Getting married | | |
| Having children | | |
| When your children leave home – "the empty nest" | | |
| Becoming a grandparent | | |
| Retirement and old age | | |

3 Share your chart with your group. Discuss differences.

4 Reread the excerpt to find three "myths" about transitions and milestones, that is, ideas people have about a period of life that aren't necessarily true. Compare the myths in the text to what people in your culture believe. For instance, do people in your culture think old age starts at 60? Discuss these myths with the class.

# HOW IT'S WRITTEN

**Learn about using references**

1 Read about one common way to cite sources in a written document.

## Citations Using APA Style

In writing a paper, when you quote or paraphrase from another source, you must acknowledge that it is not your material and tell the reader where it is from. Several different ways of providing citations exist. One of the most commonly used is American Psychological Association (APA) style. In APA style, include the last name(s) of the author(s) and the date of publication in parentheses within the sentence.

> There were 4 million Americans age 85 or older in 2000, and the Census Bureau projects that there may be as many as 31 million by 2050 (Schneider, 1999). And there will be more than 600,000 Americans. . . .

> In all societies, people evaluate their transitions according to a *social clock* that determines whether they are "on time" for their age or "off time" (Helson & McCabe, 1993; Neugarten, 1979). Cultures have different social clocks. . . .

2 With a partner, notice the references to other publications in the text of "Transitions of Life." Discuss these questions with a partner.

① How many references are there?

② What information is given in a reference and in what order?

③ Why do the authors use references?

3 Write down something you want to remember from this activity in your log.

## TOPICS FOR WRITING

### Choose one topic to write about

Whichever topic you choose, incorporate a quote from "Transitions of Life" and make sure you cite it properly.

1. Write a letter of advice to someone who is approaching young adulthood, the middle years, or old age. Tell the person what to expect – the good points and the pitfalls (likely problems).

2. Have you had the experience, or witnessed it in someone else, of being "off time" in reaching one of the major milestones of life? Write an essay describing what happened and tell what effect it had on you or the person psychologically.

3. The authors say, "In Western youth-oriented cultures, old people are typically assumed to be forgetful, somewhat senile, and physically feeble." As a result, older people are often treated disrespectfully, for example, forced to retire or put in nursing homes. Can you suggest another way of looking at old age that allows older people to continue to contribute to their families and to society? Write an essay explaining your ideas. Use examples from your experience or other reading to support your views.

## AFTER WRITING

### Share your writing

1 Exchange papers with a classmate. Use the prompts in the toolbox *Sentence Starter Feedback* on page 49 to give feedback.

2 Think about your classmate's feedback. Write a few notes to yourself about what you can change to revise your essay.

**OPENING NEW DOORS: REVISION**

## A Choose one piece of writing

1 Reread the pieces you wrote for the **Topics for Writing** sections of OPENING NEW DOORS. Also read any feedback on these pieces you received from your classmates and teacher.

2 Choose one piece to revise.

## B Revise your writing

1 Using what you learned about ARMS (see the toolbox *ARMS* on page 72) mark what you can add, remove, move, and substitute.

2 If you haven't chosen a title, do so now.

3 Does the title change the focus? If so, make necessary changes.

4 Read your writing aloud to yourself. As you read, think about how you could make the writing smoother and clearer. (See the toolbox *Reading Aloud* on page 55.)

5 Rewrite and revise.

## C Proofread

1 Read about a technique that may help you discover careless errors in your writing.

### Proofreading

Once you have revised your piece so that your ideas are clear and well organized, it is time to proofread. To proofread, go over your paper carefully with a pen in your hand, reading each word aloud so that your ear can hear it. As you do this, touch each word with your pen to help you slow down and find errors and parts that don't sound right. You may discover that words are missing or that the endings on words are not correct. If you think a word may not be correctly spelled, stop and check its spelling.

2 Proofread your writing by following the suggestions in the toolbox.

## D Share your writing

1 Form a writing circle and read your papers to each other. (See the toolbox *Writing Circle* on page 20.)

2 Choose one piece to read to the class.

## E Reflect on writing techniques

1 Write a few notes in your log about the writing techniques you have learned so far. Which ones would you like to continue using? What makes them useful to you?

2 Discuss your thoughts with your group.

## Dating and Marriage

## BEFORE READING

### Gather ideas about the topic

1 Freewrite about the dating and marriage practices of your grandparents' or parents' generation.

2 Discuss what you wrote with your group.

3 What are some nonverbal ways people use to show their romantic interest in another person? With your group, make a list.

4 Demonstrate one item on your list to the class.

 ## Pebbles
lê thi diem thúy

*lê thi diem thúy is a writer and solo performance artist. She was born in Vietnam and raised in Southern California.*

For a handful of pebbles and my father's sharp profile my mother left home and never returned. Imagine a handful of pebbles. The casual way he tossed them at her as she was walking home from school with her girlfriends. He did this because he liked her and wanted to let her know. Boys are dumb that way, my mother told me. A handful of pebbles, to be thrown in anger, in desperation, in joy. My father threw them in love. Ma says they touched her like warm kisses, these pebbles he had been holding in the sun. Warm kisses on the curve of her back, sliding down the crook of her arm, grazing her ankles and landing around her feet in the hot sand.

## AFTER READING

### A Respond to the reading

1 Reread "Pebbles" slowly as if it were a poem.

2 Write an entry in your log, answering the three response questions found in the toolbox *Response Questions* on page 9.

3 Share your responses with your group.

**B Make a personal connection**

1 Make a list of current dating and courtship practices in your culture.

2 With your group, discuss similarities and differences in these practices, according to your group's cultures, religions, or local traditions.

3 Share these practices with the class.

## HOW IT'S WRITTEN

**Appreciate poetic language**

1 With your partner, underline the words or phrases that make this passage seem like poetry. Say these words and phrases aloud several times. Discuss with the class what makes these words and phrases poetic.

2 Underline the number of times the phrase "a handful of pebbles," or part of that phrase, is used. Discuss the effect of this repetition with the class.

3 Write in your log about what you learned that you might apply to your writing.

## TOPICS FOR WRITING

**Choose one topic to write about**

❶ Throwing pebbles was the beginning of a romance and courtship between the mother and the father. The mother interpreted it as a sign of romantic interest. Find out how other courtships have begun. Ask your parents or older couples you know well about how their romance and courtship began. Pick one of the stories you hear. Write a short essay about it. Include the story and your thoughts and feelings about it. If appropriate, make the story poetic.

❷ Although the two people in the story may have known each other, it sounds like they fell in love without talking, without dating and spending time together, and that they decided to get married instantly. What do you think of that? Is it common that a person finds a husband or wife in such a quick, intuitive way, without getting to know the person through talking and dating? Is it risky or can a person trust his or her instincts about love? Write an essay in which you discuss your thoughts and feelings on how people fall in love.

❸ Have you ever made a major change based on a gesture as small as a handful of pebbles? Have you ever made a big decision based on an intuition or a feeling, but that you couldn't talk about or explain? What decision was it? What happened? Did it turn out to be right? How did you know it was probably the right thing to do? Write an essay about your experience in which you describe the experience and discuss your thoughts and feelings and the outcome.

# AFTER WRITING

## Share your writing

1 Post your essay on a wall of the classroom for everyone to read.

2 Walk around the room reading your classmates' essays. As you walk, take notes on which essays are most effective and why.

3 Discuss your thoughts with the class.

. . . . . . . . . . . . . . . . . . . . . . . . . . . . . . . . . . . . . . . . . . . . . . . . . . . . . . . . . . .

# BEFORE READING

## Gather ideas about the topic

1 Write for a few minutes in your log about some of the positive and negative aspects of dating someone from another culture.

2 Share one of your statements from your writing with your group.

3 Make a list of qualities you think are important in a person you would like to date.

4 Share your list with your group. Together make one list and see if you can agree on the three most important qualities.

5 Share the qualities your group agrees are the most important with the class. Talk about why you choose these qualities.

 Kids Talk about Dating across Cultural Lines

*The following excerpts are adapted from a PBS television show. The host talked with teenagers at two high schools that serve ethnically diverse populations – one in New Jersey and the other in Los Angeles – about dating across cultural lines.*

## Omar
*African-American*
*Born in the U.S.*
I have never, like, dated outside my own race. I wouldn't say that I would never do it, but at this point I would say that I wouldn't try it because I guess I would feel, like, out of place.

### Miriam
*Puerto Rican-American*
*Born in the U.S.*
I never really dated outside of my race until recently. I'm Puerto Rican; Kamal is my boyfriend – well, my "friend" to my parents and my family. When I mentioned the fact to my parents that I had an Egyptian "friend" and they thought we were spending a lot of time together, my mom was okay with it, but no one in my family ever dated outside their race. Everyone in my family has dated and has married a Puerto Rican; everyone has stayed in their culture. My mom was okay, but my father had somewhat of a problem, just with the fact that he's not Hispanic, period. My father feels like his babies, his daughters, should date and eventually marry an Hispanic. He's also very old-fashioned. He was brought up and raised in Puerto Rico, strong background.

Kamal, fortunately, he met my parents. My parents love him to death. . . . I'm glad I've dated him. I've learned a lot about different cultures and I'm happy. . . . And if I were to have a child, I wouldn't want to tell them, "Well, listen, you know, you're limited to dating within your race" – no. No, I'd let them choose.

### Kamal
*Egyptian-American*
*Born in the U.S.*
My mother met her, and she loves her. She approves of, like, me dating an Hispanic, because I've dated outside my race before; I've only dated one person in my race – by that, I mean Egyptian. Arab, Egyptian. So, my parents approve.

### Rafael
*Puerto Rican-American*
*Born in the U.S.*
My parents . . . no, they don't approve of me being with somebody of another culture. They want to see me with somebody who's Puerto Rican. And the thing is, I think I do, too. I think I'd prefer to be married to somebody who's Puerto Rican, but if it doesn't happen that way, I'm not gonna get all bent outta shape. . . . Love is not a matter of culture anymore. So, I wouldn't let it get in the way.

I think that when you have interracial couples and then you have a child, somehow it almost makes it harder for him to grow up into two cultures. Like, I'm not saying it's impossible, but I know that some difficulties do come up with it. And I guess I'm proud of my Puerto Rican culture, and I'd like my child to be just as proud, and not have to worry about that.

## Carolina
*Ecuadorian-American*
*Born in the U.S.*
I think I have only dated Hispanic guys, except once I did date a white male, I guess – a white guy. And it was very different because I had gotten so used to going out with Puerto Rican guys. We have a similar language, they know how to dance. Like, the white guy that I had gone out with, he didn't have like the same characteristics, the same character. And I didn't feel as comfortable, so I prefer just going out with Spanish guys.

## Shaheen
*Sierra Leonian/Indian/Scottish-American*
*Born in the U.S.*
I have dated inside and outside of my race [sees herself as black]. My first, like, two, three boyfriends were Hispanic males. And my mom was like, they're so cute, da da da. But, like, my extended family was really bothered by it. "Are you ever gonna date somebody who's black?" Or, "You have something racist against black people." And then when I finally did get an African-American boyfriend, my mom flipped out. "Oh, no, you can't date him." And I guess it was more of the life he led and his family.

But my boyfriend now, he's Dominican and his mom loves me. And I guess it's because I look like him. We pass for brother and sister, so she identifies with me more. And I appreciate her. And they're teaching me, they're re-teaching me Spanish, 'cause I kind of forgot.

## Afsaneh
*Jewish-Persian*
*Born in Iran*
Actually, my parents are kind of okay about [interracial dating]. It's not normal for a Persian girl to go out with a black person or any other person out of their race, but for me, I've talked to my parents about it and, umm, as long as they're Jewish, they're fine. It doesn't matter what race they are, I personally I don't care what race they are, it's the person inside that counts to me.

## Rawlins
*African-American and mixed European ancestry (black father, white mother)*
*Born in the U.S.*
I still hear some people say that it is okay, but "I still want to be with my culture." . . . Personally, it doesn't matter as long as you connect with that person. It's all that matters. . . . You can get caught up in boundaries. That's just where the person is at. If they're not allowing themselves to get close to a person of another race, that's just their loss. I'm just trying to keep my mind open.

# AFTER READING

## A Respond to the reading

1 Make a double entry response to at least two statements from two different young people. (See the toolbox *Double Entry Response* on page 26.)

2 Exchange logs and ask your partner to write a response to your responses. (See the toolbox *Triple Entry Response* on page 89.) Talk with your partner about your responses.

3 Share with your group your reactions to one of the teenagers' statements.

## B Find issues

1 Read the toolbox to find out what an *issue* is and how to make it a generalization that can be a starting place for a piece of writing.

> ### *Issues*
>
> An issue is a concern shared by many people. People may argue about an issue or take different points of view on it. An issue can be stated in a phrase or by questions.
>
> If an issue is stated as a phrase, it can be turned into a question.
>
> - *Issue: Interracial or intercultural marriage*
>
>   *Is it good for people of two different races or cultures to marry?*
>
>   *Should parents representing two different cultures teach their children about both parents' cultures?*
>
> Issues can be turned into generalizations that answer the questions they ask. A generalization, written as a complete sentence, can become the main idea or topic sentence of a piece of writing. Note that for each generalization you think of, someone else might think of an opposing generalization, which also could be supported in an essay.
>
> - *Question: Is it good for people of two different races or cultures to marry?*
>
>   *It is good for people of two different races or cultures to marry because their lives and the lives of their children will be richer.*
>
>   *When people of two different races or cultures marry, their lives and the lives of their children will be difficult and complicated.*
>
> *Adapted from* A Short Course in Writing, *third edition by Kenneth Bruffee.*

2 With your partner, make a list of issues about dating across cultural lines that these young people raise.

3 Together, pick one issue and write four questions about it. Then write one generalization and one opposing generalization for that issue.

4 With your group, discuss how you could support one of your generalizations in a piece of writing.

## HOW IT'S WRITTEN

### Recognize spoken and written English

1 These young people's comments are written as if they were talking. They are written as "spoken" English. The excerpts don't follow the conventions of academic "written" English. Write down two examples, from two different excerpts, of "spoken" English.

2 Work with your partner and rewrite the "spoken" English as "written" English. Put one of your examples on the board.

3 With the class, make a list of the differences you see between "spoken" and "written" English.

4 Talk with the class about when it's appropriate to write in "spoken" English.

## TOPICS FOR WRITING

### Choose one topic to write about

1 Pick one of the questions you created about an issue related to dating across cultural lines in **Find issues**. Write an essay discussing the question.

2 Write about "the perfect date." What would your perfect date be – not the place or activity, but the person? What are the most important qualities you look for in a person to date? What qualities would you overlook? Explain your choices.

3 Write about yourself, your thoughts, and your experiences on dating across cultures as though you were on this TV program. Write in "spoken" English.

## AFTER WRITING

### Share your writing

1 Read all of the essays written by people in your group. As you read, take notes on interesting ideas or expressions.

2 As a group, choose one essay to be read to the class.

## BEFORE READING

### A  Ask questions

1  Read the introductory information and the first two paragraphs of "Weddings." In your log, write down one or two questions you have.

2  Share your questions with your group.

### B  Locate the setting

1  On the map of the world on page xii, locate Togo (the capital of which is Lomé), Benin, and Nigeria.

2  With a partner, share anything you know about these two places.

### C  Write as you read

Look through the story. Note the breaks marked by [pause]. While reading, when you get to a break, stop and write what you are thinking about at that point. You can include associations, answers to your questions, more questions, or what you expect to read next.

# Weddings
Fauziya Kassindja and Layli Miller Bashir

*At the age of 17, Fauziya Kassindja left Togo, West Africa, to escape a marriage arranged by her uncle. With the help of Layli Miller Bashir, she wrote a book about her life,* Do They Hear You When You Cry? *In this excerpt from the book, she recalls her sister's wedding.*

Ayisha was the first of us girls to marry. She was to marry a man from Lomé named Abass. What a celebration that was!

We don't date in our culture. Muslims don't anyway. Couples fall in love and decide to marry in the same fashion that my parents did – that is, if they come from families that allow them to choose their own partners. Some marriages are completely arranged by the parents.

It's more customary these days, however, for a young man to select his bride. As happened with my father, he'll see a woman who captures his fancy and start watching her. Maybe he'll make a point of going to the market on the days he knows she's likely to be there. She may or may not realize she's being watched, may or may not be watching back. Eventually, the young man will approach the young woman and say some version of what my father said to my mother through her friend: "I've been watching you. I really like you. I'd like to marry you." If she doesn't share his feelings, she'll say, "I'll think about it." She won't say, "Well, I don't want to marry you." She'll be polite. Each time he approaches her, she'll say the same thing – "I'll think about it" – until he gets the message that she's not interested in him.

If the woman indicates she is interested, the prospective groom will go home and tell his family he's found the woman he wants to wed. If they don't know her or her family, his parents will do some investigating to find out if she's a good Muslim girl from a good Muslim home. Once they are satisfied with her suitability, the young man's parents will send one of his brothers or sisters to the bride's family to request a meeting. . . . The father will then go to his daughter or daughters: "Does anyone here know why this young man's family would want to come calling?"

"Yes, Daddy," one of the girls will say. "I told him to have his parents send someone to come talk to you" – a clear indication of her interest.

In families like mine, the parents may do a little prodding to make sure of their daughters' feelings. With each of my sisters my father would tease her, asking: "Is this really the man you want? Do you really love him? You can say no, sweetheart. You don't have to marry anyone you don't love." . . .

[pause]

I knew that a wedding was coming soon when a sister's husband-to-be began visiting our house. That doesn't happen until after the wedding date has been set. Once it's set, the young man is permitted to come calling on his bride-to-be. They can sit and talk and laugh together, maybe share food from the same bowl. But they're not allowed to go anywhere together, even with a chaperon.

This courtship period usually lasts a number of months, giving the couple a chance to get to know each other while the wedding itself is arranged. It takes time to arrange a wedding celebration of the size Ayisha and my sisters had. Word has to go out to friends and relatives living in different countries, to allow plenty of time for travel. Food has to be bought and prepared. . . .

My mother's three surviving sisters were always the first to arrive after a marriage announcement went out. They came about two weeks before Ayisha's wedding, from Benin and Nigeria, to help with the cooking and preparations. . . . During this time my father and brothers made themselves scarce. Weddings are women's business.

[pause]

The days of preparation passed happily, and then came Thursday, when the festivities really got started. . . . The drummers, singers, and musicians arrived after seven, and by eight the celebrating was under way.

Once the dancing in the courtyard outside had reached a certain peak, one person would announce, "It's time for the *amariya* to come and dance" for Ayisha was still in the house. . . . A great cry went out as the bride, my beautiful sister, came out of the house and entered the circle, with her maid of honor. And then Ayhisah danced. . . .

Friday night's celebrations passed in much the same way. The groom doesn't attend any of these festivities. His family may hold a separate, smaller celebration if they can afford it, but the groom is a mere phantom presence at the bride's parties. Bride and groom don't see each other until Sunday night, after they're officially married, when she's delivered to his house.

[pause]

On Saturday morning the *nachane* arrived. She's the old woman in our community who does all the ritual bathing of brides and new babies. . . .

Sunday's celebration would be the most spectacular of them all. Nobody had to wake me up that morning. My eyes popped open well before dawn. This was it! The *nachane* returned to the house to give the bride her ritual bath. . . .

The next step in the bridal ritual was the dressing and makeup. Some of Ayisha's girlfriends and a few of our female cousins came to help my sisters and aunts with this part of the ritual. . . .

Something had happened in that room while the women were dressing Ayisha, some magic. This woman standing before me, smiling back at me, wasn't just my sister Ayisha anymore. Always beautiful, she had been transformed into the most radiantly exquisite woman I had ever seen.

[pause]


## AFTER READING

### A Share responses

1 Share with a partner the writing you did while reading.

2 Discuss the similarities and differences in what you each wrote.


### B Compare cultures

1 With a partner, number the four sections of the reading (1, 2, 3, 4). Choose one section to reread. Identify one or two cultural practices related to courtship and marriage in Togo as described in your section.

2 Fill in the chart below to show a comparison between cultural practices related to courtship and marriage in Togo and in your culture.

| Cultural Practices in Togo | Cultural Practices in My Culture |
|---|---|
| | |
| | |
| | |
| | |

3 Share your chart with a partner and then with the class.

4 Discuss with the class how these activities helped you understand the story:

- Stopping and writing in your log.

- Reading your partner's log.

- Filling out the cultural practices chart.

## HOW IT'S WRITTEN

### Identify general and specific information

1 "Weddings" alternates between two kinds of writing: (1) using specific examples from personal experience, and (2) giving general information related to courtship and marriage in Togo. With a partner, look back through "Weddings" and find examples of the two types of writing – specific and general. Mark the places in the text where the information is specific (**S**) or general (**G**).

2 Share what you marked with the class. Discuss how the writer moves from specific to general.

## TOPICS FOR WRITING

### Choose one topic to write about

Whichever topic you choose, use one of these pre-writing techniques to gather ideas: freewriting (see the toolbox *Freewriting* on page 2), freewriting with kernel sentences (see the toolbox *Kernel Sentences* on page 3), clustering (see the toolbox *Clustering* on page 12), or making a list (see toolbox *Brainstorming a List* on page 7).

❶ Write an essay that describes the cultural practices of courtship and marriage in your culture. Give both general information and specific examples from personal experience, as the authors of "Weddings" did.

❷ Interview a person (or a couple) who got married at least forty years ago. What was the person's courtship like? What courtship and marriage rituals did the person go through? Was the person's courtship and marriage typical? Take notes. Write a report or prepare a report to give to the class.

❸ In Kassindja's culture, parents arranged their children's marriages. Do you know other cultures where this custom is followed? How does it work? Write an essay in which you describe the custom of arranged marriage in a specific culture. Begin or end your essay by telling readers what you think of this practice.

## AFTER WRITING

### Share your writing

1 Have at least two classmates read your first draft. Before you show them your draft, attach a sheet of paper and write down one or two questions that tell your readers the kind of feedback you would like. (See the toolbox *Asking for Feedback* on page 82.)

2 Each reader should write a response.

3 Read your classmates' comments. Mark at least two places in your writing where you need to clarify your ideas or where you could add information.

**DATING AND MARRIAGE: REVISION**

## A Choose one piece of writing

1 Reread the pieces you wrote for the **Topics for Writing** sections of DATING AND MARRIAGE. Choose two that you like and may want to revise.

2 Show your choices to a partner and talk about which one would be best to revise. Choose one.

## B Revise your writing

1 Read a writing teacher's suggestions about revision.

### Revision Tips

Here are some tips for revising your writing:

■ Add to the piece, even if you thought you were finished.

■ Add color, sound, or metaphor in at least three places.

■ Find the following words in your work: *nice, big, good, bad, old, young.* Replace each of them with a different word or words that more specifically describes the person or object.

■ Read your piece aloud. Listen to the sound. If any sentences are difficult to read, change them to make them smoother.

■ Write several different catchy beginnings for the piece. Try a question, an anecdote, a vivid description, and a statement in the present tense.

■ Choose one section and reduce it by one-third.

■ Look for anything that seems out of place or uninteresting. Whenever you lose interest, mark the passage for possible revising.

*Adapted from* Deep Revision: A Guide for Teachers, Students, and Other Writers *by Meredith Sue Willis.*

2 Talk with your group about what Willis means.

3 Follow the suggestions in the toolbox to work on your essay. Write as many drafts as you need to make the essay a strong piece of writing.

4 If you don't have a title, try several until you find one you like.

5 Proofread your final draft by following the suggestions in the toolbox *Proofreading* on page 97.

## C Share your writing

1 Attach a blank sheet of paper to your essay. Give your writing to at least three classmates to read.

2 After you read a classmate's paper, write one comment on the blank sheet of paper. The comment can be an observation (something you notice), a response (your feelings or thoughts), a compliment (something you like about the writing), or a question.

**Work**

## BEFORE READING

### Think about the topic

1 What was your first job? How did you get it? What happened on the first day? Discuss these questions with a partner.

2 With your group, make a list of first jobs held by group members. Ask each person to say one word or phrase that expresses his or her feelings about that job.

 **The First Job**
Sandra Cisneros

*"The First Job" comes from the novel* The House on Mango Street. *This novel is the story of a young girl, named Esperanza, growing up in a large city in the United States.*

It wasn't as if I didn't want to work. I did. I had even gone to the social security office the month before to get my social security number. I needed money. The Catholic high school cost a lot, and Papa said nobody went to public school unless you wanted to turn out bad.

I thought I'd find an easy job, the kind other kids had, working in the dime store or maybe a hotdog stand. And though I hadn't started looking yet, I thought I might the week after next. But when I came home that afternoon, all wet because Tito had pushed me into the open water hydrant – only I had sort of let him – Mama called me in the kitchen before I could even go and change, and Aunt Lala was sitting there drinking her coffee with a spoon. Aunt Lala said she had found a job for me at the Peter Pan Photo Finishers on North Broadway where she worked and how old was I and to show up tomorrow saying I was one year older and that was that.

So the next morning I put on the navy blue dress that made me look older and borrowed money for lunch and bus fare because Aunt Lala said I wouldn't get paid 'til the next Friday and I went in and saw the boss of the Peter Pan Photo Finishers on North Broadway where Aunt Lala worked and lied about my age like she told me to and sure enough I started that same day.

In my job I had to wear white gloves. I was supposed to match negatives with their prints, just look at the picture and look for the same one on the negative strip, put it in the envelope, and do the next one. That's all. I didn't know where these envelopes were coming from or where they were going. I just did what I was told.

It was real easy and I guess I wouldn't have minded it except that you got tired after a while and I didn't know if I could sit down or not, and then I started sitting down only when the two ladies next to me did. After a while they started to laugh and came up to me and said I could sit when I wanted to and I said I knew.

When lunch time came I was scared to eat alone in the company lunchroom with all those men and ladies looking, so I ate real fast standing in one of the washroom stalls and had lots of time left over so I went back to work early. But then break time came and not knowing where else to go I went into the coatroom because there was a bench there.

I guess it was the time for the night shift or middle shift to arrive because a few people came in and punched the time clock and an older Oriental man said hello and we talked for a while about my just starting and he said we could be friends and next time to go in the lunchroom and sit with him and I felt better. He had nice eyes and I didn't feel so nervous anymore. Then he asked if I knew what day it was and when I said I didn't he said it was his birthday and would I please give him a birthday kiss. I thought I would because he was so old and just as I was about to put my lips on his cheek, he grabs my face with both hands and kisses me hard on the mouth and doesn't let go.

## AFTER READING

### A Respond to the reading

1 Freewrite a response to what you read.

2 Share your freewriting with your group.

### B Make a visual representation

1 With your group, using a large sheet of paper, draw a series of four pictures that recreate Esperanza's story. (See **Make a visual representation** in Unit One on page 41.)

2 If the author had added one more paragraph, what do you think she would have said? Discuss this with your group. Then add a fifth picture to your visual representation.

3 Explain your group's drawings to the class.

# HOW IT'S WRITTEN

## Examine the ending

1 Reread the last paragraph and discuss the following questions with your group:

   ① How do you feel about the ending? When you first read it, what was your response?

   ② Why do you think Cisneros stopped the story in this way?

   ③ Notice the change of tense in the last sentence. Why do you think the author switched tenses?

2 Summarize your group's discussion for the class.

# TOPICS FOR WRITING

## Choose one topic to write about

   ❶ Write an essay about your first job or about a job you have had. Tell how you got the job and what you did on the job. Give enough details so readers understand how you felt about it. You may want to include one specific incident on one particular day that will show readers what the job was like for you.

   ❷ Have you ever had the experience of being taken advantage of because of your age, your gender, or your newness to a place? Write an essay about the experience. Give enough details so readers understand how you felt about it.

   ❸ In this story, Esperanza was a teenager in high school when she got her first job. At what age do young people typically go to work in your culture? What jobs do young people have? Write an essay in which you describe a typical job of young people in your culture and give your thoughts and feelings about it. Include the personal story of someone you know, or yourself, as an example.

# AFTER WRITING

## Share your writing

1 Look back at the three toolboxes on giving feedback: *Reader's Response Feedback* on page 15, *Sentence Starter Feedback* on page 49 and *Asking for Feedback* on page 82. Choose the feedback method you would like your partner to use.

2 Find a partner and ask him or her to give you feedback, using the method you chose.

3 Afterwards, discuss with your partner why you chose this feedback tool.

## BEFORE READING

### Test your knowledge

1 In "Behind the Counter," you will read about the teenage workforce in the United States. Before you read, decide whether the following statements are true (**T**) or false (**F**). The correct answers are given in the text.

_____ ① Most workers in fast food restaurants are teenagers.

_____ ② Places such as fast food restaurants like to hire young workers mostly because of their high energy.

_____ ③ Teenagers gain experience, job skills, and self-esteem from working.

_____ ④ Young people who work too many hours a week tend to skip classes and drop out of school.

_____ ⑤ Most teens who work save their money for college.

_____ ⑥ Teenagers often work late at night or work longer hours than they are supposed to according to federal and state employment laws.

_____ ⑦ Most teenagers who work in fast food restaurants prefer working at the counter with customers rather than working in the kitchen.

2 Compare your answers with those of a partner.

# Behind the Counter
Eric Schlosser

*While doing research for a book called* Fast Food Nation, *Eric Schlosser interviewed many teenagers who work in fast food restaurants. This is an excerpt from one chapter of the book.*

Every Saturday Elisa Zamot gets up at 5:15 in the morning. . . . By 5:30, Elisa's showered, done her hair, and put on her McDonald's uniform. She's sixteen, bright-eyed and olive-skinned, pretty and petite, ready for another day of work. Elisa's mother usually drives her the half-mile or so to the restaurant, but sometimes Elisa walks, leaving home before the sun rises. Her family's modest townhouse sits beside a busy highway . . . in a largely poor and working-class neighborhood.

When Elisa arrives at McDonald's, the manager unlocks the door and lets her in. . . . For the next hour or so the two of them get everything ready. They turn on the ovens and grills. They go downstairs into the basement and get food and supplies for the morning shift. They get the paper cups, wrappers, cardboard containers, and packets of condiments. They step into the big freezer and get the frozen bacon, the frozen pancakes, and the frozen cinnamon rolls. . . .

The restaurant opens for business at seven o'clock, and for the next hour or so, Elisa and the manager hold down the fort, handling all the orders. . . . Elisa works behind the counter. She takes orders and hands food to customers from breakfast through lunch. When she finally walks home, after seven hours of standing at a cash register, her feet hurt. She's wiped out. . . . And the next morning she gets up at 5:15 again and starts the same routine.

No other industry in the United States has a workforce so dominated by adolescents. About two-thirds of the nation's fast food workers are under the age of twenty. Teenagers open the fast food outlets in the morning, close them at night, and keep them going at all hours in between. Even the managers and assistant managers are sometimes in their late teens . . . Instead of relying upon a . . . well-paid, and well-trained workforce, the fast food industry seeks out part-time, unskilled workers who are willing to accept low pay. Teenagers . . . are less expensive to hire than adults, [and] . . . easier to control.

**PROTECTING YOUTH**
*Protecting Youth at Work*, a report on child labor published by the National Academy of Sciences in 1998 . . . concluded that the long hours many American teenagers now spend on the job pose a great risk to their future educational and financial success. Numerous studies have found that kids who work up to twenty hours a week during the school year generally benefit from the experience, gaining an increased sense of personal responsibility and self-esteem. But kids who work more than that are far more likely to cut classes and drop out of high school. Teenage boys who work longer hours are much more likely to develop substance abuse problems and commit petty crimes. . . .

Elisa Zamot is a junior in high school. In addition to working at McDonald's on the weekends, she also works there two days a week after school. All together, she spends about thirty to thirty-five hours a week at the restaurant. She earns the minimum wage. Her parents, Carlos and Cynthia, are loving but strict. They're Puerto Rican and moved to Colorado Springs from New Jersey. They make sure Elisa does all her homework and impose a midnight curfew. Elisa's usually too tired to stay out late, anyway. Her school bus arrives at six in the morning. . . .

Elisa had wanted to work at McDonald's ever since she was a toddler – a feeling shared by many of the McDonald's workers I met in Colorado Springs. But now she hates the job and is desperate to quit. Working at the counter, she constantly has to deal with rude remarks and complaints. Many of the customers look down on fast food workers and feel entitled to treat them with disrespect. Sweet-faced Elisa is often yelled at by strangers angry that their food's taking too long. . . . One elderly woman threw a hamburger at her because there was mustard on it. Elisa hopes to find her next job at a Wal-Mart, at a clothing store, anywhere but a fast food restaurant.

After graduating, Elisa hopes to go to Princeton. She's saving most of her earnings to buy a car. The rest is spent on clothes, shoes, and school lunches. A lot of kids at her school don't save any of the money earned at their fast food jobs. They buy beepers, cellular phones, stereos, and designer clothes.

During my interview with local high school kids, I heard numerous stories of fifteen-year-olds working twelve-hour shifts at fast food restaurants and sophomores working long past midnight. The Fair Labor Standards Act prohibits the employment of kids under the age of sixteen for more than three hours on a school day, or later than seven o'clock at night. Colorado state law prohibits the employment of kids under the age of eighteen for more than eight hours a day. . . .

Most of the high school students I met liked working at fast food restaurants. They complained that the work was boring . . . but enjoyed earning money, getting away from school and parents, hanging out with friends at work, and goofing off as much as possible. Few of the kids liked working the counter or dealing with customers. They much preferred working in the kitchen, where they could talk to friends and fool around. . . .

None of the fast food workers I met in Colorado Springs spoke of organizing a union. The thought has probably never occurred to them. When these kids don't like the working conditions or the manager, they quit. Then they find a job at another restaurant, and the cycle goes on and on.

## AFTER READING

### A Check your answers

1 With your partner, go back to your true/false answers in **Test your knowledge** on page 116. Check your answers against what the author said in the text. How accurate were your guesses?

2 Discuss and compare your answers with your group.

### B Annotate the reading

1 Read about a useful technique to use when reading difficult material, for example, from a textbook.

### Annotating

Annotating is a way of reading with a pencil in hand. As you read, you mark up the text in any way that makes sense to you. If you don't want to mark directly on the text, you can make a photocopy and write on it.

- Underline, circle, highlight, or bracket important or interesting words, phrases, and sentences.

- Draw arrows to connect related ideas.

- Write comments and questions in the margins.

- Number points.

- Make any other markings that are meaningful to you.

> Most people who annotate read a text several times and make more annotations each time they read it. Rereading helps readers see things in a new way and with fresh understanding.

2 Reread the text and annotate it.

3 Explain your annotations to a partner.

## C Find advantages and disadvantages

1 In this text, Schlosser presents both positive and negative aspects of teenagers working in fast food restaurants. With a partner, make a list of the advantages and the disadvantages he presents. Which list is longer?

| Advantages | Disadvantages |
|---|---|
| | |

2 Share your lists with your group. If you can think of any other advantages or disadvantages of teenagers working in fast food restaurants from your own experience, add them to your lists.

## HOW IT'S WRITTEN

### Identify general and specific information

1 This reading gives two kinds of information: specific information about Elisa's work experience and general information about teenagers working in fast food restaurants. With a partner, number the paragraphs and then label each paragraph with **S** if it contains mainly specific information and **G** if it contains mainly general information.

2 Compare your findings with your group.

3 Reread only the parts of the text that present general information, skipping the parts about Elisa. What effect does that have on you as a reader? What does Elisa's story add? Discuss this with the class.

# TOPICS FOR WRITING

## Choose one topic to write about

Whichever topic you choose, make sure you support your opinion with facts and examples from this reading, from your own experience, or from your observations of other people. Include both personal stories and general information.

1. Write a letter to parents of a teenager giving them advice about whether or not they should let their child work in a fast food restaurant.

2. What is your opinion of teenagers as "perfect candidates" for fast food jobs? Write an essay explaining your point of view.

3. According to this article, U.S. law says that children under the age of 16 should not work more than three hours a day on a school day, nor should they work after 7:00 P.M. What is your opinion of this law? Write an essay explaining your point of view.

# AFTER WRITING

## Share your writing

1 Attach a blank sheet of paper to your writing. Join a group of classmates who wrote on the same topic you did. Exchange papers and read at least three other essays. On each blank paper, write at least one comment, reaction or question.

2 Read your classmates' feedback about your writing.

3 As a group, choose one essay to be read to the class.

# BEFORE READING

## Think about the topic

1 Read the title. What kinds of jobs do you think are significant, important, and meaningful? Make a list and freewrite about your list.

2 Discuss what you wrote with a partner.

# To be of use
Marge Piercy

*This poem is from a collection called* The Art of Blessing the Day: Poems with a Jewish Theme. *Marge Piercy is the author of over twenty-five novels and books of poetry.*

The people I love best
jump into work head first
without dallying in the shadows
and swim off with sure strokes almost out of sight.
They seem to become natives of that element,
the black sleek heads of seals
bouncing like half-submerged balls.

I love people who harness themselves, an ox to a heavy cart,
who pull like water buffalo, with massive patience,
who strain in the mud and muck to move things forward,
who do what has to be done, again and again.

I want to be with people who submerge
in the task, who go into the fields to harvest
and work in a row and pass the bags along,
who are not parlor generals and field deserters but move in a common rhythm
when the food must come in or the fire be put out.

The work of the world is common as mud.
Botched, it smears the hands, crumbles to dust.
But the thing worth doing well done
has a shape that satisfies, clean and evident.
Greek amphoras for wine or oil,
Hopi vases that held corn, are put in museums
but you know they were made to be used.
The pitcher cries for water to carry
and a person for work that is real.


## AFTER READING

### A Read and respond

1 With a partner, read the poem aloud to each other several times.

2 Freewrite for a few minutes about what you noticed the second and third times you heard the poem.

## B Make a personal connection

1 Look back at what you wrote in **Think about the topic** on page 120. Freewrite about how Piercy describes meaningful work and people who do it. Is her description similar to or different from yours?

2 Share your freewriting with a partner.

## C Act out the poem

1 Sometimes powerful images in poetry can be acted out. In your group, have one person read the poem aloud while the others act out what is happening. Use the words of the poem to guide your actions, and use your imagination!

2 Act out your version of the poem for the whole class.

# HOW IT'S WRITTEN

## A Find metaphors and similes

1 Piercy uses many metaphors and similes to describe the work of the world, the people who do it, and things worth doing well. With a partner, reread the poem and list all of the metaphors and similes. (See the toolbox *Metaphors and Similes* on page 86.)

2 Put the metaphors and similes into categories. For example, how many of them have to do with animals?

3 Summarize your findings for the whole class.

## B Listen to the sounds

1 Poets pay a lot of attention to the sounds of the words in their poems. Poetry is meant to be read aloud. In your group, have one person read the poem aloud while the rest of the group listens with their eyes closed, letting the sounds of the poem fill their minds.

2 One way poets create poetry is through alliteration. Read about this technique.

### Alliteration

Alliteration is the repetition of the same letter or sound at the beginning of words that are close together. One example of alliteration is the common phrase "calm, cool, and collected."

3 With a partner, go back through the poem and mark places where there is alliteration. What effect does the alliteration have on you?

4 Report your findings to the class.

## TOPICS FOR WRITING

### Choose one topic to write about

Whichever topic you choose, include words that appeal to the reader's senses (see the toolbox *Using Your Senses* on page 10) and metaphors and similes (see the toolbox *Metaphors and Similes* on page 86). Experiment with alliteration.

1. Write a poem about the work of the world, the people who do it, and things that are worth doing well. Use your freewritings in **Think about the topic** on page 120 and **Read and respond** on page 121 as a way to get started. Divide the poem into three or four stanzas.

2. At the end of her poem, Piercy says "The pitcher cries for water to carry and a person for work that is real." Write an essay about how you interpret her statement, answering one or more of these questions:
   - What does this statement and the whole poem say about the work of the world?
   - How does this statement relate to you and your own life?
   - Why do you think Piercy said it?
   - How would you change your life if you took this poem seriously?
   - Why do you think it's important for people to read this poem?

3. Write a short essay that begins with one of these sentence starters:
   - *I want to work with people who . . .*
   - *I like to share responsibilities with people who . . .*

## AFTER WRITING

### Share your writing

1 Read what you wrote to a partner. Ask your partner to restate what he or she understood and what he or she liked best about the writing.

2 Make notes in your log.

> ## Writer's Tip
>
> *Read poetry every day of your life. Poetry is good because it flexes muscles you don't use often enough. Poetry expands the senses and keeps them in prime condition. It keeps you aware of your nose, your eye, your ear, your tongue, your hand.*
>
> **Ray Bradbury**

## BEFORE READING

### Think about the topic

1 Read the title and introductory information. With your group, make a cluster of words and phrases you associate with the word *paramedics*.

2 Read your group's associations to the class.

 # The Model Medic
Sarah Freeman

*This profile of a New York City paramedic (or emergency medical technician) appeared in the newspaper* The Irish Echo *in December, 2002. It is based on interviews.*

Rhona Chambers has been spat on, vomited on and urinated on yet claims that such experiences are better than the treatment she received at the hands of the fashion industry. As a paramedic in New York City, this former model puts up with a lot in the line of duty. She has relinquished all contact with the modeling world and the life of glamour and privilege that goes with it. She doesn't regret it for one minute. "I love going to work as a paramedic. I never liked going to work as a model," she said last week.

Chambers grew up in a sheltered Mormon Community in Utah. . . . By the time she was 16, Chambers knew that she wanted to go to New York. She and a friend had long talked about moving there. She wanted to be a model, he wanted to be a makeup artist. Finally, they took the step and left Utah.

"We were so young, we didn't really think about what we were doing," Chambers said. They shared an apartment in the East Village and Chambers got her first job in the fashion industry. . . . Now 36, Chambers recalls her early missteps with laughter.

The first step in a modeling career is to build up a portfolio of work in Europe. Models are sent to Paris and Milan where there is a constant demand for fresh faces. As Chambers describes the experience: "You are sent to France at 17 and you don't speak French. The agency doesn't provide chaperones, because they don't give a damn. Their concern is that you work hard and earn money for them. As a young girl you are very vulnerable."

Chamber's experience in Italy was not much better. "My first job was for Italian *Vogue*," she recalled. "That sounds glamorous but the reality is different. We were all housed in a hotel together. The agencies would give our telephone number to all the playboys that hung around the fashion scene." . . .

Chambers knew the work would not last forever. "Magazine work dries up once a model reaches her early 20s and her skin is not as young. . . . Chambers knew she wanted out of the business when she found herself dressed as a green bean for a vitamin advertising campaign. . . .

Once Chambers turned 28, she realized that the work was not going to improve and she started to look at other options. She had been fascinated by medicine since she was 10. "I cut my finger and needed stitches. The doctor explained the procedure to me and I was so interested," she recalled.

She started to do an Emergency Medical Training course and really enjoyed the challenge. The next logical step was to do the paramedic training. "That involved a very intense course, two years' work squeezed into one," she said. . . .

Chambers completed the training and soon found herself immersed in the work. "Despite the dangers, I love it," she said. "Most of us are adrenaline junkies. We love the more exciting jobs where people have been shot or someone has fallen under a train." . . .

Chambers enjoys the down-to-earth nature of the job, an atmosphere in which colleagues are close. . . . One of the first partners she had on the job was Eddie Cabellero. They worked together in Brooklyn. Caballero was surprised at first that a fashion model would want to work as a paramedic. . . . Caballero said, "Rhona may not fit the typical description of a paramedic, but she epitomizes all the important qualities of what makes an excellent paramedic. She is knowledgeable and loves helping people." . . .

Chambers admits that there are unsavory aspects to the job, and distressing incidents, such as when she was punched when she was pregnant. . . . "People get angry with us if they think we are not doing enough to help the victim," she said. "I can understand that. They are frightened and don't realize that we have all the same equipment as an emergency room. . . .

Chambers clearly relishes the work, and does not miss the fickle world of fashion. "We are making a difference and helping people," she said. "I have no interest in clothes designers now, no interest at all." . . .

Chambers is aware of the hectic nature of her job and the toll it can take. "The burnout factor is high for paramedics," she said. "You can't really be a full-time paramedic at 50, but if I could, I would like to do this for the rest of my life."

# AFTER READING

## A Respond to the reading

1 Choose one of the following ways to respond to a reading:
   - *Freewriting* (see page 2)
   - *Response Questions* (see page 9)
   - *Double Entry Response* (see page 26)

2 Share your response with your group. Afterwards, explain why you chose the particular reading response you did.

**B** Find positive and negative points

1 Using information from the reading, fill out the chart below with positive and negative features of being a model and being a paramedic.

| Occupation | Positive Points | Negative Points |
| --- | --- | --- |
| Model | | |
| Paramedic | | |

2 Compare your chart with those of members of your group. Discuss whether or not you would agree with Rhona Chambers's career choice.

## HOW IT'S WRITTEN

### Discover how writers use questions

1 Read about a strategy writers may keep in mind when writing about a topic.

### The Reporter's Formula

Newspaper reporters try to answer several questions to give their readers the information they need. This is called the "reporter's formula." Other writers use this formula, too. The questions begin with these words:

*Who? What? When? Where? Why? How?*

Answering these questions can help you as both a reader and as a writer. As a reader, the questions can help you find and organize the important information from a piece of writing. As a writer, the questions help you gather ideas and make sure you include the essential points about a topic.

2 With your group, discuss what questions Freeman asked and answered to develop "The Model Medic."

3 What would you like Freeman to tell you more about? Write down two or three questions you would like to ask her.

4 Share your questions with the class.

# TOPICS FOR WRITING

## Choose one topic to write about

Whichever topic you choose, you are going to interview someone. You will need to find out about the type of work the person does, the kinds of equipment or tools he or she uses, how the person came to do this work, how the person feels about the work, and difficulties the person has had to overcome. When you write, make sure you include a description of the person and your thoughts about what he or she does. Include quotes in your essay. When doing the interview, follow the steps given in the toolbox *Interview Tips*.

1 Write about a person who is doing a dangerous or highly skilled job.

2 Write about a person who is doing a job you would like to do some day.

3 Write about a person who is doing volunteer work that is helping to make people's lives better.

## Interview Tips

- Make a list of questions. Use questions in the reporter's formula to get started. (See the toolbox *The Reporter's Formula* on the opposite page.)

- Share your questions with someone else and see if you can think of other questions you could add to your list.

- Put your questions in a logical order.

- Think of ways to encourage the person to tell you one or two anecdotes (stories).

- Choose a person to interview that you can go back to in case you want to do a follow-up interview.

- If you can, record the interview on tape; otherwise, make sure you take good notes.

# AFTER WRITING

## Share your writing

1 Share your writing with classmates who chose the same topic as you.

2 Report back to the class about what was similar or different about each person's writing, both in *what* they wrote and *how* they wrote it. Tell the class about any memorable quotes in your classmates' writings.

## Writer's Tip

*Get people talking. Learn to ask questions that will elicit answers about what is most interesting or vivid in their lives . . . Whatever form of nonfiction you write, it will come alive in proportion to the number of "quotes" that you can weave into it naturally as you go along.*

**William Zinsser**

3 Exchange papers with a classmate who wrote on a different topic. Read your partner's essay. Then write down two or three questions that will help your partner add more information or details to the essay.

4 Write some notes to yourself about how to further develop your essay. Include a list of additional information you need from the person you interviewed.

## Writer's Tip

*There are an enormous number of people out there with invaluable information to share with you, and all you have to do is pick up the phone. They love it when you do, just as you love it when people ask if they can pick your brain about something you happen to know a great deal about.*

**Anne Lamott**

# WORK: REVISION

## A Choose one piece of writing

1 Reread the pieces you wrote for the **Topics for Writing** sections of WORK. Also read any feedback from classmates and notes you wrote for yourself for each piece.

2 Pick one piece to revise.

## B Improve the beginning

1 Read about what beginnings should do.

### Beginnings

Smart writers try to write an opening that "hooks" the reader right away. Many writers write this opening after they have written their first draft and know what they are going to say. They then go back to the beginning and revise the opening, looking for a way to catch the reader's attention.

Once you have the reader's attention, you have to hold it. You want to make the reader continue to read. Writers do this in many ways. Essay writers usually reveal the message, main point, or topic in a general way and then focus the reader's attention on a particular aspect of the subject. Story writers may describe a place, a mood, and a character that reveal where the story is going.

In summary, a good beginning should do two things:

■ **Get the reader's attention:** Ask a question. Tell a relevant anecdote. Start with a story that is an example of your point. Use a quote.

■ **Focus the readers' attention:** Let the reader know what you're going to write about and the aspect of the subject you want him or her to think about. Don't give too much general information; you may bore the reader. Get quickly to your own focus or the perspective you're presenting. But don't be too blunt; don't say, "I'm going to tell you about . . ."

2 With a partner, reread the first sentences of each of the pieces in this section, WORK ("The First Job," "Behind the Counter," "To be of use," and "The Model Medic"). Discuss whether or not the writers succeeded in hooking you into the texts. If you think they did, discuss how they did it.

3 Now look at the beginning of your essay. Does it make your reader want to read more? Ask your partner for an opinion.

4 Think of at least three different ways to begin your essay. Try them out on your partner. Finally, choose one and include it in your final draft.

## C Share your writing

1 Read your writing to your group.

2 With your group, choose one piece of writing to read to the class.

**Writer's Tip**

[T]he lead must capture the reader immediately and force him [or her] to keep reading. It must cajole him [or her] with freshness or novelty or paradox, or with humor, or with surprise, or with an unusual idea, or an interesting fact, or a question.

**William Zinsser**

## Exploring Emotions

# BEFORE READING

## A Gather ideas about the topic

1 Read about a technique that can help you organize your thoughts before reading or writing.

> ### *Venn Diagram*
>
> Making a Venn diagram is a way to help you see how two concepts are similar and different. To make a Venn diagram, draw two slightly overlapping circles, like this:
>
>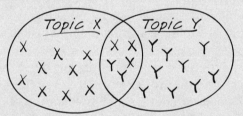
>
> Label one circle with a word or phrase showing one of the concepts and label the other circle with a word or phrase showing the other concept. In the first circle, put words that only apply to the first concept. In the second circle, put words that only apply to the second concept. In the part where the two circles overlap, write down any words that apply to both concepts. The overlapping of the circles shows you what words and phrases connect to both of the concepts.
>
> This technique is useful when preparing to write about a topic that has two aspects to it, like two ideas or two points of view.

2 Use the instructions above to create a Venn diagram with the concepts *hope* and *success*.

3 Write your definition of *hope*.

## B Write as you read

Where you see [pause] in the reading, stop reading and write one thing you understood about what you read and any questions you have at that point.

# Hope Emerges As Key to Success in Life

## Daniel Goleman

*Psychologist Daniel Goleman has published many articles on stress, meditation, and relaxation, and has written a number of books on psychology. This article appeared in the* New York Times.

Psychologists are finding that hope plays a surprisingly potent role in giving people a measurable advantage in realms as diverse as academic achievement, bearing up in onerous jobs and coping with tragic illness. . . .

"Hope has proven a powerful predictor of outcome in every study we've done so far," said Dr. Charles R. Snyder, a psychologist at the University of Kansas who has devised a scale to assess how much hope a person has.

For example, in research with 3,920 college students, Dr. Snyder and his colleagues found that the level of hope among freshmen at the beginning of their first semester was a more accurate predictor of their college grades than were their S.A.T. scores or their grade point averages in high school, the two measures most commonly used to predict college performance.

"Students with high hope set themselves higher goals and know how to work to attain them," Dr. Snyder said. "When you compare students of equivalent intellectual aptitude and past academic achievements, what sets them apart is hope."

In devising a way to assess hope scientifically, Dr. Snyder went beyond the simple notion that hope is merely the sense that everything will turn out all right. "That notion is not concrete enough, and it blurs two key components of hope," Dr. Snyder said. "Having hope means believing you have both the will and the way to accomplish your goals, whatever they may be."

Despite the folk wisdom that "where there's a will there's a way," Dr. Snyder has found that the two are not necessarily connected. In a study of more than 7,000 men and women from 18 to 70 years old, Dr. Snyder discovered that only about 40 percent of people are hopeful in the technical sense of believing they typically have the energy and means to accomplish their goals, whatever those might be.

The study found that about 20 percent of the people believed in their ability to find the means to attain their goals, but said they had little will to do so. Another 20 percent have the opposite pattern, saying they had the energy to motivate themselves but little confidence that they would find the means.

The rest had little hope at all, reporting that they typically had neither the will nor the way.

"It's not enough just to have the wish for something," said Dr. Snyder. "You need the means, too. On the other hand, all the skills to solve a problem won't help if you don't have the willpower to do it."

[pause]

## TRAITS AMONG THE HOPEFUL

Dr. Snyder found that people with high levels of hope share several attributes:

- Unlike people who are low in hope, they turn to friends for advice on how to achieve their goals.

- They tell themselves they can succeed at what they need to do.

- Even in a tight spot, they tell themselves things will get better as time goes on.

- They are flexible enough to find different ways to get to their goals.

- If hope for one goal fades, they aim for another. "Those low in hope tend to become fixated on one goal, and persist even when they find themselves blocked," Dr. Snyder said. "They just stay at it and get frustrated."

- They show an ability to break a formidable task into specific, achievable chunks. "People low in hope see only the large goal, and not the small steps to it along the way," Dr. Snyder said.

People who get a high score on the hope scale "have had as many hard times as those with low scores, but have learned to think about it in a hopeful way, seeing a setback as a challenge, not a failure," said Dr. Snyder.

[pause]

## NURTURING A BRIGHTER OUTLOOK

He and his colleagues are trying to design programs to help children develop the ways of thinking found in hopeful people. "They've often learned their mental habit of hopefulness from a specific person, like a friend or teacher," Dr. Snyder said.

"Hope can be nurtured," he said. Dr. Snyder has made a videotape for that purpose, showing interviews with students who are high on hope, to help freshmen better handle the stress of their first year.

[pause]

# AFTER READING

## A Respond to the reading

1 Compare your definition of *hope* with the author's. Discuss differences and similarities with a partner.

2 Read to your partner what you wrote after each section of "Hope Emerges As Key to Success in Life."

3 Freewrite a reaction to one or two of the ideas you understood from the article. Share your freewriting with your group.

**B Understand the reading**

1 With a partner, do the following:

   ① Find one paragraph both of you had trouble understanding. Reread it and discuss what you think it means.

   ② In the section "Traits among the Hopeful," find the sentence that says, "Dr. Snyder found that people with high levels of hope share several attributes." Reread the six points that follow the sentence and restate each point in your own words.

2 Share your ideas with the class.

## HOW IT'S WRITTEN

### A Think about headings

1 Notice the headings in the article. How did these headings help you as a reader? Discuss with a partner.

2 Share your findings with the class.

### B Observe references to experts

1 Writers often incorporate information from other sources in their writing. In this article, Goleman writes mainly about the research of another psychologist, Dr. Charles R. Snyder. Reread the article with a partner and answer the following questions:

   ① How does Goleman introduce the psychologist Dr. Snyder? What information does he include? What effect does this information have on you as a reader?

   ② Which paragraphs describe Snyder's findings and/or restate something Snyder said? What words and expressions tell the reader that the ideas are not Goleman's but Snyder's? Write down these words and expressions.

   ③ At times, Goleman uses direct quotes from Snyder. At other times, he summarizes or restates Snyder's ideas. Write down all the differences between the direct quotes and the restatements. Why does Goleman use both?

2 Share your findings with the class.

3 Read a summary of differences between quoting and paraphrasing.

## Quoting and Paraphrasing

In an essay, if you use other people's ideas, always state where they come from. You must name the author, the title of the work, the place and date of publication, and the publisher or the Web site (if found on the Internet). When you use someone else's words or ideas without citing the source, it is called **plagiarism**. This is not acceptable in academic writing and may result in a serious punishment if discovered by your teacher. In professional writing, it is illegal.

When writers use the exact words someone has said or written, they use quotation marks (" ") to set the words off and to show readers that the words belong to someone else. These are called quotes, or quotations.

> "It's so hard to tell someone about what you think," said Gil in
> A *Gathering of Old Men* (Ernest J. Gaines, NY; Vintage Books, 1992,
> p. 111). It reminded me of when I was a little kid.

When writers want to report what someone has said without using the person's exact words, they tell about the ideas that were expressed using their own words. This is called a paraphrase. In this case, no quotation marks are needed.

> In the article "They're Home Alone" in November 29, 1999,
> *Newsweek* (pp. 105–106), Annetta Miller talks about children who,
> around the age of 11 to 13, have been left home alone after school.

## TOPICS FOR WRITING

### Choose one topic to write about

Whichever topic you choose, include information from "Hope Emerges As Key to Success in Life." Make sure that you cite the article appropriately.

1. Pick one statement from "Hope Emerges As Key to Success in Life" that you find especially meaningful. Copy it exactly as it's written. Use this quotation as the beginning of a piece of writing in any form – a short essay, a story, a memoir, a poem, or a letter.

2. Write an essay in response to the article "Hope Emerges As Key to Success in Life." Include a summary of the article, your reaction to its ideas, and a conclusion that offers your readers advice. In your essay, cite the article.

3. Write a letter of advice to a student in his or her first year of college. Tell the student what Dr. Snyder discovered about the connection between hope and success in college. Give the student some suggestions about how to nurture hope.

## AFTER WRITING

### Share your writing

1 Form a group with people who chose the same writing topic. Read one another's papers and write several comments for the writer. Your comments should be supportive and helpful. You could do one or more of the following:

- Ask a question for more information.

- Tell about a part that confused you.

- Make a suggestion to make the writing clearer.

- Write a comment about the beginning or the ending.

- Comment on the organization.

- Tell the writer something else that you noticed.

2 After you read your classmates' comments, think about what you might add or change when you revise this. Write a few notes to yourself.

. . . . . . . . . . . . . . . . . . . . . . . . . . . . . . . . . . . . . . . . . . . . . . . . . . . . . . . . . . . . . . . . . . . . . . .

## BEFORE READING

### Think about the topic

1 In your group, make a list of situations in which you or someone you know cried. Share your list with the class.

2 Freewrite about how people react to crying in your culture. When is crying acceptable? When is crying unacceptable?

3 Share your writing with your group.

# It's O.K. to Cry: Tears Are Not Just a Bid for Attention

Jane Brody

*Jane Brody is a medical journalist and the author of seven popular books, including the bestselling* Jane Brody's Good Food Book. *She currently serves as the personal health columnist for the* New York Times. *Also a highly respected fitness and nutrition expert, Brody has appeared on hundreds of television and radio programs.*

Crying is hardly an activity encouraged by society. Tears, be they of sorrow, anger, or joy, typically make Americans feel uncomfortable and embarrassed.

The shedder of tears is likely to apologize, even when a devastating tragedy was the provocation. The observer of tears is likely to do everything possible to put an end to the emotional outpouring. But judging from recent studies of crying behavior, links between illness and crying and the chemical composition of tears, both those responses to tears are often inappropriate and may even be counterproductive.

People are the only animals definitely known to shed emotional tears. Since evolution has given rise to few if any purposeless physiological responses, it is reasonable to assume that crying has one or more functions that enhance survival.

Although some observers have suggested that crying is a way to elicit assistance from others (as a crying baby might from its mother), the shedding of tears is hardly necessary to get help. Vocal cries, whines or whimpers such as animals use would have been quite enough, more likely than tears to gain attention. So, it appears, there must be something special about tears themselves.

Indeed, the new studies suggest that emotional tears may play a direct role in alleviating stress. University of Minnesota researchers who are studying the chemical composition of tears have recently isolated two important chemicals, leucine-enkephalin and prolactin, from emotional tears. The first of these may be an endorphin, one of the body's natural pain-relieving substances.

Both chemicals are found only in tears that are shed in response to emotion. Tears shed because of exposure to a cut onion would contain no such substance.

Researchers at several other institutions are investigating the usefulness of tears as a means of diagnosing human ills and monitoring drugs.

At Tulane University's tear and analysis laboratory Dr. Peter Kastl . . . and his colleagues report that they can use tears to detect drug abuse and exposure to medication, to determine whether a contact lens fits properly or why it may be uncomfortable, to study the causes of "dry eye" syndrome and the effects of eye surgery, and perhaps even to measure exposure to environmental pollutants.

At Columbia University Dr. Linsy Farris and colleagues are studying tears for clues to the diagnosis of diseases away from the eyes. Tears can be obtained painlessly without invading the body and only tiny amounts are needed to perform highly refined analyses.

Tears are produced continuously by the tiny lacrimal glands in the upper, outer corners of the eyes, under the lids. Every time you blink (on average 13 times a minute) your eyelids carry a film of tears across the corneas. . . . The windshield-wiper effect of the blink also helps to cleanse the eyes of debris and irritating chemicals and perhaps even to fight infection, since tears contain anti-bacterial enzymes.

Tears that do not evaporate leave through the lacrimal canal and sac at the inner corner of the eye. From there they drain through the nose, which is why you usually have to blow your nose when you cry. Tears shed down the face represent an overflow of the lacrimal ducts, as might happen to gutters during a downpour.

Crying behavior and sounds may also be useful in diagnosing abnormalities in infants. Two California researchers found that ailing babies typically have high-pitched, shrill cries.

Crying also seems to serve as a means of communication for babies before they learn to talk; mothers soon learn to distinguish between cries of pain, fear and hunger, and those of crankiness.

As for adults, Dr. [William] Frey's studies of more than 200 men and women who kept "crying diaries" for a month found that 85 percent of the women and 73 percent of the men said they felt better after crying. On average, the participants reported a 40 percent reduction in stress after crying.

Despite this reported relief, men do not cry often – only one-fifth as often as women. Forty-five percent of the men, but only 9 percent of the women, shed no emotional tears during the monthlong study. Furthermore, when men do cry they often fail to shed tears; the tears well up in their eyes but do not spill over.

Dr. Frey suggests that the holding back of tears may be a reason why men develop more stress-related diseases than women do. Dr. Margaret Crepeau of the Marquette University College of Nursing found that people with stress-related disorders – for example, ulcers and colitis – were more likely than healthy people to view crying as a sign of weakness or loss of control. The ill people also reported that they cried less often.

If the theory that tears relieve stress is correct, how does one account for tears of joy? Traditional explanations are that crying at graduations, weddings and happy endings really reflects unhappy feelings, such as the "loss" of a child to a new spouse or anxiety about the child's future. However, a more likely reason is simply that tears of joy are a response to intense emotion, which is stressful whether the feeling is sad or happy.

In any event Dr. Frey believes the evidence gathered is sufficiently convincing to warrant a change in attitude toward crying. It's time, he says, for adults to stop telling children things like "Now, now, don't cry" and "Big boys don't cry." Crying is a natural phenomenon and the withholding of tears appears to be a danger to health.

# AFTER READING

## A Respond to the reading

1 Working with your group, reread the article and underline the benefits of crying.

2 What did you underline that you did not know before you read this article? Did learning this new information change your opinion about crying? Discuss these questions with your group.

3 Write two or three sentences about what you thought and felt before and after you read the article.

## B Observe references to experts

1 The author uses scientific research to support her argument. With a partner, reread the article and make a list of the experts Brody cites. Write a brief summary of each expert's research finding next to that person's name.

2 Compare your summaries with those of others in the class.

3 Explain why you think the author uses so many experts' opinions.

# HOW IT'S WRITTEN

## A Examine the beginning

1 Work with a partner. Reread the first four paragraphs. Why do you think Brody chose to start her essay this way? Is the introduction effective? Why or why not?

2 Share your thoughts with the class.

## B Notice how research is reported

1 Work with your group. Look at where Brody refers to scientific research in her article. What words and expressions does she use to report research findings? Make a list of these words and expressions.

2 Share your findings with the class.

# TOPICS FOR WRITING

## Choose one topic to write about

● Despite the facts that there are benefits to crying, many people never cry. Write an essay in which you argue the benefits of crying. Convince your readers that it's O.K. to cry. Use examples from your own experience to show why you feel this way. Cite a passage from "It's O.K. to Cry" to support your argument.

2 Think of a time when someone you know was crying. Describe the situation. Write a letter to this person now. Explain what you used to think about crying. Tell how your opinion has changed after reading "It's O.K. to Cry." Quote something from the article that you think will be particularly helpful to this person.

3 Write an essay in two parts. In the first part, summarize Brody's article "It's O.K. to Cry." In the second part, include your reaction (opinions, thoughts, and feelings) to the article. Add an ending that ties the two parts together.

## AFTER WRITING

### Share your writing

1 Proofread your paper by reading it aloud and touching each word with a pen. (See the toolbox *Proofreading* on page 97.) Find at least three things to change.

2 Form a group with two or three people in the class who wrote about the same topic. Read your papers aloud to one another. Notice the different ways in which you approached the same topic. Make a list of the similarities and differences in your papers.

3 Report to the whole class on what your group wrote about, giving a one- or two-sentence summary of each person's ideas about crying. Explain what the members of your group agree on and disagree on.

· · · · · · · · · · · · · · · · · · · · · · · · · · · · · · · · · · · · · · · · · · · · · · · · · · · · · · · · · ·

## BEFORE READING

### Think about the topic

1 Read the title and introductory material. Freewrite about one of the following topics:

■ A time when you broke up with someone you loved.

■ A time when someone you loved broke up with you.

■ A time when a friend or someone you were close to went through the breakup of a relationship.

2 Exchange a few ideas with a partner.

# Going Through the House

Claire Braz-Valentine

*Claire Braz-Valentine is a widely published poet, award-winning playwright, and journalist. She has worked with youth at risk and incarcerated adults for many years. She is one of the few writers who is approved to work in maximum security prisons in the state of California. This poem appears in a collection called* Breaking Up Is Hard to Do, Stories by Women.

I don't care
really I don't.
I can remove you from my life
throw you out
like last year's calendar.

So you want another woman.
So fine.
I'll start with the refrigerator,
remove your peanut butter,
your hot sauce,
that stupid stuff you put on your steaks,
and the last piece of the cake I made for your birthday
I'll put them,
no I'll throw them,
I will smash them to smithereens in the garbage can.

I'll go through the closet,
grab that shirt of yours
that I used to wear in the garden
the sock you forgot in the corner
wad them up
tear them up
shred them
take them into the street and
drive my car over them
get them out of my sight.

I'll yank that smart ass teddy bear
you bought me for Christmas
right off of my bed pillow
rip its seedy little eyes out
wipe that wise ass grin off its face
hang its skin from a nail
on the tree you planted
Then I'll kill the tree.

I'll take every card you ever gave me
not read those dumb sappy lies anymore
about how you'll love me forever,
burn them up,

pulverize them into cat litter.
I can do it with my eyes closed.

I'll get that picture from the living room
that you bought at the flea market
and rip it up
flush it down the toilet.
You always had rotten taste anyway.

I'll yank clothes that you liked me to wear
off of their hangers,
go to Goodwill.
Go to hell.
Give them to her, the new woman,
but as you say,
she's so much smaller than I.
Who gives a shit?
I sure don't.

I'll get all my cleaning supplies
scrub the whole house
get your prints off.
Take a hot bath,
no a scalding one,
get your prints off me,
cut my hair,
paint my fingernails.
You always hated that,
wear the big earrings you said are flashy,
and lots of the perfume that made you sneeze,
get your smug scumsucking voice off my answering machine,
not forward your mail,
return it to sender,
tell them you died.

I'll do these things
I really will.
I don't care
really I don't.


## AFTER READING

### A Read and respond

1 Read the poem aloud to a partner.

2 A good way to respond to a poem is to explain how it makes you feel and
   what it reminds you of in your own life. Freewrite in your log about this for
   five minutes.

3 Share what you wrote with your partner.

## B Analyze the author's feelings

1 The author says, "I don't care really I don't." Is she telling the truth? How do you know? Underline two or three places in the poem to support your opinion.

2 Share your findings with your group.

# HOW IT'S WRITTEN

## A Notice specific details

1 The poet is very specific about what her lover has left behind. With a partner, reread the poem and underline the items that were left behind. What do these items tell us about the person that left? Which items make the poet the angriest? How do you know? Talk about your answers to these questions.

2 Summarize your discussion for the class.

## B Study the verbs

1 The poet uses strong active verbs to tell what she will do to the things her lover left behind. Reread the poem and underline the strong active verbs she uses. If you are unsure of the meanings of some of the verbs, look them up in the dictionary.

2 With a partner, make a list of the verbs you underlined. Put a plus (+) sign beside the ten verbs you think are strongest.

3 Beside each verb on your list of the ten strongest verbs, write what senses each verb appeals to. For example, "flush" may appeal to your sense of hearing and of sight, as you can imagine hearing the water in the toilet bowl and seeing it drain away.

# TOPICS FOR WRITING

Choose one topic to write about

1 Remember a time when you got really angry. What did you do to express your anger? What images, colors, and sensations come to mind when you remember this experience? Write a poem about your anger. Use as many sensory details as you can to express your anger.

> ## Writer's Tip
>
> *Look for verbs of muscle, adjectives of exactitude.*
>
> Mary Oliver

**②** Since anger is such a difficult emotion to deal with, some people have found it helpful to write a letter to the person they are angry at, but not send the letter. Think about a time when you were angry at someone. Write a letter to this person starting with "I don't care really I don't." Tell what you would like to do to show your anger. Be as specific as possible. Use strong, active verbs.

**③** Tell the true story of an experience of breaking up. It could be a story about you breaking up with someone or about someone breaking up with you. Or you could write about someone you know who went through this experience. Show the emotions in the situation by using specific details and active verbs.

## AFTER WRITING

### A  Make your verbs effective

1 Underline your verbs. Which ones could be stronger?

2 Using a thesaurus, change at least three of the verbs.

> ## Writer's Tip
>
> *Verbs are very important. They are the action and energy of a sentence. Be aware of how you use them.*
>
> **Natalie Goldberg**

### B  Make your images effective

1  Look back at your writing. Make a list of the sensory details you have already used. Which ones have you left out? Include at least two images for each of the senses: two for sound, two for taste, two for touch, two for sight, and two for smell.

2 Add these images to your writing.

### C  Share your writing

1 Read your writing to people in your group. Ask your group members to listen for your verbs and your images.

2 Ask your group members to tell you which verbs they remember and which images they thought were most effective.

3 Take notes on what your listeners said about your writing. You may also want to write down some effective verbs and images you heard in your classmates' writing.

# BEFORE READING

## Relate to the setting

1 With your group, look at the picture below showing the kind of geography described in the story. Label parts of the picture with these words from the story: **mesa**, **cliff**, **canyon**, **slope**, **juniper tree**, and **desert**. If you don't know the meanings of these words, look in a dictionary or ask for help.

2 Discuss these questions with your group:

&#9312; Does this place look like any place you've ever been? Where? What did it feel like to be there?

&#9313; If you were in the place in the photo, what animals and plants do you think you might you encounter?

&#9314; What would it be like to be there? Think about sights, sounds, smells, climate, air quality, and temperature.

# Black Steer Canyon

Terry Tempest Williams

*This excerpt from Williams's book called* Refuge *tells the experience the author and her husband had while hiking with friends in a wilderness area in Utah, in the western United States.*

Brooke and I with a few good friends decided to go south for the Fourth of July: Dark Canyon, a remote area in southeastern Utah. On the map it appears without character. For years, I had dreamed of entering this primitive area where one can walk barefoot on slickrock for days, finding cool, midday soaks in hidden potholes. But first, we had to descend into Black Steer Canyon. Dark Canyon was one day away.

Somewhere between thoughts of rattlesnakes and finding the safest route down the steep, talus slope, I lost my footing. Skin, bone to stone, my head hit on rock and with my hands in my pockets I tumbled down the cliff until I was caught and saved by an old, juniper tree.

One of my companions, who was hiking behind me, yelled to see if I was all right. I answered yes, but as soon as I rolled over and tried to stand up with my pack still on, he said, "No, Terry – you're not all right. Lie down."

The river of blood that dyed my white shirt red was not from a nosebleed, but rather a long, deep pressure wound on my forehead, which had popped open like a peach hitting pavement. Lying down on the scree slope, I couldn't get two thoughts out of my mind: How badly am I hurt? And who will take care of me? I could feel myself losing consciousness.

Brooke hiked back up the slope to reach me. Fortunately, one of the members of our group was an emergency medical technician, with a well-supplied first-aid kit. I looked into her eyes as she was trying to stop the bleeding and asked, "Am I going to die?"

"Yes," she said. "But not today."

I relaxed.

"All you need when you get home," one friend said, "is some long bangs."

We had been joking all morning about how the only good part of this hike down Black Steer Canyon (now christened "Bum Steer Canyon") was that we wouldn't have to climb back out. The good news that I was going to live was now dampened by the view of the cliff before me. I was the only person who could carry me out.

With a tightly bandaged head, after some water and a twenty-minute rest, Brooke and I climbed out of the canyon. Once atop the mesa, where the going was flat, we traversed the desert in hundred-degree heat, pushed on by a shot of energy only adrenaline can produce. It took us four hours to get back to the car.

Ten hours later, we arrived in Salt Lake City and met Brooke's brother-in-law, a plastic surgeon at the LDS Hospital. He reopened the cut, which I saw with a mirror in hand, for the first time. It ran from my widow's peak straight down my forehead across the bridge of my nose down my cheek to the edge of my jaw. I saw the boney plate of my skull. Bedrock.

I have been marked by the desert. The scar meanders down the center of my forehead like a red, clay river. A natural feature on a map. I see the land and myself in context.

A blank spot on the map is an invitation to encounter the natural world, where one's character will be shaped by the landscape. To enter wilderness is to court risk, and risk favors the senses, enabling one to live well.

The landscapes we know and return to become places of solace. We are drawn to them because of the stories they tell, because of the memories they hold, or simply because of the sheer beauty that calls us back again and again.

I will return to Dark Canyon.

The unknown Utah that some see as a home for used razor blades, toxins, and biological warfare, is a landscape of the imagination, a secret we tell to those who will keep it.

"It's no secret among tradition peoples," Mimi said sitting next to me on my bed. "Many native cultures participate in scarification rituals. It's a sign that denotes change. The person who is scarred has undergone some kind of transformation."

The next time I looked into the mirror, I saw a woman with green eyes and a red scar painted down the center of her forehead.


## AFTER READING

### A  Find the main events

1 Reread the excerpt and underline the phrases or sentences in each paragraph that tell the main events.

2 Show what you underlined to your partner. Make any necessary changes until you and your partner agree.


### B  Respond to the reading

1 Reread the excerpt again. As you read, stop three or four times to make a double entry in your reading log. (See the toolbox *Double Entry Response* on page 26.)

2 Share your double entry with your group. Discuss similarities and differences in your responses.


### C  Understand the lessons learned

1 Reread the last seven paragraphs, starting with "I have been marked . . ."

2 With a partner, write down three conclusions the writer draws from her experience.

3 Explain to your group in your own words what one of the conclusions means.

# HOW IT'S WRITTEN

## Examine the ending

1 With a partner, reread the story and find where you think the ending begins.

2 With your partner, analyze the ending, using the following questions:

① What makes you think this is the ending? What words or sentences signal the ending?

② What technique does the author use in the ending? Does Williams summarize, generalize, draw conclusions, say something new, look to the future, find something positive, or do something else?

3 Discuss and share your thoughts about the ending with the class.

# TOPICS FOR WRITING

## Choose one topic to write about

❶ Choose one sentence from "Black Steer Canyon" to use as the first sentence of an essay or story of your own. Be sure to put the sentence in quotation marks and cite your source.

❷ Does this story remind you of a similar experience, for example, a hike, a mountain climb, a risky adventure, or a time someone you were with got hurt? Write an essay about what happened and what lessons you learned. Use details so that readers can visualize the place and experience the emotions.

❸ Pretend you are a newspaper reporter for the *Black Steer Canyon News* and you have just interviewed the plastic surgeon at LDS Hospital about Williams's accident. You are aware that local people are concerned about the dangers of hiking in this remote area and know that they would be interested in reading about it. Write an article that describes what happened. (See the toolbox *The Reporter's Formula* on page 126.)

# AFTER WRITING

## Share your writing

1 Exchange papers with a classmate. Write a response to your classmate's writing. Tell what you like best about the piece and give the writer one or two suggestions to make the images in his or her writing more powerful.

2 Read your partner's comments. Write a note to yourself about how you could revise this piece.

## Writer's Tip

*There's no such thing as a born writer. It's a skill you've got to learn.*

Larry Brown

**EXPLORING EMOTIONS: REVISION**

## A Choose one piece of writing

1 Reread the pieces you wrote for the **Topics for Writing** sections of EXPLORING EMOTIONS. Pick two pieces you might want to work on.

2 Show your choices to a partner. Have your partner help you choose one to revise.

## B Add to your writing

1 Read about techniques you can use to get additional information on your topic.

### Adding Information to Essays

If your essay seems too short or underdeveloped, here are some suggestions on how to add more information to your writing.

- Do a computer or library **search** for an article on your topic. Read the article, take notes of useful or interesting ideas, and use one or more of these ideas in your essay. Remember, if you use exact words from your reading, use quotation marks; otherwise, restate the information in your own words. In both cases, be sure to tell the title of the piece, author, and so on. (See the toolboxes *Citations Using APA Style* on page 95 and *Quoting and Paraphrasing* on page 135.)

- Do a **survey** on your topic. Write out a question or set of questions. Then survey people and record their answers, either in writing or on tape. Summarize your results; use percentages, charts or graphs, if possible. Add some quotations and the data to your essay.

- Read **other students' papers** on the same topic. Even if they took a different point of view, you can get ideas for your writing. Sometimes thinking about opposing points of view can help you better defend yours.

- Find some **statistics** that help support your point of view. Include these as evidence.

- Use **examples** that relate to the topic from what you read (anything you read, including novels). Or ask other people if they know "stories" to tell about this issue.

2 Use one or more of these techniques to add to your essay.

3 Revise and rewrite your piece.

## C Get feedback

1 Ask one or more readers to fill out the Peer Feedback Form on page 216 after they read your essay.

2 Use readers' comments from the form to help you improve your essay. Write a final draft.

## D Share your writing

1 Post your revised essay on a wall of the classroom. Walk around the room and read as many essays as you can. Take notes on interesting ideas and expressions.

2 Talk with the class about what you learned from reading your classmates' writing.

# UNIT 3
## A Changing World

Health

Environment

Gender Roles

Into the Future

# A Changing World

As I looked down, I saw a large river meandering slowly along for miles, passing from one country to another without stopping. I also saw huge forests, extending across several borders. And I watched the extent of one ocean touch the shores of separate continents. Two words leaped to mind as I looked down on all this: commonality and interdependence. We are one world.

John-David Bartoe

## A  Make connections

1  Read the quotation aloud with a partner.

2  Discuss with a partner where you think Bartoe might have been when he made these observations. After your discussion, look on page 224 to see the source of this quotation.

3  Together, discuss connections between what you read and the title of this unit: **A Changing World**.

4  Look at the photograph below and talk about any additional connections you see.

5  Share your ideas with your partner.

## B Gather ideas about the topic

1 Read about another way to gather ideas on a topic before writing.

### Looping

Looping is useful for finding your ideas on a given topic. Put the topic at the top of a page. Then freewrite without stopping for five to ten minutes. Read over what you have written. Pick out the main point you seem to be making and, below your freewrite, write a sentence stating it. It doesn't have to be what you wrote the most about. It can be something you like or even something you didn't quite say, but want to. It is like a kernel sentence.

Now do another loop. Start by using the sentence you just wrote. Again, write for five to ten minutes without stopping. Read what you wrote and determine the main idea of what you just wrote. Write a sentence about it. Now use this sentence to start your third loop. Repeat the process so that you have three loops. By this time, you will probably find that you have an idea you can develop into a longer piece of writing.

2 Choose one idea you and your partner discussed in **Make connections** on the opposite page. Follow the instructions in the toolbox to write about the idea. Do three loops.

3 Reread your freewriting. Find an idea that you can share with your group.

## C Preview Unit 3

1 Read the section headings and titles for the readings in this unit. With your group, choose a title and predict how it will connect with the title of the unit: **A Changing World**.

2 Share your prediction with the class.

Health

## BEFORE READING

### A Gather ideas about the topic

1 What connections do you see between chemicals and health? What illnesses might be caused by chemicals? What effect might chemicals in the environment (home, garden, school, playground, etc.) have on children's health? Write your answers in your log.

2 Share your answers with your group and see how many different ideas your group has.

3 With your group, define these words: **insecticides**, **pesticides**, **herbicides**, and **toxins**.

### B Ask questions

1 Read the title and introductory information. Write down one or two questions you think the article will answer.

2 Share your questions with your group.

## Kids and Chemicals
Elizabeth Guillette

*Elizabeth Guillette is a research scientist in anthropology at the University of Florida. "Kids and Chemicals," published in* Yes! *magazine, describes research Guillette conducted to try to answer the question: What do our choices about toxins mean for our children?*

The people of the Yaqui Valley of Mexico underwent a split when modern farming and pesticides were introduced in the early 1950s. Those in the valley floor embraced the use of insecticides, herbicides, and other agricultural chemicals. Spraying for insects also became common in their homes.

In the foothills, farmers preferred the traditional ranching and agricultural methods. This group shunned pesticides. Today, these communities are similar in terms of modernization, diet, and lifestyle, although the difference in their use of pesticides continues. What have these choices meant for their children?

I recognized a research opportunity when I heard of the Yaqui Valley, where these distinctive paths highlighted consequences from the use of chemicals that otherwise are difficult to isolate.

At first I wanted to study cancer. I was still thinking in terms of dramatic, obvious disaster, like that found in laboratory rats subjected to huge amounts of chemicals. But the mothers in the valley insisted that I look at broader, more subtle effects. They suspected chemicals were affecting their children, but could not identify specifics. To uncover hidden impacts, I asked children, ages four and five, to perform a series of play activities representative of developmental levels. I found that the pesticide-exposed children were less proficient at catching a ball, reflective of poor eye-hand coordination. They had lower stamina levels, measured by jumping contests. When asked to recall a gift of a balloon and its color, many could not remember the gift, and very few remembered the color. The children who had grown up without exposure to agricultural chemicals always remembered the gift and usually its color.

Most striking were their drawings of people. The pesticide-exposed four-year-olds of the valley made scribbles and the five-year-olds frequently made a circle at the bottom of the paper and a line upward to represent the body. Others drew odd shapes with abstract divisions, where dots represented eyes and enclosed areas were body parts. The drawings of the children who lived in the foothills, on the other hand, accurately placed body parts and facial features.

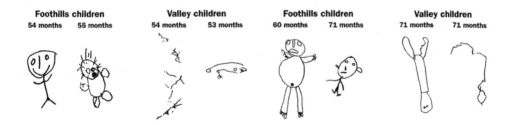

| Foothills children | | Valley children | | Foothills children | | Valley children | |
|---|---|---|---|---|---|---|---|
| 54 months | 55 months | 54 months | 53 months | 60 months | 71 months | 71 months | 71 months |

Two years later, at ages six and seven, the children exposed to pesticides continued to lag behind. Their drawings were commensurate to those of four-year-olds who had not been exposed. Their stamina remained low, their coordination poor. Simple problem-solving, easy for the foothill group, was difficult for the valley children. The exposed children exhibited symptoms of illness at a rate three to four times that of the others. They had a high rate of upper respiratory infection and other symptoms such as allergies and rashes.

The children who have grown up exposed to pesticides may never reach their full potential as functioning members of society. In this, the Yaqui Valley is not unique. Contamination is global; every child is exposed to various pesticides to some degree. While the children I studied are highly exposed to a few toxins, probably more than the average American child, American children are exposed to multiple toxins. These can add up and interact, causing significant effects that we don't yet recognize.

## AFTER READING

### A Find answers to your questions

1 Think back to the questions you wrote in **Ask questions** on page 154. Which questions were answered by the reading? Discuss with your group.

2 How did asking questions before reading change the way you read? Discuss this with the class.

### B Respond to the reading

1 Reread the text and annotate it. (See the toolbox *Annotating* on page 118.)

2 Tell a partner what you learned that surprised you.

### C Understand the reading

1 With a partner, look at the children's drawings above the reading. Explain them to each other, telling how they connect with the reading.

2 Then together make a list of the effects of agricultural chemicals on the pesticide-exposed children in Guillette's research study.

3 With the class, discuss some of the differences between the two groups of children as described in "Kids and Chemicals."

## HOW IT'S WRITTEN

### Appreciate the structure

1 Reread paragraphs one and two. With your group discuss what each paragraph says and does. (See the toolbox *Descriptive Outlining* on page 35.)

2 Reread the toolbox *Beginnings* on page 129. Do you think Guillette has found an effective way to begin this article? Discuss this question with the class.

3 Reread the toolbox *Writing Endings* on page 42. Talk with the class about whether the ending in "Kids and Chemicals" is effective and if so, why.

## TOPICS FOR WRITING

### Choose one topic to write about

1 Choose a specific illness affected by an environmental problem (for example, asthma, other respiratory illnesses, allergies, rashes, cancer, and so on). Do research in the library or on the internet to find out what specific environmental conditions trigger or cause this health problem. Write an essay explaining your findings. End your essay with one or two suggestions that parents might follow to insure better health for their children.

② With a group, investigate an environmental hazard that might be affecting the health of the people living near your home or school. Do some active research: go out and observe, interview experts, go to the library or do Internet research. Write a report describing the problem. Find out if you can send your report to some relevant authority to bring attention to this problem.

③ If your school has a cafeteria, with a partner, find out the rules and health regulations that the cafeteria has to follow in the purchase, storage, preparation and disposal of food. You may want to interview the person in charge of the cafeteria and an official who has oversight. Write a report to your classmates on your findings. In your conclusion, state whether you believe your cafeteria is a safe place to eat or not.

## AFTER WRITING

### Share your writing

1 Form a group with two or three other people in the class who wrote on the same topic you did. Read your papers aloud to one another. Notice the different ways in which you approached the same topic.

2 Briefly describe each person's approach to the class.

3 Hearing others' papers can give you ideas about how to change yours. Make notes about what you can change when you revise this piece of writing.

........................................................................

## BEFORE READING

### Think about the topic

1 The title of the reading that follows is "War on Disease." What kinds of diseases can you think of that the world has to battle? With your group, list some.

2 For each disease, discuss what you think some causes are and where you think the disease is most common.

3 Compare your group's list with those of your classmates.

## War on Disease
Rick Weiss

*This excerpt from* National Geographic *magazine is the first in a series of articles titled "Challenges for Humanity in the 21st Century." This particular article is about the global effort to control disease. Other articles in the series report on keeping food safe and water clean in urban areas.*

Just a few years ago medicine seemed to be winning the fight against disease. But now old adversaries are coming back and new infections are emerging, exposing us all to serious, sometimes unexpected, threats.

GLOBAL ENEMIES

Six maladies alone account for 90 percent of the deaths from infectious diseases worldwide. Spread in different ways and influenced by different factors, they continue to resist control. Aggravating social, economic, and political instability, these diseases have increasingly become global security threats. Large, densely populated cities in developing countries, where most of the world's people now live, are especially vulnerable.

| Influenza | Influenza viruses continually appear in different forms, requiring the production of a new vaccine each flu season. In some years the symptoms are mild; in others they can be lethal. Three episodes were especially virulent: the influenza pandemic in 1918–19, the Asian flu in 1957–58, and the Hong Kong flu in 1968–69. |
|---|---|
| HIV/AIDS | Passed on through bodily fluids, human immunodeficiency virus, or HIV, almost invariably leaves the body defenseless against the infections that define full-blown acquired immunodeficiency syndrome, or AIDS. Sub-Saharan Africa, with one-tenth of the world's population, has more than 70 percent of all HIV cases. |
| Diarrheal Diseases | Waterborne bacteria, viruses, and parasites produce about four billion cases of diarrhea a year. Those at highest risk include the 1.1 billion people lacking access to safe drinking water and the 2.4 billion without adequate sanitation facilities. Cholera, an acute diarrheal disease, claims more than 5,000 lives a year. |
| Tuberculosis | Propelled by a cough or sneeze from an infected person, tuberculosis bacteria can begin to grow in the lungs and throat of anyone who breathes them in. Drugs discovered in the 1940s beat back the disease, but the bacteria have recently begun to develop resistance, and tuberculosis has reappeared with a vengeance. |
| Malaria | Caused by microscopic parasites transmitted by the bites of infected mosquitoes, malaria attacks red blood cells. Global warming has expanded the range of malaria-carrying mosquitoes, putting more than 40 percent of the world's population at risk. In addition, warmer weather makes mosquitoes breed faster and bite more often. |
| Measles | A highly contagious viral disease that can lead to pneumonia or encephalitis, measles was an inevitable rite of childhood until an effective vaccine became available in 1963. Still striking more than 30 million a year and killing some 900,000, it is the world's leading cause of vaccine-preventable death in children. |

# AFTER READING

## A Make a personal connection

1 Reread the passage and mark facts you find most surprising or meaningful to you.

2 Quote two or three of these facts in your log. After each one, freewrite your thoughts and feelings about it.

3 Read one of your freewritings to your group.

## B Understand the reading

1 With your group, write a one-sentence summary of the main point of each of the opening paragraphs of "War on Disease."

2 Read your summaries to the class.

3 With a partner, choose one disease found in the chart. Paraphrase the information about it.

4 Read your paraphrase to the class.

## C Acquire new vocabulary

1 This selection contains many words and phrases related to health and illness. With a partner, circle all of these words.

2 Choose five that are new to you and write a definition or find a synonym for each.

3 Teach your group the vocabulary words you chose.

4 Make a class list of health-related vocabulary. Be sure everyone understands the meaning of all the words and phrases on the list.

# HOW IT'S WRITTEN

## Notice words of attitude

1 The title of this article, "War on Disease," and the title of the whole series, "Challenges for Humanity in the 21st Century," use words that express a sense of extreme importance or urgency. Underline other words and phrases in the article that express this same attitude.

2 Compare your words with that of your group and discuss how they affect the reader.

3 Summarize your discussion for the class.

## TOPICS FOR WRITING

### Choose one topic to write about

Whichever topic you choose, make sure that you include information from other sources. Be sure to cite your sources appropriately. See the toolboxes *Citations Using APA Style* on page 95 and *Quoting and Paraphrasing* on page 135.

1 Choose one of the diseases listed in this article to research. Find out what people can do to prevent or fight the disease.

2 Think of another health-related challenge for the twenty-first century. Do some research in the library or on the Internet. Write an essay explaining what the challenge is, what has caused or causes it, and what we might do to prevent or fight it.

3 At the beginning of this article, the author says, "Just a few years ago medicine seemed to be winning the fight against disease." Think of one health problem or illness that medicine has succeeded in treating or curing, for example high blood pressure, polio, diabetes, and so on. Do some research on it. Write an essay explaining the history of how this treatment or cure came about.

## AFTER WRITING

### A Add to your essay

1 Reread the toolbox *Adding Information to Essays* on page 149. Since you have already done some research for your essay, follow one of the toolbox's other techniques (2–5).

2 Add the new information to your essay.

### B Share your writing

1 Find someone who wrote on the same topic you did. Ask the person to read your essay and fill out the **Peer Feedback Form** on page 217.

2 Read your partner's comments and make notes on changes you might make.

# BEFORE READING

## Preview the reading

1 Read the title and introductory information. With the class, discuss what connections laughing might have with health.

2 Read about *skimming*, a technique that helps you get an overall idea of a text before starting to read it.

> ## *Skimming*
>
> It is often helpful to get a general idea of a piece of writing before you actually start reading it. One way to do this is to skim it. This is how it works:
>
> ■ Read the title and subtitle(s), if there are any.
>
> ■ Read the first sentence of all the paragraphs.
>
> ■ Read the entire first and last paragraphs if the piece is long.
>
> This process will help you get the main idea and familiarize you with the overall organization of the reading. It is especially useful for reading long or difficult material.

3 Skim the reading, "No Laughing Matter."

4 Write one point you think the person interviewed will make.

5 Read your prediction to your group.

# No Laughing Matter
Sophie Petit-Zerman

*This interview was first published in the British journal* New Scientist. *When it was reprinted in the* Utne Reader *in September–October 2002, it had the subheading:* Too Few Laughs Can Have Consequences for Your Health.

Humans don't have a monopoly on laughter, says Silvia Cardoso, a behavioral biologist at the State University of Campinas in Brazil. Cardoso says laughing is a primitive reflex common to most animals. Even rats laugh. In this interview with British weekly *New Scientist*, she discusses other discoveries from her research with laughter.

### SO WHY DO PEOPLE LAUGH SO MUCH?

Only 10 to 20 percent of laughing is a response to humor. Most of the time it's a message we send to other people – communicating a joyful disposition, a willingness to bond, and so on.

### DOES LAUGHTER DIFFER BETWEEN THE SEXES?

Women smile more than laugh, and are particularly adept at smiling and laughing with men as a kind of "social lubrication." It might even be possible that this has a biological origin, because women don't or can't use their physical size as a threat, which men do, even if unconsciously.

### AND BETWEEN CULTURES?

Cultural differences are certainly part of it. Loud, raucous laughter with exaggerated movements and expressions is considered "unfeminine" in most cultures, and is much more common among men, particularly if they're with other men. Socially dominant individuals, from bosses to tribal chiefs, use laughter to control their subordinates. When the boss laughs, their minions laugh too. Laughter might be a form of asserting power by controlling the emotional climate of the group, and it also has a dark side. There are theories that laughter and aggression have common origins; some kinds of laughter in primates apparently are threatening – just look at the way they bare their teeth. That might explain why being laughed at is so unpleasant.

### IS IT TRUE THAT LAUGHING CAN MAKE US HEALTHIER?

It's undoubtedly the best medicine. For one thing, it's exercise. It activates the cardiovascular system, so heart rate and blood pressure increase, then the arteries dilate, causing blood pressure to fall again. Repeated, short, strong contractions of the chest muscles, diaphragm, and abdomen increase blood flow into our internal organs, and forced respiration – the *ha! ha!* – makes sure that this blood is well oxygenated. Muscle tension decreases, and indeed we may temporarily lose control of our limbs, as in the expression, "weak with laughter."

It may also release brain endorphins, reducing sensitivity to pain and boosting endurance and pleasurable sensations. Some studies suggest that laughter affects the immune system by reducing the production of hormones associated with stress, and that when you laugh, the immune system produces more T-cells. But no rigorously controlled studies have confirmed these effects.

Laughter's social role is definitely important. I'm very concerned that today's children may be heading for a whole lot of social ills because their play and leisure time is so isolated, and they lose out on lots of chances for laughter.

**WHY?**

Staring at computer screens rather than laughing with each other is at odds with what's natural for children. Natural social behavior in children is playful, and in such situations laughter indicates that make-believe aggression is just fun, not for real. This is an important way in which children form positive emotional bonds, gain new social skills, and generally start to move from childhood to adulthood. Parents need to be careful to ensure that their children play in groups, with both peers and adults, and laugh more.

## AFTER READING

### A Respond to the reading

1 Reread the interview. As you read, stop at least three times and write a double entry response in your log. (See the toolbox *Double Entry Response* on page 26.)

2 Exchange logs with a partner and read one another's responses.

3 Discuss similarities and differences.

### B Answer questions

1 Each group should choose one question from the following list to answer orally. Base answers on information from the reading.
   ① Why do humans laugh?
   ② How does laughter differ between males and females and between cultures?
   ③ What can laughter tell us about social relations?
   ④ How can laughing make us healthier?
   ⑤ What connection does laughter have to childhood development?

2 Report your question and answer to the class.

### C Connect with another reading

1 Recall what you read about the benefits of crying in "It's O.K. to Cry" on page 137. Do you see any connections with what you read in "No Laughing Matter"? Discuss this with your group.

2 Together, write one generalization you can make about crying and laughing.

## HOW IT'S WRITTEN

### Notice form

1 "No Laughing Matter" and "The Model Medic" (see page 124) are both based on interviews. With the class, compare the way the information is presented in each article and list differences you notice.

2 Discuss the effect on readers of these two ways of writing about an interview.

## TOPICS FOR WRITING

### Choose one topic to write about.

❶ Pick a sentence or an issue from the reading that jumps out at you, that relates to you in some way. Write an essay about it. First state the sentence or describe the issue, explaining what it means in "No Laughing Matter." Then tell why it's meaningful to you. If it reminds you of something in your own life, explain.

❷ Cardoso says that it's unnatural and unhealthy for children to spend their time at computers when they should be playing. What do you think about this idea? Write an essay giving your opinion. Use your own experience, your observation of others, and your reading to explain what you think.

❸ Cardoso writes that laughter is "undoubtedly the best medicine." Many people do not like to take drugs, not even aspirin or other over-the-counter medicines. They prefer alternative remedies, for example, medicines made from plants or other long-standing traditional practices, such as acupuncture. Write an essay in which you state your views about the effectiveness of conventional medicine as opposed to alternative remedies.

## AFTER WRITING

### Share your writing

1 Attach a blank sheet of paper to your writing. Join a group of classmates who wrote about the same topic. Exchange papers and read at least three other essays. On each blank page, write at least one comment, reaction, or question about the attached essay.

2 Read your classmates' comments about your essay.

3 As a group, choose one piece of writing to read to the class.

4 In your log, write about what made the writing your group chose the best one to read to the class.

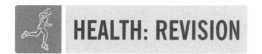

# HEALTH: REVISION

## A  Choose one essay

1  Reread the pieces you wrote for the **Topics for Writing** sections of HEALTH. Choose two that you like and may want to revise.

2  Show your choices to a partner and talk about which essay would be best to revise.

3  Finally, choose one.

## B  Learn more about endings

1  Read about different ways writers can bring a piece of writing to its conclusion.

### Types of Endings

Here are several different ways you can end a piece of writing. You can use just one of these ways or combine two or more.

- Remind your readers of your **main idea**.

- Give a **summary** of what you've said, but don't repeat everything or use the same words.

- Offer a **solution** or **resolution** to the conflict or problem you've discussed. This works especially if you've made the topic into a problem.

- Give **advice** to the readers. You may even address the readers as if you're talking to them.

- Use a **quotation** from an expert or a famous person if that seems appropriate.

- Draw a **conclusion** or a lesson from what you've written. If you've done some research or made a strong argument, the conclusion should come easily.

- Give the readers **something to think about** – a related topic, another solution, or a new thought. Show the reader that you know there is more to discuss.

2 With your group, read the examples below and decide which kind of ending these writers have used. Choose from the list in the toolbox *Types of Endings* on page 165.

① Parents, school officials, and government officials should do everything possible to educate young people about the dangers of drug abuse. Society, as a whole, must change its attitude toward the careless use of all drugs. If people reexamine their attitudes toward this problem, drugs may stop destroying our cities and our youth.

② To conclude, an intelligent, mature individual will always value love more than money because that person knows that love, rather than money, is the ultimate source of happiness. There is great wisdom in the Biblical warning: "The love of money is the root of all evil."

③ In conclusion, although television has both advantages and disadvantages, its advantages for people worldwide far outweigh its disadvantages. Television has done a lot to help shrink the globe and to bring the human race closer to understanding each other. We should not try to get rid of television. Instead, we should consider how to use this great invention wisely.

3 Discuss your answers with the class.

4 With the class, reread the endings of "It's O.K. to Cry" (page 137), "On Turning Fifty" (page 88), and "Kids and Chemicals" (page 154). Refer to the toolbox *Types of Endings* on page 165, and discuss how the writers ended their pieces.

## C Revise your essay

1 Read the ending of the essay you are going to revise. Did you use one of the types of endings described in the toolbox *Types of Endings* on page 165? Are you satisfied with your ending?

2 Rewrite your ending using one of the ways in the toolbox.

3 Now rewrite it another way. Choose the one you like best.

4 Make any other changes you want to the rest of the essay.

## D Share your writing

1 In your group, pass the revised essays around until everyone has read all of them.

2 As a group, choose one essay to read to the class.

## Writer's Tip

*The perfect ending should take the reader slightly by surprise and yet seem exactly right to him (or her).*

**William Zinsser**

## Writer's Tip

*The best part of all, the absolutely most delicious part, is finishing it and then doing it over . . . I rewrite a lot, over and over again, so that it looks like I never did.*

**Toni Morrison**

# Environment

## BEFORE READING

### Gather ideas about the topic

1 What is "global warming"? As a class, answer the question.

2 What do you know about penguins? What is their habitat? What characteristics do they exhibit? Are they threatened? Discuss these questions with a partner.

3 What would happen if the water in the lakes, rivers, or ocean near where you live rose about a foot? Discuss the consequences with your group.

 ## The Mercury's Rising
Sharon Begley

*This excerpt and the map on page 168 are taken from* Newsweek, December 4, 2000.

You might assume that "global warming" means what it says, involving nothing more complex than a rise in the world's temperature. But notice the penguins. Over the last several months, hundreds of Magellanic penguins have been washing ashore near Rio de Janeiro, 2,000 miles north of their usual haunts. The wayward birds may be signs of a massive climate shift in the South Atlantic: warming may have altered ocean circulation so as to nudge the cold-water currents (which the penguins follow for chow) thousands of miles off course. As it happens, one of the greatest worries about global warming is that it will shift Atlantic Ocean currents that warm northern Europe. If that happens, temperatures could plunge 20 degrees in 10 years. Lost penguins, warn some scientists, may be harbingers of such catastrophes – which the benign-sounding "global warming" doesn't even hint at.

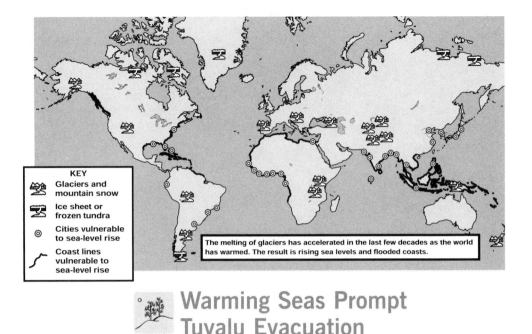

**KEY**

- Glaciers and mountain snow
- Ice sheet or frozen tundra
- Cities vulnerable to sea-level rise
- Coast lines vulnerable to sea-level rise

The melting of glaciers has accelerated in the last few decades as the world has warmed. The result is rising sea levels and flooded coasts.

# Warming Seas Prompt Tuvalu Evacuation

*This article tells about Tuvalu, an island country located between Hawaii and Australia. The article appeared in* Co-op America Quarterly. *For more information, see* www.earth-policy.org.

Rising sea levels caused by climate change have resulted in the first evacuation of a Pacific island nation. The leaders of Tuvalu, which is located between Hawaii and Australia, announced in November that the island country's citizens will abandon their homeland.

During the 20th century, sea level rose 8–12 inches. As sea level has risen, Tuvalu has experienced lowland flooding. The salt-water intrusion has adversely affected the country's drinking water and food production, and coastal erosion is decimating Tuvalu's nine islands.

Paani Laupepa, a Tuvaluan government official, reported to the Earth Policy Institute that the nation suffered an unusually high number of hurricanes during the last decade. Many scientists link higher surface water temperatures resulting from global warming to greater and more destructive storms.

Laupepa criticized the United States for its March 2001 abandonment of the Kyoto Protocol, an international agreement calling for industrialized nations to reduce their greenhouse gas emissions, which are a main cause of global warming. "By refusing to ratify the Protocol, the U.S. has effectively denied future generations of Tuvaluans their fundamental freedom to live where our ancestors have lived for thousands of years," Laupepa told the BBC.

Tuvalu has asked Australia and New Zealand to allow the gradual relocation of the country's population.

Although Tuvalu is the first island nation to succumb to rising sea levels, it is not the only one imperiled by them. In 1987, Maumoon Abdul Gayoom, president of the Maldives, told the United Nations General Assembly that global warming has made his country of 311,000 an "endangered nation."

# AFTER READING

## A Understand the readings

1 What is the relationship between penguins and global warming? Write a two-sentence answer to this question.

2 Compare your answer to those of other members of the class.

3 With a partner, look back through the text and find several consequences of climate change on Tuvalu. Make a list.

## B Acquire new vocabulary

1 With your group, make a list of the words or phrases from the readings that are important to someone studying or writing about environmental science.

2 Divide the words among the members of your group. Research your words and explain their meaning to the rest of your group.

## C Read a map

1 With your group, look at the key to the map. Read what the symbols stand for and then find examples of each symbol on the map. Look especially at the geographic areas that represent you and members of your group.

2 As a group, pick one continent. Write one sentence summarizing the information given on the map for that continent.

3 Write in your log about what you've learned from reading the texts and the map.

# HOW IT'S WRITTEN

## Notice negative connotation

1 With your partner, reread "Warming Seas Prompt Tuvalu Evacuation" and underline the words or phrases that give off negative connotations, that is, negative feelings, attitudes, or meanings. Compare your list with others in the class.

2 Take one of the sentences that uses words with negative connotations. Rewrite the sentence, substituting neutral words and phrases for the negative words. See the example below:

Original sentence:

... that the nation *suffered* an *unusually high number* of hurricanes during the last decade.

Altered sentence:

... that the nation *experienced more* hurricanes *than usual* during the last decade.

3 Discuss with a partner the effect of changing the negative words in the example sentence and in your rewritten sentence.

4 Discuss with the class why this article was written with a number of negatively charged words. Consider these questions.

① What effect does the author want to have on the reader?

② Where would this kind of writing appear?

## TOPICS FOR WRITING

### Choose one topic to write about

Whichever topic you choose, read the toolbox *Cubing* below and then use this technique to gather ideas before writing.

❶ Where does your water come from? Many people are not aware of the source of their water. Do some research to find out – visit your city's Web site or water department. Trace the pipes in your house to the street and beyond. Follow a drop of water from its source to your faucet. How is it kept clean and how is it protected from contamination? Write a report for your community on the water supply.

❷ Write a report about the successful cleanup of a body of water, like a river, a lake, a stream, or a reservoir. What happened? Who was involved in the story? What were the effects of the cleanup? Do some research if necessary. Write about the cleanup to bring it to people's attention.

❸ Look at the Web site, www.onesweetwhirled.com. Read about what you can do to fight global warming. Write an article or an editorial, as if for a student newspaper, giving advice on what individuals can do to slow down global warming.

### Cubing

Cubing allows you to look at a topic from six different perspectives, instead of one. Each side of the cube instructs you to take a different perspective (see the illustration below). You should freewrite for three to five minutes on your topic in each of these ways. By the end of this process, you will have gathered many different ideas to include in your writing.

■ **Describe it:** What does it look like? What are its characteristics? What are the first things you notice about it?

■ **Compare it:** What is it similar to? What is it different from?

■ **Associate it:** What does it remind you of? How does it connect with you, with your family, or with your community?

- **Analyze it:** Look deeper. What is it really made of? How does it work?

- **Apply it:** What is it used for? Who uses it?

- **Argue for or against it:** Is it a good thing or a bad thing? Explain why.

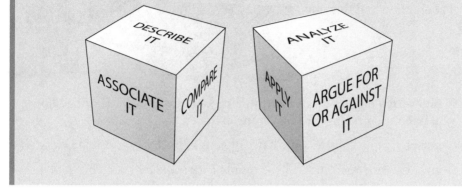

## AFTER WRITING

### A Check citations

1 Reread the toolboxes *Citations Using APA Style* on page 95 and *Quoting and Paraphrasing* on page 135.

2 Make any changes needed to cite your sources properly.

### B Share your writing

1 Ask a classmate to read your writing. The reader should write comments by following the suggestions in the toolbox *Reader's Response Feedback* on page 15.

2 Read your classmate's comments. Write down at least three changes you can make to revise this writing.

## BEFORE READING

### Pool your knowledge

1 Match each animal's name with its definition and drawing.

    ① bird with a dark body and a white head and tail,        a. armadillo
       at one time in danger of becoming extinct

    ② any of various vultures; any hawk of genus "buteo"    b. bald eagle

    ③ any of several mammals of the family *Dasypodidae*,    c. buzzard
       having a covering of armor-like, jointed bony plates

2 Check your answers with your group. Find out if anyone in your group knows anything more about each animal.

 **Buzzard**
Bailey White

*Bailey White is one of America's best-loved storytellers. She writes commentaries about relatives and rural life in her native Georgia. Her stories are collected in several books including* Mama Makes Up Her Mind and Other Dangers of Southern Living, *from which "Buzzard" is taken.*

There was something in the road. I drove closer to it. It was a buzzard eating a dead armadillo. I got closer. It was a big buzzard. And I'd never seen a buzzard's tail feathers so bleached and pale.

That buzzard better move, I thought. I'd never had to slow down for a buzzard before. They always lope out of the way. I got closer.

The buzzard turned his head and looked at me. He stood up on his big yellow legs. His head was snow white. His eyes were gold. He wasn't a buzzard. He was a bald eagle.

Then, not until after I had brought the car to a full stop, he spread his wings and with a slow swoop lifted himself into the air. He turned his head and gave me a long look through the car windshield with his level yellow eyes. Then he slowly wheeled up into the sky until he was just a black dot against the blue.

I turned the car off. I thought about the glare he had given me: What are *you* doing here? it had said. When I got started again, I drove slower and felt smaller. I think it does us all good to get looked at like that now and then by a wild animal.

# AFTER READING

## A Respond to the reading

1 Freewrite for a few minutes in your log about what you just read.

2 Share your freewriting with your group.

## B Understand the main idea

1 With your group, find one sentence in the text that you think expresses White's main idea. Restate it in your own words.

2 Share your findings with the class.

# HOW IT'S WRITTEN

## A Notice sentence length

1 With a partner, compare the sentences in the first three paragraphs with the sentences in paragraphs four and five. Discuss why you think White chose to use short sentences in the first part of the essay. Discuss what effect they have on the reader.

2 Summarize your discussion for the class.

## B Appreciate the structure

1 With a partner, make a descriptive outline of "Buzzard." (See the toolbox *Descriptive Outlining* on page 35.)

2 Compare your outline with those of two other people.

3 With the class discuss which part of this essay tells a story and which part gives White's opinion or main idea. Discuss whether you think White is effective in placing her opinion where she does.

# TOPICS FOR WRITING

## Choose one topic to write about

1 White said she "drove slower and felt smaller" after her encounter with the bald eagle. Write about a similar experience you have had with an animal. Tell what happened to you and how it made you feel. Use White's story as a model, making a generalization or point at the end of your essay.

❷ The bald eagle is an endangered species. Choose another animal that is endangered by human activity, pollution, or disease. Do some research on the animal, using the Internet, a library, or a museum. Write an essay about the animal. Tell where the species lives, why it is endangered, and some possible ways to save it. In your writing, convince readers of your point of view.

❸ Write a composition in any form (poem, story, essay, and so on) using the name of an animal or plant as the title.

## AFTER WRITING

### Share your writing

1  Using your pen to touch each word, proofread your paper. (See the toolbox *Proofreading* on page 97.)

2  Exchange papers with a classmate. Ask your reader to write answers to these questions:
   ①  What details stand out for you?
   ②  What point does the piece make?
   ③  Do the details illustrate the point?
   ④  Did the writer vary the sentence length to make a point?

3  Make some notes on how you could revise this writing.

• • • • • • • • • • • • • • • • • • • • • • • • • • • • • • • • • • • • • • • • • • • • • • • • •

## BEFORE READING

### A  Gather ideas about the topic

1  With your group, read this list of facts about what is happening to the earth today.
   ①  By 2025, the demand for water around the world is expected to exceed supply by 56 percent.
   ②  More than a billion people have no access to clean drinking water.
   ③  Nearly three billion people live without basic sanitation.
   ④  It takes 725 gallons of water to make one quarter-pound hamburger with cheese.
   ⑤  Unless raised organically, cotton, tobacco, and coffee use the most pesticides of any crops grown. Pesticides harm farmworkers, birds, wildlife, and the soil.

⑥ Every day, thirty-three thousand children die of hunger-related causes.

⑦ At least 1.5 million tons of hazardous waste are released into the air, water and land every day.

⑧ Every day 116 square miles of tropical rain forest are destroyed.

2 Many of these facts were taken from a newsletter called "Green Guide: Environmental Change Begins at Home." With your group, suggest one thing people could do at home to help conserve resources in two of the situations described above.

3 Share your suggestions with the class.

## B Prepare for the reading

1 With a partner, read the introductory information and the author's way of introducing "The Brave Little Parrot."

2 With your group, discuss what connections you see between the eight facts in **Gather ideas about the topic** and Martin's idea about what is happening to the earth today and Martin's idea that the world is "burning."

# The Brave Little Parrot
Rafe Martin

*Rafe Martin is an award-winning author and storyteller. He has been featured at many prestigious storytelling events around the United States and has performed in Japan. When Martin tells this story, he introduces it with the following words:*
"This is my retelling of a 2,500-year-old Buddhist tale, whose message seems entirely contemporary. Our world is burning, and each of us can help do something about it. Small deeds, done wholeheartedly, may have the potential to change everything – in ways we might never guess. For many of us, telling stories is such a way. Fly on, little parrot!"

Once a little parrot lived happily in a beautiful forest. But one day without warning, lightning flashed, thunder crashed, and a dead tree burst into flames. Sparks, carried on the rising wind, began to leap from branch to branch and tree to tree.

The little parrot smelled the smoke. "Fire!" she cried. "Run to the river!" Flapping her wings, rising higher and higher, she flew toward the safety of the river's far shore. After all, she was a bird and could fly away.

But as she flew, she could see that many animals were already surrounded by the flames and could not escape. Suddenly a desperate idea, a way to save them, came to her.

Darting to the river, she dipped herself in the water. Then she flew back over the now-raging fire. Thick smoke coiled up, filling the sky. Walls of flame shot up, now on one side, now on the other. Pillars of fire leapt before her. Twisting and turning through a mad maze of flame, the little parrot flew bravely on.

Having reached the heart of the burning forest, the little parrot shook her wings. And the few tiny drops of water that still clung to her feathers tumbled like jewels down into the flames and vanished with a hiss.

Then the little parrot flew back through the flames and smoke to the river. Once more she dipped herself in the cool water and flew back over the burning forest. Once more she shook her wings, and a few drops of water tumbled like jewels into the flames. Hiss.

Back and forth she flew, time and time again from the river to the forest, from the forest to the river. Her feathers became charred. Her feet and claws were scorched. Her lungs ached. Her eyes burned. Her mind spun as dizzily as a spinning spark. Still the little parrot flew on.

At that moment some of the blissful gods floating overhead in their cloud palaces of ivory and gold happened to look down and see the little parrot flying among the flames. They pointed at her with their perfect hands. Between mouthfuls of honied foods, they exclaimed, "Look at that foolish bird! She's trying to put out a raging forest fire with a few sprinkles of water! How absurd!" They laughed.

But one of those gods, strangely moved, changed himself into a golden eagle and flew down, down toward the little parrot's fiery path.

The little parrot was just nearing the flames again, when a great eagle with eyes like molten gold appeared at her side. "Go back, little bird!" said the eagle in a solemn and majestic voice. "Your task is hopeless. A few drops of water can't put out a forest fire. Cease now, and save yourself before it is too late."

But the little parrot continued to fly on through the smoke and flames. She could hear the great eagle flying above her as the heat grew fiercer. He called out, "Stop, foolish little parrot! Stop! Save yourself!"

"I didn't need some great, shining eagle," coughed the little parrot, "to tell me that. My own mother, the dear bird, could have told me the same thing long ago. Advice! I don't need advice. I just" – cough, cough – "need someone to help!"

Rising higher, the eagle, who was a god, watched the little parrot flying through the flames. High above he could see his own kind, those carefree gods, still laughing and talking even as many animals cried out in pain and fear far below. He grew ashamed of the gods' carefree life, and a single desire was kindled in his heart.

"God though I am," he exclaimed, "how I wish I could be just like that little parrot. Flying on, brave and alone, risking all to help – what a rare and marvelous thing! What a wonderful little bird!"

Moved by these new feelings, the great eagle began to weep. Stream after stream of sparkling tears began pouring from his eyes. Wave upon wave they fell, washing down like a torrent of rain upon the fire, upon the forest, upon the animals and the little parrot herself.

Where those cooling tears fell, the flames shrank down and died. Smoke still curled up from the scorched earth, yet new life was already boldly pushing forth – shoots, stems, blossoms, and leaves. Green grass sprang up from among the still-glowing cinders.

Where the eagle's teardrops sparkled on the little parrot's wings, new feathers now grew: red feathers, green feathers, yellow feathers too. Such bright colors! Such a pretty bird!

The animals looked at one another in amazement. They were whole and well. Not one had been harmed. Up above in the clear blue sky they could see their brave friend, the little parrot, looping and soaring in delight. When all hope was gone, somehow she had saved them.

"Hurray!" they cried. "Hurray for the brave little parrot and for this sudden, miraculous rain!"

## AFTER READING

### A Respond to the reading

1 Choose one of the following activities:

① Freewrite in your log for a few minutes about what you read. Read your writing to your group.

② Write answers to the three response questions found in the toolbox *Response Questions* on page 9.

2 Read your writing to your group.

### B Understand the vocabulary

1 With a partner, pick one paragraph you had trouble understanding because of the vocabulary.

2 Learn the meaning of the most important words by looking at the context. (See the toolbox *Context Clues* on page 85.) If necessary, use a dictionary.

3 Tell what the paragraph says by restating it in your own words, replacing each difficult word or phrase with a synonym.

4 Share your work with your group and then with the class.

### C Find the main idea

1 Discuss with your group the message of this story.

2 Write a sentence that expresses Martin's message and then share your sentence with your group.

3 Choose the sentence you like best to share with the class.

# HOW IT'S WRITTEN

## Learn about fables

1 Read about a kind of story that teaches a lesson.

> ### Fables
>
> A fable is a story, often told orally, that usually uses animals that speak and act as human beings. Writers use stories, like fables, to help make a point or to teach a lesson. Such stories make writing colorful, interesting, and memorable. Here is an example of a fable from Aesop, a sixth-century creator of Greek fables.
>
> #### The Widow and the Hen
> A widow had a plump hen who laid an egg every day, without fail. The widow thought to herself: If I give the hen twice as much barley, she will lay twice as many eggs. So she fed the hen twice a day. But after a few days, the hen became so fat that she stopped laying eggs at all.
>
> LESSON: You can't bribe nature.

2 In what way does "The Brave Little Parrot" fit the above description of a fable? Discuss this with a partner.

3 What is a popular fable in your culture? What lesson does it teach? Tell the fable to your group.

4 Choose the fable you like best to share with the class.

# TOPICS FOR WRITING

## Choose one topic to write about

1 In the introduction to "The Brave Little Parrot," Martin says: "Small deeds, done wholeheartedly, may have the potential to change everything." Write about a small deed that has changed things. Begin your essay with this quotation from Martin's introduction and use your story to prove and illustrate his idea.

2 Think of a fable or tale that was told to you as a child or that you have heard or read as an adult. Write the story as though you are going to tell it at a national storytelling festival. Begin with an introduction, telling something about the origin of the story and its message.

3 Write an essay explaining what steps people can take at home to help conserve the earth's resources. Think about such things as water, food, the products we buy and use, transportation, and so on. If your school has a newspaper, submit the essay for publication.

# AFTER WRITING

## Share your writing

1 Give your paper to a classmate. Ask your reader to write two or three feedback comments.

2 Read your classmate's responses. Circle any ideas you may be able to use in revising.

# ENVIRONMENT: REVISION

## A Choose one piece of writing

1 Reread the pieces you wrote for the **Topics for Writing** sections of ENVIRONMENT. Also read any comments from classmates and notes you made.

2 Choose one piece to revise.

## B Revise your writing

1 On your draft, mark and number places where you will make changes. On another piece of paper, for each number describe the changes you plan to make.

2 Rewrite the parts that need revising.

## C Get the words right

1 Once your essay says what you want it to say, you can pay closer attention to the words. Read about a strategy that may help you "get the words right."

> **Writer's Tip**
>
> *The beautiful part of writing is that you don't have to get it right the first time, unlike, say, a brain surgeon. You can always do it better, find the exact word, the apt phrase, the leaping simile.*
>
> **Robert Cormier**

### Getting the Words Right

Imagine you are the boss of a factory and the words you have written are your employees. If the workers are productive, they stay. If they are not doing their job well, or are not needed, they are fired or are let go. The word boss must also recognize when to hire new workers, like when there is a job to be done and no one is doing it.

Go through your piece of writing again as the "word boss." Look at each word in each sentence and ask yourself these questions:

■ Is this word doing its job well? Are there stronger, more specific, more concrete words that could do the job better?

■ Do I need to hire any "new workers" for this sentence? Could I add any words to make the meaning clearer?

■ Are there any unnecessary words in this sentence that need to be "fired"?

*Adapted from* The Writing Workshop *by Alan Ziegler.*

2 Follow the steps in the toolbox to improve your writing.

3 Write as many drafts as necessary.

## D  Get feedback

1  Ask one or more readers to read your essay and fill in the **Peer Feedback Form** on page 217.

2  Use your readers' comments to help you improve your essay. Write a final draft.

## E  Share your writing

1  Post your essay on a wall of the classroom. Walk around the room and read as many essays as you can. Take notes on interesting ideas and expressive language.

2  With the class, discuss what you learned from reading your classmates' writing.

### Writer's Tip

Hemingway: *I rewrote the ending to* Farewell to Arms, *the last page of it, thirty-nine times before I was satisfied.*

Plimpton: *Was there some technical problem there? What was it that had you stumped?*

Hemingway: *Getting the words right.*

**Ernest Hemingway and George Plimpton**

Gender Roles

# BEFORE READING

**A Gather ideas about the topic**

1 The Swedish International Development Agency outlined a typical day for a man and a woman in an African family that grows both cash crops and its own food supply. Read the list of activities.

| A Woman's Day | A Man's Day |
|---|---|
| Rises first and kindles the fire | |
| Breast-feeds the baby | |
| Fixes breakfasts and eats | Rises when breakfast is ready |
| Washes and dresses children | Eats |
| Walks 2 kms to fetch water | Walks 1 km to the field |
| Gives livestock food and water | |
| Washes cooking utensils, etc | Works in the field |
| Walks 2 kms to fetch water | |
| Washes clothing | |
| Breast-feeds the baby | |
| Walks 1 km to bring food to husband | |
| Walks 1 km back home | Eats when wife arrives with food |
| Walks 1 km to her field | |
| Weeds field | Works in the field |
| Breast-feeds the baby | |
| Gathers firewood on the way home | |
| Walks 1 km home | Walks 1 km home |
| Pounds maize | Rests |
| Walks 2 kms to fetch water | |
| Kindles the fire | |
| Prepares meal and eats | Eats |
| Breast-feeds the baby | Walks to village to visit other men |
| Puts house in order | Goes to bed |
| Goes to bed last | |

2 Talk with a partner about the differences between a woman's day and a man's day as shown in the chart. Do their days seem equal?

3 How does this list compare to men's and women's work in your culture? Discuss this question with your group.

## B Write as you read

Look through the story. Note the breaks marked by [pause]. While reading, when you come to a break, stop and write down one thing you understood in that section and your response to it.

 **Taming Macho Ways**
Elvia Alvarado

*This selection is taken from* Don't be Afraid Gringo, *the true story of Elvia Alvarado, who worked as an organizer of the peasant women* (campesinas) *in her community in Honduras for the National Congress of Rural Workers (CNTC). In the process, she changed from passively accepting her poverty-stricken life to actively changing the conditions of her life and community. In this passage, she talks about wanting to change the way men and women treat each other.*

When I started working with the mothers' clubs in the Catholic church, it was the first time I realized that we women work even harder than the men do.

We get up before they do to grind the corn and make tortillas and coffee for their breakfast. Then we work all day – taking care of the kids, washing the clothes, ironing, mending our husband's old rags, cleaning the house. We hike to the mountains looking for wood to cook with. We walk to the stream or the well to get water. We make lunch and bring it to the men in the field. And we often grab a hoe and help in the fields. We never sit still one minute.

It's true that there are some jobs that require a lot of strength and that women can't do as well as men. For example, when we have to clear a piece of forest, it's the men who go out with the axes and cut down the trees. Other work we consider "men's work" is chopping firewood and plowing the land with a team of oxen. These are things that men do better than women, because they're stronger. I don't know if it's a physical difference from birth, but the fact is that here in Honduras women are usually either pregnant or nursing, and that takes a lot of energy out of you.

Men may be out working during the day, but when they come home they usually don't do a thing. They want their meal to be ready, and after they eat they either lie down to rest or go out drinking. But we women keep on working – cooking the corn and beans for the next day's meal, watching the children.

Even when we go to sleep, we don't get to rest. If the babies wake up crying, we have to go take care of them – give them the breast if they're still breast-feeding, give them medicine if they're sick.

The next morning, we're up before the sun, while our husbands are still sleeping.

In some families, like the workers in the city, I've seen men help women in the house. But I've never seen it in a campesino home. Even if the man has no work and sits at home, he won't help out.

I have a friend in the city who works in a factory. If he comes home from work and the meal isn't ready – maybe his wife is busy watching the children or washing clothes – he just grabs the pots and pans and gets to work. I've seen it with my own eyes. He actually cooks the meal for the whole family. You'd never see that in a campesino house!

I don't think it's fair that the women do all the work. Maybe it's because I've been around more and I've seen other relationships. But I think that if two people get together to form a home, it should be because they love and respect each other. And that means that they should share everything.

The problem some campesina women have is even worse. Not only do their husbands refuse to help, but they don't even support the family. They don't give her money to put food on her children's plates.

[pause]

Another problem women have is that their husbands often beat them. Say a campesino comes home late after drinking or sleeping with a woman he has on the side. If his wife yells at him, he hits her. Sometimes he leaves her all black and blue or with a bloody nose, a black eye, or a busted lip.

The neighbors can hear everything. But since it's a fight between the two of them, no one interferes. Unless the woman starts to yell, "Help! So-and-so's trying to kill me." Then the neighbors come over and tell him to stop hitting the poor woman.

"No," the campesino says. "This no-good woman is yelling about things she has no right to stick her nose into. I'm the man in this family, and nobody tells me what to do."

He usually stops hitting her when the neighbors get involved. But if no one comes to help her, she wakes up the next morning all black and blue.

The woman never says what really happened. She's too embarrassed. So she says she fell down or had an accident. She doesn't even tell her friends or her own mother what happened. Because if she tells her mother, her mother says, "You knew what he was like when you went to live with him. So why did you go with him in the first place?" Or if the mother tells her to come home and live with her and she does, a few days later they get back together again and the mother's the one that looks bad.

If the woman can't take it any more, she leaves him. But even after the woman leaves, the man usually follows her and keeps harassing her.

We know it's against the law to beat someone like that, but the police don't get involved in fights between couples. They say it's none of their business. They say it's something for the man and wife to figure out by themselves.

[pause]

Machismo is a historical problem. It goes back to the time of our great-grandfathers, or our great-great-grandfathers. In my mind it's connected to the problem of drinking. Drinking is man's worst disease. When men drink, they fight with everyone. They hit their wives and children. They offend their neighbors. They lose all sense of dignity.

How are we going to stop campesinos from drinking? First of all, we know the government isn't interested in stopping it, because it's an important source of income. Every time you buy a bottle of liquor, part of that money goes to the government.

That's why the government doesn't let the campesinos make their own liquor, because the government doesn't make any money off homemade brew. So a campesino can go into town any time, day or night, spend all his money, and drink himself sick. But if he gets caught making *choruco* – that's what we call homemade spirits made from corn and sugar – they throw him in jail. The government wants the campesinos to drink, but only the liquor that they make money off of.

If we're ever going to get campesinos to stop drinking, we first have to look at why so many campesinos drink. And for that we have to look at what kind of society we have. We've built up a society that treats people like trash, a society that doesn't give people jobs, a society that doesn't give people a reason to stay sober. I think that's where this vice comes from.

I've seen what happens when campesinos organize and have a plot of land to farm. They don't have time for drinking any more, except on special occasions. They spend the day in the hot sun – plowing, planting, weeding, irrigating, cutting firewood for the house, carrying the produce to market. Most of them are very dedicated to their work and their families.

So I've noticed that once the campesinos have a purpose, once they have a way to make a living and take care of their families, they drink less. And they usually stop beating their wives, too. And I've seen that once the women get organized, they start to get their husbands in line.

[pause]

I know that changing the way men and women treat each other is a long process. But if we really want to build a new society, we have to change the bad habits of the past. We can't build a new society if we are drunks, womanizers, or corrupt. No, those things have to change.

But people *can* change. I know there are many things I used to do that I don't do any more, now that I'm more educated. For example, I used to gossip and criticize other women. I used to fight over men. But I learned that gossip only destroys, it doesn't build. Criticizing my neighbors doesn't create unity. Neither does fighting over men. So I stopped doing these things.

Before, whenever I'd see the slightest thing I'd go running to my friends. "Ay, did you see so-and-so with what's-his-face?" I'd go all over town telling everyone what I saw. Now I wouldn't say anything. That's her business.

If someone is in danger, then, yes, we have to get involved. For example, I heard a rumor that a landowner was out to kill one of the campesino leaders I work with. I made sure to warn the campesino so he'd be careful. That kind of rumor we tell each other – but not the idle gossip.

I also used to flirt with married men, just for the fun of it and to make their wives jealous. Now I'm much more responsible, much more serious. That doesn't mean I don't joke around and have a good time. I just make it clear that we're friends.

We all have to make changes. Campesino men have to be more responsible with their women. They have to have only one woman. Because they have a hard enough time supporting one family, let alone two. Campesinos who drink have to stop drinking. And campesinos who fight with their wives have to stop fighting. Our struggle has to begin in our own homes.

[pause]

## AFTER READING

### A Share your responses

1 Exchange logs with a partner and read each other's writing.

2 Discuss similarities and differences.

### B Make connections

1 Alvarado describes several problems Honduran women have. With your group, list four of them.

2 Think about problems women in your culture have. List them.

3 In your group, compare the problems in each of your cultures with the problems Alvarado describes. Find three or four problems common to all the cultures represented by your group.

4 Share your lists with the class.

## HOW IT'S WRITTEN

### Think about examples

1 One way of supporting a point of view in writing is to give examples from your own experience or from your observation of others. Reread the essay noticing Alvarado's use of examples. Circle each example. Put **P** next to each example that is personal and **O** next to each example that is an observation of others.

2 Discuss these questions with your group: Which kind of example does Alvarado use most often? What effect do these examples have on you as a reader?

# TOPICS FOR WRITING

### Choose one topic to write about

Whichever topic you choose, make sure you give examples from your personal experience as well as your observations of others.

**1** Describe a typical day in the life of a man and a woman in your culture.

**2** What problems do women in your culture have because of machismo or male dominance? In your opinion, what can be done to change the way men treat women?

**3** Alvarado says "people *can* change." Do you agree or disagree with the idea that people can change?

# AFTER WRITING

### Share your writing

1 Exchange papers with another person. Analyze your partner's composition using the following questions as a guide:

① Which sentence best expresses the writer's main idea?

② Do the other paragraphs relate to the main idea? Explain.

③ Are the examples clear? Do they help support the main idea? Explain.

2 Discuss your analysis with your partner.

3 Write a note to yourself in your log or on your paper about some changes you might make to improve your writing.

......................................................................

# BEFORE READING

**A Think about the topic**

1 Read the following statements and decide whether you **Agree (A)** or **Disagree (D)** with each one.

_____ ① Women work harder than men.

_____ ② There are more advantages to being female than being male.

_____ ③ Women are usually better than men at nurturing and taking care of children.

_____ ④ There are some jobs that men are better at than women.

_____ ⑤ Women belong at home, taking care of the house and the children.

_____ ⑥ Men and women should always earn the same pay when they do the same work.

_____ ⑦ There are some jobs that women are better at than men.

_____ ⑧ Men make better managers than women.

2 Compare your answers with your group.

## B Write as you read

As you read, underline the facts related to women with one color pen and the facts related to men with another color.

## Women and Work: Around the World, Women Earn Less
### Newsweek Education Program

*The following materials appeared in a special supplement to* Newsweek *magazine called "The Status of Women Around the World." It was published in February, 2000. The source was* <u>www.aflcio.org/women</u>.

**ON EVERY CONTINENT, MORE WOMEN ARE WORKING FOR PAY THAN EVER BEFORE**

■ In industrial countries, by 1990, 60 percent of women of working age were in the work force compared to 53 percent in 1980.

**BUT ON EVERY CONTINENT, WOMEN'S PAY LAGS WELL BEHIND MEN'S PAY**

■ In Asia, women in Bangladesh earn as little as 42 percent of what men earn, and in Vietnam it's 92 percent.

■ Women in the Syrian Arab Republic earn only 60 percent of what men earn, and women in Tanzania earn 92 percent of men's earnings.

■ In South America, Chile's women earn 61 percent of what men earn, and Colombian women earn 85 percent of men's earnings.

■ Much of women's work (caring for children and the elderly or doing agricultural work) is unpaid. In fact, around the world women receive no wages for 66 percent of the work they do.

**WOMEN HOLD JOBS AT THE BOTTOM OF THE PAY SCALE**

■ In Japan, about 37 percent of working women hold low-wage jobs – compared to only 6 percent of men.

■ In the United States, about 33 percent of working women hold low-wage jobs – compared with 20 percent of men.

- In the United Kingdom, about 31 percent of working women hold low-wage jobs – compared with 13 percent of men.

- In France, 25 percent of working women hold low-wage jobs – 9 percent of men do.

- In Sweden, about 8 percent of working women hold low-wage jobs – 3 percent of men do.

- Worldwide, women hold only 14 percent of administrative and managerial jobs and less than 6 percent of senior-management jobs.

**ONE KEY RESULT? AROUND THE WORLD, MORE WOMEN THAN MEN LIVE IN POVERTY**
- Females account for 70 percent of the more than 1 billion people who live in poverty.

**THE UNITED STATES LAGS BEHIND OTHER INDUSTRIALIZED COUNTRIES**
- In the United States, equal pay has been the law since 1963, but women still earn only 74 percent of men's pay. The U.S. wage gap for women is worse than the gap in Australia, Austria, Germany, Italy, Norway, and Sweden.

- The United States and [South] Korea are the only industrialized nations that have failed to sign a 1961 international resolution endorsing the principle of equal pay for work of equal value.

- The United States has also failed to ratify the 1979 UN Convention for the Elimination of All Forms of Discrimination against Women.


# AFTER READING

## A  Respond to the reading

1 Write a double entry response in your log. (See the toolbox *Double Entry Response* on page 26.)

2 Exchange logs with a partner and read each other's writing. Discuss similarities and differences.


## B  Understand the reading

1 With a partner, choose three statements from the text to paraphrase or restate using different words.

2 Share your paraphrases with your group.

**C Make a graph from the reading**

1 With your group, create a graph to show some of the statistics that appear in the reading. You can use any kind of graph you wish, for example, a bar graph or a pie graph.

2 Show and explain your graph to the class.

## HOW IT'S WRITTEN

**Appreciate the format**

1 The subheadings in this reading are statements. How would you describe the differences between these statements and the ones in the rest of the text? Which would you label as main idea? Supporting detail? Generalization? Example? Talk about these questions with a partner.

2 Summarize your discussion for the class.

## TOPICS FOR WRITING

**Choose one topic to write about**

1 Do women and men in your community have the same job opportunities? Are certain careers or jobs typically associated with men and others with women? Have these things changed over the past 30 years? Write an essay that describes changing attitudes toward gender and work in your culture. Give your opinion on these changes.

2 Write a family history of women working. Describe the kinds of jobs and work situations of the women of several generations in your family, including today's.

3 Choose one of the statements you discussed in **Think about the topic** on page 187. and explain your point of view. Support your opinion with examples from your experience or your reading.

## AFTER WRITING

**Ask a partner for feedback**

1 Exchange papers with a partner. Use the information in the toolbox *Sentence Starter Feedback* on page 49 to write comments about your partner's essay.

2 Read your partner's comments. Mark places in your essay where you can make your meaning clearer and where you can add more information.

# BEFORE READING

## Gather ideas about the topic

1 What jobs in your culture are typically done only by men? What jobs are typically done only by women? Make two lists.

2 Share your lists with your group. Discuss their similarities and differences. Discuss changes that have been occurring in the past 10–20 years.

3 Read the title, the introductory information, and the first sentence of the article below. What do you think is meant by the word "chauvinism" in the title? Discuss this with the class.

# Battling Chauvinism to Do a Man's Job

InfoChange

*The Web site www.infochangeindia.org was set up in the year 2000 to distribute information about positive changes occurring in India, especially at grassroots levels. This is one of the site's "Stories of Change."*

Chamela, a tribal woman of Banda (Shahuji Maharaj district, Uttar Pradesh, India) is an excellent hand pump mechanic. Every day, she cycles from village to village, wielding a wrench, dismantling pumps and putting them back in perfect order. Though illiterate, Chamela and several other Dalit and Kol tribal women learned the intricacies of hand pump repair through the intervention of a voluntary group called Vanangana. Founded by Madhavi Kuckreja in 1994, Vanangana, derived from van (forest) and angan (courtyard), seeks to impart non-conventional skills to women, enabling them to manage their daily lives more effectively.

Banda's low water table and indifferent irrigation facilities led to a heavy reliance on hand pumps, which never seemed to work. Training the women in repair has changed the character of this dry and hard land. "There was some doubt whether illiterate women could understand the mechanics involved, but they surprised all of us by learning quickly," recalls Ashok Mishra, junior engineer of Jal Nigam, a government agency that trained the women initially.

In the Manickpur block to which the women were first assigned, nearly half the pumps were inoperative. Villages had to wait for days for the two Jal Nigam mechanics who attended to nearly 930 pumps spread over an area of 1,000 square kilometers. The newly acquired skills of the women, however, have now ensured that almost 90 per cent of the pumps work all through the summer.

The lives of the women have simultaneously changed. Many have chosen this as a profession. While Chamela fought with her mother-in-law to be allowed to do the job, others have battled chauvinism, scorn and apathy to become mechanics themselves. In some villages, the men would drive them away, saying they didn't trust women to do a man's job. Their 'low' caste status too worked against them. In Bauri village, the hand pump was outside the home of an upper-caste village headman, who prevented the women from touching it. He only agreed after the villagers coerced him.

The achievements of the women mechanics have prompted the Uttar Pradesh (UP) state government to replicate the scheme in other regions too. Vanangana was also chosen by the Uttar Pradesh government as one of the participant NGOs (non-governmental organizations) in the World Bank-funded Swajal Project. This rural water supply and environmental sanitation project works in over 1,000 villages in 19 districts of the state.

## AFTER READING

### A Annotate and summarize the reading

1 Reread the text and annotate it. (See the toolbox *Annotating* on page 118.)

2 Using your annotations as a guide, write a short summary of the article.

3 Read your summary to your group.

### B Understand the reading

1 With a partner, underline phrases or sentences that show how the women fought chauvinism and what changes the women made.

2 Why was the story of these women included in a series called "Stories of Change"? Discuss this with your group.

## HOW IT'S WRITTEN

### Examine the use of stories

1 Reread the article and put brackets [ ] around the parts that tell Chamela's story.

2 Compare your findings with your group. Then discuss in your group how a personal story adds interest to the reading.

3 Write a note to yourself about this technique of using a personal story or example in informative writing.

# TOPICS FOR WRITING

## Choose one topic to write about

Whichever topic you choose, make sure you include one or more personal stories as examples.

**1** Do you know about a situation in which women have been successful in learning to do a man's job? Write an essay that describes how their success came about.

**2** Just as women are starting to do jobs that used to be thought of as "men's work," men are also starting to do jobs that used to be considered only "women's work." Write an essay about these changes in tradition.

**3** Write an essay that could be included in a Web site titled "Stories of Change." Your essay can be about any group in any country or culture that has succeeded in making some kind of social change at the grassroots level.

# AFTER WRITING

## Share your writing

1 Write down two or three questions that will guide your readers' feedback. (See the toolbox *Asking for Feedback* on page 82.) Ask at least two classmates to read and write comments about your essay.

2 Read your readers' comments and think about how you can revise this essay.

. . . . . . . . . . . . . . . . . . . . . . . . . . . . . . . . . . . . . . . . . . . . . . . . . . . . . . . . . . . . . . . . . . .

# BEFORE READING

## Think about the topic

1 Would you want to know the sex of your child before it is born? Why or why not? Freewrite your response to these questions.

2 Share some of your freewriting with a partner.

 **First Lullabye**
Patricia Kirkpatrick

*This poem appeared in a collection of poetry called* Minnesota Writes: Poetry.
*Kirkpatrick is a poet who teaches at Hamline University in Saint Paul and is the*
*author of the children's book,* Plowie: A Story from the Prairie. *She wrote this*
*poem to celebrate the birth of her daughter.*

Someone knows the sex of our child.
"Don't tell us," we said.
The child swims in the sea of the womb.
Let her be a boy now if this is his time.

Let him sleep on the crescent moon
of her spine in the dark without learning
the ways of this world too soon.
Let the spring tulips open, red or yellow

no matter to the trembling
waterdrop beating inside her.
Let the world's first word for our child
be the world's secret a little longer.


## AFTER READING

### A Understand the reading

1 Reread the poem aloud to a partner.

2 With your partner, discuss these questions:

   ① Does the writer of the poem want to know the sex of the baby?
   Why or why not?

   ② Notice Kirkpatrick's use of pronouns. What, if anything, do they tell you
   about what she wants?

3 Summarize your discussion for the class.


### B Respond to the reading

1 Reread the poem and stop at least two times to make a double entry
response. (See the toolbox *Double Entry Response* on page 26.)

2 Exchange logs and ask your partner to write a response to your responses.
(See the toolbox *Triple Entry Response* on page 89.) Talk with your partner
about your responses.

3 With your group, discuss your reaction to the poem.

## HOW IT'S WRITTEN

### Appreciate the images

1 Reread the poem and find an image you like. What feeling does it evoke?

2 Explain to your group how this image helps you understand the poem.

## TOPICS FOR WRITING

### Choose one topic to write about

❶ Through medical progress, parents are now able to know the sex of their child before it is born. What do you think of this practice? Should parents learn the sex of their child before its birth? Write an essay explaining your point of view.

❷ In many countries, boy babies are preferred to girl babies. Is this true in your culture? What do you think about this attitude? Write an essay explaining your point of view.

❸ "First Lullabye" was written for the writer's unborn child. What would you want to say to your unborn child? Write a letter or a poem to express this.

## AFTER WRITING

### Share your writing

1 Post your writing on a wall of the classroom for everyone to read.

2 Walk around the room reading your classmates' pieces. As you walk, take notes on which writing is most effective and why.

3 Discuss your thoughts with the class.

# GENDER ROLES: REVISION

## A Choose one essay

1 Reread the pieces you wrote for the **Topics for Writing** sections of GENDER ROLES. Pick two you would like to develop.

2 Show your choices to a partner. Discuss which one you would most like to revise. Explain why. Choose one to work on.

## B Think about examples

1 Read about the use of examples as a way to enhance your writing.

### Choosing Examples

Here are some criteria for helping you choose and check your examples:

- **Sufficient:** Do you have enough examples – or details or facts or evidence – to make your point strongly? Is your support sufficient? Of course, sometimes one strong, detailed example is enough.

  > People who get exercise tend to live longer than those who don't. For example, my father walks five miles every day, and he is 90 years old.

- **Typical:** Is the example typical? Does it represent the type of situation you want to make a point about? You should choose examples that people expect to see. Be careful though; if you choose an example that's too common, it may seem stereotypical.

  > Single parents can raise children just as well as two parents. A good example is a 7-year-old boy whose parents both died, leaving him an orphan. His 20-year-old, unmarried brother then raised him successfully.

- **Authentic:** Is the example true? All your examples should sound true to the reader.

  > Television can influence children to do harmful or dangerous things. I once read about a young boy who watched a superhero show, then, with a cape tied around his neck, jumped off a roof in imitation.

- **Relevant:** Is the example relevant to your point? Will the reader see a logical connection?

  > One way to reduce the number of cars in cities might be to outlaw single passenger cars in the city center during peak hours. For example, some people in New York City propose that cars entering the center of the city in the morning hours be required to carry two or more passengers.

> How can you remember these criteria? Perhaps you've guessed – the first letter of each word forms an acronym: STAR. Use STAR to check your essay to see if you need to change any of your examples.

2 Reread your essay. If the essay includes any examples, see if they fit the criteria above. Add to, remove, or substitute any that don't. If your essay contains no examples, you may want to add one or more.

3 Explain to your partner what changes you plan to make. Get your partner's opinion.

## C Revise your essay

1 Where does your essay need "cleaning house, getting rid of the junk, getting things in order, tightening things up?" (See the **Writer's Tip** on this page.) Make the necessary changes in your essay as you rewrite it.

2 If you don't yet have a title, try several until you find one you like.

3 Proofread your final draft by following the suggestions in the toolbox *Proofreading* on page 97.

## D Share your writing

1 Form a group of three or four. Pass your papers around the circle until everyone has read all the essays.

2 As a group, choose one essay to read to the class.

## Writer's Tip

*What makes me happy is rewriting. In the first draft you get your ideas and your theme clear . . . But the next time through it's like cleaning house, getting rid of the junk, getting things in order, tightening things up. I like the process of making writing neat.*

**Ellen Goodman**

Into the Future

## BEFORE READING

### Gather ideas about the topic

1 In your group, work out the average number of hours per week your group watches TV. Also, find out what programs your group watches and put them into categories.

2 The title of this reading is "Kill Your Television." How would "killing your TV" change your lives? Discuss this with your group.

3 Summarize your discussions for the class.

 **Kill Your Television**
Bill Duesing

*Bill Duesing is an organic farmer and environmental artist. He and his wife, Suzanne, operate the Old Solar Farm near Bridgeport, Connecticut. This essay appeared in a book called* Living on the Earth: Eclectic Essays for a Sustainable and Joyful Future. *It was first aired on WSHU Public Radio in Fairfield, Connecticut.*

For several years an essay has been lurking around my computer, waiting to be written. Named after a bumper sticker that always makes me smile, it's called "Kill Your Television." Suzanne (my wife) objects to that title because she feels it is too violent. But here goes, anyway.

The catalyst for this writing is a fascinating book called *The Age of Missing Information* by Bill McKibben. In it he compares the information he got by watching all of one day's programming on a 93-channel cable system, with the information he experienced during a 24-hour camping trip in the Adirondack Mountains. It brought a lot of things into focus.

Since 1977, Jerry Mander's book, *Four Arguments for the Elimination of Television*, has impressed me. His first argument is that TV confines, narrows, and controls what we are capable of experiencing and knowing. Most of our senses are *not* engaged by television. Smell, touch, taste, and peripheral vision begin to atrophy as sight and sound command our attention. The second argument posits that it was inevitable that TV would be used as an instrument of "psychic colonization" and human domination. Our neuro-physiological responses to electrons beamed into our eyes, which may include physical damage as well as suppression of conscious thinking and creative imagination, comprise his third argument. The fourth is that the very nature of television means that it hardens the edges of any information that is present, creating narrow minds receptive to the simplification of consumer culture. The technology itself is *not* neutral.

More recently in *Sports Illustrated* and *Business Week*, I've seen articles about television's future. The human male sits in an easy chair with a remote control, commanding a giant screen that accesses 500 channels and has the ability to switch or mix them at the touch of a control. The sports buff can create his own instant replays or watch several games simultaneously. Surround-sound, TV shopping and other wonders abound.

But no matter how big the screen, or how many channels there are, TV . . . puts somebody else's program into your head. And the bottom line of any TV program is to make us want something we didn't want before. As the chief executive of the world's largest ketchup maker said, "Once television is there, people of whatever shade, culture, or origin want roughly the same things."

Almost every program on the tube is there because it is successful at getting people to watch commercials. The average American child will see between 350,000 and 640,000 commercials by the time she reaches 18. The national average of 30 hours of viewing per week was borne out recently by an informal survey of fifth-graders in Bridgeport (Connecticut). That's 5–10 hours per week of commercials alone.

This is the reason why many of us who carry out real processes such as gardening, measuring, or cooking with school children, are so opposed to the trend toward more TV in schools. One of the main problems in education is that our children watch too much TV already. And they have too few direct, real experiences. They have seen everything on TV and think they know and can do everything. Like TV itself, this is a dysfunctional illusion.

Our appreciation of the richness and pleasure of life without TV keeps growing. Try it yourself.


## AFTER READING

### A Understand the reading

1 Reread the essay, and annotate it. (See the toolbox *Annotating* on page 118.) Mark all the ways the author supports his argument.

2 With your group, write a summary of the essay, stating the author's point of view. (See the toolbox *Writing a Summary* on page 53.)

3 Show your summary to another group to see if the summaries are similar or different. If necessary, rewrite your summary.

4 With the class, make a list of all the reasons Duesing uses to convince readers not to watch TV.

**B Acquire new vocabulary**

1 Find five words that are new to you and that you think will be useful to know.

2 Write a definition, either by guessing the meaning from the context (see the toolbox *Context Clues* on page 85) or by using a dictionary.

3 Use each of the five words in a sentence of your own.

4 Teach your five words to your group.

## HOW IT'S WRITTEN

### A Notice words that show order

1 Reread paragraph three. What words or phrases tell you that a new idea is being introduced? Underline them.

2 With your group discuss how using such words and phrases helps the reader.

### B Observe references to other writers

1 The author both quotes and paraphrases the ideas of others. (See the toolbox *Quoting and Paraphrasing* on page 135.) With a partner, find three examples of either quotes or paraphrases and mark them **Q** (quotation) or **P** (paraphrase).

2 Describe how the author cites sources. Note the punctuation used.

### C Paraphrase a paragraph

1 There are eight paragraphs in this essay. Divide the class into eight groups. Each group should work on one paragraph. With your group, paraphrase or restate the ideas in the paragraph using your own words.

2 Write your paraphrase on the chalkboard or a transparency for the class to read.

3 Examine each rewritten paragraph for accuracy and clarity. Revise if necessary.

### D Examine the title

1 What do you think of the title? Is it effective? (See the toolbox *Titles* on page 38.) Freewrite your response. Tell your group what you think and why.

2 With the class, make a list of other titles Duesing could have used instead of this one. Which one do you like best? Why?

# TOPICS FOR WRITING

### Choose one topic to write about

Whichever topic you choose, make sure to include some words or ideas from other people, either from your reading or from people that you talk to about the issue. Be sure to cite properly. (See the toolbox *Citations Using APA Style* on page 95.)

1 Write an essay arguing for or against television.

2 Drawing on the points made in this reading about the dangers of television, imagine what the future will be like if people continue to watch too much television. What will people be like? Look like? What will school, work, play, and home life be like? Write an essay describing the effects of too much television on the world and people of the future.

3 Conduct a survey of a group of people – students, children, elderly people, families, or a mixed group – about how much television they watch every day. Ask about the number of hours, the type of shows, their feelings and attitudes toward television, why they watch, and what they think they gain or lose from watching. Report and analyze your findings.

# AFTER WRITING

### Share your writing

1 Give your essay to a classmate who chose the same topic you did. Write a descriptive outline of your partner's essay. (See the toolbox *Descriptive Outlining* on page 35.)

2 Read your partner's descriptive outline of your essay. See if there are any parts that need to be clarified or expanded.

· · · · · · · · · · · · · · · · · · · · · · · · · · · · · · · · · · · · · · · · · · · · · · · · · · · · · · · · · · ·

# BEFORE READING

### Preview the reading

1 What does "vs." in the title of the first reading mean? Discuss with the class.

2 Skim the reading "Lectures vs. Laptops." (See the toolbox *Skimming* on page 161.)

3 In your log, freewrite for five minutes about what you think the essay will be about.

4 After freewriting, write one sentence that states the opinion you think the author will express in this essay. Share your statement with your group and then with the class.

# Lectures vs. Laptops
Ian Ayres

*Ian Ayres is a professor of law at Yale University in New Haven, Connecticut. This essay appeared in the* New York Times.

Something alarming happened in my contract law class. I asked that laptop computers be used only for note taking, and my students went ballistic.

Solitaire and Minesweeper are everywhere now in university classes. At Yale, where classrooms are wired to the Internet, students can also surf the Web, send e-mail or even trade stock. Soon the wireless Internet will make this possible at all schools.

Not all students do this sort of thing. But the abusive use of laptops is getting to be increasingly prevalent. Students toggle between windows during any part of the class they deem to be boring – often when their fellow students are asking questions or answering them. Seeing the person in the next seat playing a video game while you are trying to puzzle out a law question is demoralizing. And students who surf are not fully present to ask or answer questions themselves.

Admittedly, students can mentally check out of class in other ways – for instance, by daydreaming or doodling. But not all activities are equally addictive. I should know. I might be the only law professor to have asked for cybersitter filtering software to keep me from surfing the Web too much at my office.

Still, I was surprised at how brazenly my own students resisted my laptop restrictions, both in class discussion and in virtual chat room (which, perversely, they could post to during their other classes.) They argued that they were multi-tasking, staying productive during dead or badly taught portions of class. They said classroom surfing reduces sleepiness, increases their willingness to attend class, allows them to research legal questions being discussed, and so on. They said the professor has an incentive to teach more effectively when he or she must compete against other more interesting claims on students' attention.

Their arguments could apply equally well to the opera hall, the jury box, or the church pew. Will the lure of technological stimulation someday overwhelm current mores about paying attention in those places, too? At least, we should try to stem the tide in the classroom. Few students say on their admissions applications, after all, that they intend classroom solitaire to be a central part of their educational experience.

# Letters

*Ian Ayres's essay* "Lectures vs. Laptops" *provoked many letters from readers of the* New York Times.

To the Editor:

No teacher should allow laptop computers in the classroom. The classroom should be a quiet place where students can pay full attention to the words of the instructor without getting distracted by the noise of clicking keys.

Let the policy of "no laptops in my class" be stated clearly in the teacher's syllabus and that's that. Students can either live with it or drop the class.

**Patricia Reyes**
Boston, Mass

To the Editor:

Ian Ayres, a Yale law professor, says he dislikes students using laptops in his class, even for note taking. I don't understand where he's coming from. Maybe he'd better join the 21st century.

I would say more, but I'm too busy. I'm in my business ethics class at Brooklyn Law School catching up with my e-mail.

**James J. Haggerty**
Brooklyn, NY

To the Editor:

It's no news to me that Ian Ayres's law students are playing solitaire and writing e-mails in his class. I've seen students in my history class at our university place bids on eBay. It seems unbelievable, yet we see people multitasking every day. How many times have you noticed someone load a grocery cart while talking on a cell phone? Or open "snail mail" during a conversation with a colleague? No longer is it considered rude. Now it's considered productive.

**Marcia Wolf**
Minneapolis, MN

To the Editor:

As a law student, I would like to add to Professor Ayres's complaint: cell phones. Students' phones are constantly beeping or burping or singing or tooting during classes, interrupting the professor's lecture and the students' concentration. We need to return to the respect and quiet that teachers used to get in the law schools of my father's time.

**Matteo Capone**
Chicago, IL

# AFTER READING

## A Find pros and cons

1 Ayres thinks laptop computers should be used only for taking notes in the classroom. Not all agree. Working with a partner, make a list of the pros and cons, as explained in Ayres's essay and the letters, of using laptop computers in the classroom.

2 Choose one of the pros or cons and explain it fully to the others in the class.

## B Understand the reading

1 Reread the last paragraph of Ayres's essay. Restate it in your own words. What attitude is the author expressing? Discuss this with your group.

2 Summarize your discussion for the class.

3 Form groups of four people. As a group, choose one letter in response to Ayres's essay, reread it, and restate the important points the writer makes.

4 Split your group into pairs and find another pair that read a different letter. Make a new group of four. Explain to the other pair what the letter you read said.

5 Work with a partner. Write one sentence that expresses the main point of each letter.

6 Are the main points of the letters similar or different? Do the writers agree or disagree? Discuss this with the class.

## C Acquire new vocabulary

1 This essay and the letters that follow it contain a number of words and phrases related to computers. With a partner, circle five such items. Try to figure out the meaning from the context (see the toolbox *Context Clues* on page 85) or use a dictionary to help you.

2 Make a class list of computer-related vocabulary. Be sure everyone understands the meaning of all the words on the list.

# HOW IT'S WRITTEN

## A Notice words of attitude

1 Ayres uses a number of words and phrases in his essay that show his attitude or point of view about the issue of laptops in classes, for example, the word "alarming" in the first sentence. With a partner, find other such attitude words and circle them.

2 How do these words affect you as a reader? What do they communicate? Discuss these questions with your group.

## B Outline the text

1 With a partner, write a descriptive outline of Ayres's essay. (See the toolbox *Descriptive Outlining* on page 35.) Explain your outline to your group.

2 In which paragraph does Ayres give students' reasons for using laptops in class? Why do you think he does this? Discuss this with your group.

3 Summarize your discussion for the class.

## TOPICS FOR WRITING

### Choose one topic to write about

Whichever topic you choose, make sure that you state your opinion clearly and give examples to support your point of view.

**1** The essay by Ayres appeared in the *New York Times*. Write a letter to the editor of this newspaper giving your reactions to Ayres's essay.

**2** Think of an aspect of modern technology or a piece of equipment that you do not like or wish to have. Write an essay called "X vs. X" (for example, "Snail mail vs. e-mail") or "Against X" (for example, "Against Dishwashers").

**3** Many people think they can do two things at once. Some people call this "multitasking." Write an essay giving your opinion about "multitasking" and people's ability to do this.

## AFTER WRITING

### Ask for feedback

1 Reread your piece with ARMS in mind. (See the toolbox *ARMS* on page 72.) Make any changes necessary.

2 Ask a classmate to read your writing and give you some feedback. (See the toolbox *Asking for Feedback* on page 82.)

3 In your log or on your paper, write your plans for revising your writing.

> ## Writer's Tip
>
> *Push yourself beyond when you think you are done with what you have to say. Go a little further. Sometimes when you think you are done, it is just the edge of beginning.*
>
> **Natalie Goldberg**

## BEFORE READING

### Gather ideas about the topic

1 Read the title and introductory information. What "inventions, ideas, and social trends" do you think are worth saving from the past 100 years? Make a list.

2 Share your list with your group. Which items are on more than one list? Choose five that your group considers the most important.

3 With your group, take turns reading the headings of the article aloud. Did your group's list of inventions, ideas, and social trends include any of these items? What do you think of the list in the article? Do you agree that each item is important? Why or why not?

# The 20th Century: What's Worth Saving?

### Jay Walljasper & Jon Spayde

*Near the end of the twentieth century, two writers for a magazine called the* Utne Reader *decided to ask readers for their opinions about what we should keep from the past 100 years. To start the discussion, they published a list of items from the twentieth century that they considered worth taking into the twenty-first century. Their items included inventions, ideas, and social trends. Eleven of the items appear below, in alphabetical order.*

Let's face it: The 20th century has been rough going. Auschwitz. Hiroshima. The Gulag. Chernobyl. AIDS. . . . Yet at the same time great strides have been made in many fields, from social justice to medicine to pop music. Perhaps the century's most important lesson is this: No technology, no ideology, no social trend can dictate the future; it's the outcome of the choices we make, both personally and as a society. Only when everyone has a voice will we be able to decide which choices are the best ones.

To start the discussion, we've drafted a list of things from the past 100 years we think are worth taking into the 21st century. We hope you'll add ideas of your own.

#### ANTIBIOTICS

When Scottish bacteriologist Alexander Fleming went on vacation in 1928 and left his staphylococci sample uncovered, he returned to find a mold attacking it. That mold – penicillin – launched the first of several families of antibiotics. . . . The least complex and least expensive of life-sustaining technologies, antibiotics have their dark side – but continue to save lives and restore health to millions.

## BIRTH CONTROL

The concept of *birth control* – that women [and men] have the right to choose how many children they raise – goes beyond oral contraceptives (introduced in 1960) to the idea that the purpose of sex is more than reproduction.

## BLOOD BANKS

Dr. Oswald Robertson created blood depots during World War I, and a Leningrad hospital established the first blood bank in 1932. Five years later, Cook County Hospital in Chicago created the first U.S. version. [The U.S. government] adopted a nationwide blood-collection program in 1940.

## EARTH DAY

The first Earth Day, on April 22, 1970, pulled together public support for cleaning up the environment. The results were almost immediate: The Nixon administration [in the U.S.] soon founded the Environmental Protection Agency, and Congress passed landmark legislation to clean up America's air and water. Now celebrated in 140 nations with rallies, street fairs, and television specials, Earth Day is an annual reminder that environmental quality depends upon all of us doing our part.

## GANDHI'S SATYAGRAHA

Literally "the power of truth," *satyagraha* is Mahatma Gandhi's term for his resistance tactics. [These tactics] not only drove the British empire out of India but also guided Martin Luther King Jr.'s civil rights struggle. Gandhi conceived *satyagraha* in 1906 in South Africa, where he was a lawyer fighting for the rights of Indians. He drew largely upon India's *ahimsa* tradition, Tolstoy's writing, and Jesus' Sermon on the Mount. As historian William Shirer noted, Gandhi "taught us all that there was a greater power in life than force."

## HUMAN RIGHTS

In a century in which slavery was still legal until 1962 in Saudi Arabia . . . and an outright white supremacist government ruled until 1994 in South Africa, the campaign for basic human rights is surprisingly young. The 1948 United Nations Universal Declaration on Human Rights and global organizations such as Amnesty International and Human Rights Watch continue to inspire activists to stand up to tyranny in courageous ways.

## INTERNET

[T]he Internet [was] born in 1969 as ARPANET, a decentralized military communications system. Created by computer firm Bolt, Beranek, and Neumann in Cambridge, Massachusetts, the system had 15 sets of computers online by 1971, and 37 by 1973. But in 1983, the system converted to the Internet as we know it. Five years later, 60,000 computers were plugged in; today millions of civilians have global access to uncensored, nearly instant, and almost-free information.

### OVERSEAS AIR TRAVEL

The first round-trip transatlantic flight occurred in 1919 when British fliers captained a dirigible from England to New Jersey and back. But the real breakthrough in travel came in the late 1950s, when Boeing's new 707 jet brought down the price of overseas airline tickets. . . . Although shorter trips are better left to speedy trains, affordable air travel transformed our culture.

### PAPERBACK BOOKS

What began as a risky venture in 1935 for Britain's Penguin Books turned into a cultural revolution by the 1950s, largely due to the genius of Robert de Graff, who invented the mass-market book and founded Pocket Books in 1939. Paperbacks were printed on huge presses in large quantities at reasonable prices and sold in drugstores and bus stations. They democratized reading by putting more books into more people's hands than ever before.

### SOLAR POWER

As early as 1904, a power plant in St. Louis was converting sunlight into electricity, but high costs meant that fossil fuels, hydroelectric dams, and nuclear plants dominated the 20th-century energy supply. Due to the recent advances in photovoltaic solar cells, invented in 1954, and increasing awareness of the environmental price of other energy sources, sales of solar cells jumped 40 percent in 1997 alone. Half a million homes, mostly in remote Third World villages, use them for all their electrical needs.

### UNIVERSAL SUFFRAGE

At the turn of the century, no country on earth offered women the right to vote. Norway was the first nation to do so, in 1913. It wasn't until 1920 that most American women could step into a voting booth. And for blacks of both genders, polling places [in the U.S.] were off-limits in many states until passage of the Voting Rights Act of 1965.

## AFTER READING

### Create a time line

1  With a partner, choose one paragraph to reread. After reading, restate the important facts in the paragraph.

2  Place the important events from your paragraph on the time line below. (See the toolbox *Time Lines* on page 46.)

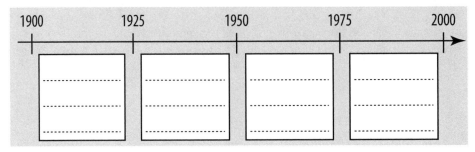

3 Find classmates who chose the same paragraph you did. Compare what you added to the time line.

4 Report your findings to the class. Then create a class time line based on all the paragraphs. Add more details to the time line on the opposite page.

## HOW IT'S WRITTEN

**Notice the details**

1 Quickly reread the text. As you reread do the following:
  ① Circle the dates.
  ② Underline the names.
  ③ Bracket [ ] the important events..

2 What effect do these kinds of details have on you as a reader? Discuss this with your group.

## TOPICS FOR WRITING

**Choose one topic for writing**

Whichever topic you choose, use the toolbox *The Reporter's Formula* on page 126 to help you.

❶ Choose one item from the list that you wrote in **Gather ideas about the topic** on page 206. Write a letter to the editors of the *Utne Reader* about it. Convince them that this item is worth taking into the twenty-first century. Address your letter to 21st Century, *Utne Reader*, 1624 Harmon Place, Minneapolis, MN, 55403 or e-mail it to editor@utne.com. Include some history about the item and explain its value to the world. You may have to do some research to support your opinion. Include specific dates and names.

❷ Choose one of the headings from the article and write an essay about it. Do some research to gather more information. Include some history about the topic as well as its value to the world. Include specific dates and names.

❸ In their introduction to this reading, the authors argue, "No technology, no ideology, no social trend can dictate the future; it's the outcome of the choices we make, both personally and as a society." Do you agree or disagree with this statement? Do an individual's choices help determine our future? Explain and illustrate your opinion using your own experience, your observation of others, or your reading. Include examples to support what you say.

## AFTER WRITING

### Share your writing

1 Exchange essays with a partner. Read your partner's essay. Circle the dates, underline the names, and bracket [ ] the important information. Then write a comment about the type and amount of information given in the essay. If there is something more you want to know, ask about it.

2 Read what your partner wrote. Make notes about what you can add to make your essay more informative and interesting.

• • • • • • • • • • • • • • • • • • • • • • • • • • • • • • • • • • • • • • • • • • • • • • • •

## BEFORE READING

### A Gather ideas about the topic

1 With the class, make a cluster around the words "The twenty-first century." Then make another cluster around the words "A changing world." What words appear in both clusters? What connections do you see?

2 In your log, create a Venn diagram. (See the toolbox *Venn Diagrams* on page 131.) Label one circle "The twenty-first century," label the other "A changing world." Use the words from your clusters to fill in the diagram.

3 Share your diagram with your group.

### B Write as you read

As you read, pause for a minute after each paragraph to let an image come to your mind. Jot down the image in your log.

## Entering the Twenty-First Century
### Thich Nhat Hanh

*Thich Nhat Hanh was born in Vietnam in 1926. He left home as a teenager to become a Zen Buddhist monk. Since 1966 he has lived in exile in France, where he writes, teaches, gardens, and helps refugees worldwide. This essay is taken from his book entitled* Peace Is Every Step.

The word "policy" is very much in use these days. There seems to be a policy for just about everything. I have heard that the so-called developed nations are contemplating a garbage policy to send their trash on huge barges to the Third World.

I think that we need a "policy" for dealing with our suffering. We do not want to condone it, but we need to find a way to make use of our suffering, for our good and for the good of others. There has been so much suffering in the twentieth century: two world wars, concentration camps in Europe, the killing fields in Cambodia, refugees from Vietnam, Central America, and elsewhere fleeing their countries with no place to land. We need to articulate a policy for these kinds of garbage also. We need to use the suffering of the twentieth century as compost, so that together we can create flowers for the twenty-first century.

When we see photographs and programs about the atrocities of the Nazis, the gas chambers and the camps, we feel afraid. We may say, "I didn't do it; they did it." But if we had been there, we may have done the same thing, or we may have been too cowardly to stop it, as was the case for so many. We have to put all these things into our compost pile to fertilize the ground. In Germany today, the young people have a kind of complex that they are somehow responsible for the suffering. It is important that these young people and the generation responsible for the war begin anew, and together create a path of mindfulness so that our children in the next century can avoid repeating the same mistakes. The flower of tolerance to see and appreciate cultural diversity is one flower we can cultivate for the children of the twenty-first century. Another flower is the truth of suffering – there has been so much unnecessary suffering in our century. If we are willing to work together and learn together, we can all benefit from the mistakes of our time, and, seeing with the eyes of compassion and understanding, we can offer the next century a beautiful garden and a clear path.

Take the hand of your child and invite her to go out and sit with you on the grass. The two of you may want to contemplate the green grass, the little flowers that grow among the grasses, and the sky. Breathing and smiling together – that is peace education. If we know how to appreciate these beautiful things, we will not have to search for anything else. Peace is available in every moment, in every breath, in every step. . . .

## AFTER READING

### A  Respond to the reading

1  Choose one activity:

① Write for a few minutes in your log about what you read. Use the response questions to guide you. (See the toolbox *Response Questions* on page 9.)

② Write a double entry response as you reread the essay. (See the toolbox *Double Entry Response* on page 26.)

2  Look over what you wrote and underline any sentences or phrases you like.

3  Read your underlined sentences to your group.

## B Understand the reading

1 With a partner, write two or three questions you have about what the author says.

2 Discuss these questions with your group.

3 Based on your discussion, write a one-sentence statement that expresses the main point of the reading.

4 Share your statement with the class.

## C Acquire new vocabulary

1 With a partner, circle three words or phrases that are unfamiliar to you and that you think will be useful to know.

2 Learn the meaning from the context or use a dictionary to help you define the words and phrases. Find a synonym for each word or phrase.

3 Share your work with your group.

# HOW IT'S WRITTEN

## Appreciate the language

1 The author uses the metaphor of a garden in this essay by using words like "compost" and "flower." (See the toolbox *Metaphors and Similes* on page 86 for information on metaphors.) With a partner, find and circle all the words that can be associated with a garden.

2 With your group discuss how this metaphor helps organize the essay.

3 Find one sentence in the essay that you like or that you find especially expressive or meaningful. Copy the sentence on the left side of a page in your log. On the right side of the same page, write about why you like the sentence or what makes the sentence well written.

4 Read what you wrote to your group.

5 Summarize your group's discussions for the class.

# TOPICS FOR WRITING

## Choose one topic to write about

1 Thich Nhat Hanh writes, "The flower of tolerance to see and appreciate cultural diversity is one flower we can cultivate for the children of the twenty-first century." Do we need to help our children develop the tolerance to see and appreciate cultural diversity? Explain your point of view, writing to convince a reader of your opinion. Think of one or two

authors of the readings in this unit. Which one(s) do you think would agree with you? If appropriate, quote them or restate some of their ideas in your essay.

2 In the last paragraph, Thich Nhat Hanh describes his idea of peace education for children. What are your ideas for educating children in ways of creating peace in their world? What can parents or teachers do to help children make peace?

3 Using the title "Entering the Twenty-First Century," write an essay about things you would like to change as we enter this new century, for example, attitudes, behaviors, cultural practices, and so on. In your essay, you might try to use a metaphor to help you express your ideas.

## AFTER WRITING

### A  Share your writing

1 With a pen in your hand, proofread your paper. (See the toolbox *Proofreading* on page 97.) Make any changes needed.

2 Give your paper to at least two other people. Ask for written comments on whatever you want help with. (See the toolbox *Asking for Feedback* on page 82.) Readers should also find one sentence they like or find especially well written and explain why.

3 Read your classmates' comments on your piece.

4 Make notes on what changes you can make to revise this essay.

> ## Writer's Tip
>
> *I don't have any idea how to get something right; I just know when it is. . . . The whole thing is a process of trial and error, and then looking at it as a reader, making changes, then rereading it again.*
>
> **Kathryn Lance**

### B  Reflect on writing techniques

1 Think about how your way of writing has changed since you began to use this book. For example, what do you do now to get started on a composition? To make your writing clearer and more developed? To get feedback? How are these strategies different from what you used to do? Freewrite for a few minutes.

2 Discuss your discoveries with the class.

# INTO THE FUTURE: REVISION

## A Choose one piece to revise

1 Read the pieces you wrote for the **Topics for Writing** sections of INTO THE FUTURE. Choose one to revise.

2 Read any comments from classmates or notes you made with ideas for revising.

## B Revise your writing

1 Read all the **Revision** pages in the book to remind yourself of what to think about when revising. Use these suggestions to make notes about what changes to make.

2 Read some tips on how to create logical development and to engage the reader.

## Writer's Tip

*I remember learning three specific, helpful things that might qualify as rules [for writing]. They were:*

- *Your first sentence (or paragraph) makes a promise that the rest of the story (or novel) will keep.*

- *Give your readers a reason to turn every page.*

- *Keep a very large trash can beside your desk.*

**Barbara Kingsolver**

## Logical Development

You need to keep your reader engaged and enable him or her to follow your thinking. Use the following questions to help you ensure that your writing flows from one idea to the next in a logical or coherent way:

- Does your essay fulfill the promise made in the first sentence or first paragraph? If not, what changes can you make, either in the beginning or in the rest of the essay?

- Do the ideas in each sentence lead logically to the ideas in the next? If not, what changes can you make to show a logical development of ideas?

- Does one paragraph lead logically to the next? If not, what changes can you make to show a logical movement?

- Does the entire piece hold the reader's interest? If not, what changes can you make to keep reader's interest from section to section?

3 Revise your writing according to the questions in the toolbox.

## C Share your writing

1 Read your writing to your group.

2 With your group, discuss how this piece of writing was influenced by what you have learned about writing in this book.

# PEER FEEDBACK FORM

Writer _____ Responder _____

Title/topic _____ Date _____ Draft _____

........................................................................................................................

*Beginning:*

| | | | |
|---|---|---|---|
| Attracts the reader's attention | Yes | No | Partly |
| Tells the writer's main point or attitude | Yes | No | Partly |
| Tells the reader where the essay is going | Yes | No | Partly |

*Comments/suggestions:*

........................................................................................................................

*Development (Middle):*

| | | | |
|---|---|---|---|
| Uses information from reading(s) | Yes | No | Partly |
| If yes, properly cites source(s) | Yes | No | Partly |
| Includes personal example(s) or observation of others | Yes | No | Partly |
| Gives enough support to convince readers of writer's opinion/attitude | Yes | No | Partly |

*Comments/suggestions:*

........................................................................................................................

*Ending/conclusion:*

| | | | |
|---|---|---|---|
| Pulls the essay together at the end | Yes | No | Partly |
| Leaves the reader with something new to think about | Yes | No | Partly |

*Comments/suggestions:*

........................................................................................................................

*Language and Organization:*

| | | | |
|---|---|---|---|
| Expresses meaning clearly throughout | Yes | No | Partly |
| Organizes the essay logically | Yes | No | Partly |

*Comments/suggestions:*

# INDEX OF TOOLBOXES

# INDEX OF READINGS

# INDEX OF AUTHORS

# ACKNOWLEDGEMENTS

Page x, Natalie Goldberg. From *Writing Down the Bones: Freeing the Writer Within*, p. 5-6. (Boston: Shambhala Publications, 1986).

Page 2, Joan Sauro. From *Whole Earth Meditation: Ecology for the Spirit*, by Joan Sauro, C.S.J. Innisfree Press. Philadelphia, PA, 1992. Printed by permission of Joan Sauro, C.S.J.

Page 4, Brett Lott, "Brothers." Copyright © 1993 by the *Antioch Review*, Inc. First appeared in the Antioch Review, Vol. 51, no. 1. Reprinted by permission of the Editors.

Page 6, Meredith Sue Willis. From *Blazing Pencils: A Guide to Writing Fiction and Essays*, p. 4 (NY: Teachers and Writers Collaborative, 1990).

Page 7, Esmeraldo Santiago, "The Brown Hen." From *When I Was Puerto Rican*. Copyright © 1993 by Esmeralda Santiago. Reprinted by permission of the author through Copyright Clearance Center.

Page 13, Amy Tan, "Memory: My Mother." From *The New Yorker*, December 24 & 31, 2001, p. 83. Copyright © 2001 by Amy Tan. First appeared in THE NEW YORKER. Reprinted by permission of the author and the Sandra Dijkstra Literary Agency.

Page 16, Eric Koji Stowe, "There Was Rice at Every Meal." From *What Are You: Voices of Mixed Race Young People*, pp. 103-104, edited by Pearl Fuyo Gaskins. Copyright © 1999 by Pearl Fuyo Gaskins. Reprinted by permission of Henry Holt and Company, LLC.

Page 19, Paul Heilker. From *The Essay: Theory and Pedagogy for an Active Form* (National Council of Teachers of English, 1996).

Page 21, Donald Murray. From *Shoptalk: Learning to Write with Writers* (Boynton/Cook, 1990).

Page 22, Cherylene Lee, "Safe." From *Charlie Chan Is Dead: An Anthology of Contemporary Asian-American Fiction*, edited by Jessica Hagedorn. Penguin Books, 1993.

Page 25, Elaine Mar, "I Answer to Elaine." Excerpt from pages 158-160 from *Paper Daughter: A Memoir by Elaine Mar*. Copyright © 1999 by Elaine Mar. Reprinted by permission of HarperCollins Publishers Inc.

Page 28, Natalie Goldberg. From *Writing Down the Bones: Freeing the Writer Within*, p. 70 (Boston: Shambhala Publications, 1986).

Page 30, Misha Kratochvil, "Translating for Parents Means Growing Up Fast." From "Urban Tactics" section of *The New York Times*, Sunday, August 26, 2001. Copyright © 2001, The New York Times. Reprinted by permission.

Page 34, Barbara Mujica, "No Comprendo." From *The New York Times* Op-Ed page, January 3, 1995. Copyright © 1995, The New York Times. Reprinted by permission

Page 39, Donald M. Murray. From *Learning by Teaching*, p. 99 (Montclair, NJ: Boynton/Cook, 1982).

Page 40, Yu-Lan (Mary) Ying, "Five New Words at a Time." From *The New York Times* Op-Ed page, Saturday, March 6, 1993. Copyright © 1993 (1995), The New York Times. Reprinted by permission.

Page 42, Elizabeth Cowan. From *Writing: Brief Edition*, p. 86-87 (Glenview, IL: Scott, Foresman and Company, 1983).

Page 44, Katarzyna McCarthy, "My Family Hero." Reprinted by permission of the author.

Page 50, Ian Frazier, "An Act of Courage." Excerpted from *On the Rez* by Ian Frazier, as it appeared in The Atlantic Monthly, December 1999, pp. 53-84. Published by Farrar, Straus and Giroux, 2000. Copyright © 2000 by Ian Frazier. Reprinted by permission of the author.

Page 55, Richard Marius. From Susan Shaughnessy, *Walking on Alligators: A Book of Meditations for Writers* (San Francisco: Harper, 1993).

Page 55, Achibald MacLeish. From Donald M. Murray, *Shoptalk: Learning to Write with Writers* (Boynton/Cook, 1990).

Page 56, Gloria Steinem, "Believing in the True Self." From *Revolution from Within* by Gloria Steinem. Published by Little, Brown and Company, 1992. Copyright © 1992 by Gloria Steinem. By permission of Little, Brown and Company, (Inc.).

Page 59, Russell Baker, "Becoming a Writer." From *Growing Up* by Russell Baker. Published by Congdon & Weed, Inc. and Contemporary Books, Chicago, 1982. Reprinted by permission of Don Congdon Associates, Inc. Copyright © 1982 by Russell Baker

Page 63, Lucille Clifton, "homage to my hips." First appeared in *Two-Headed Woman*, published by The University of Massachusetts Press. Reprinted by permission of Curtis Brown, Ltd. Copyright © 1980 by Lucille Clifton.

Page 65, Laurence Steinberg & Ann Levine, "The Search for Identity." Excerpted from pages 300-302 from *You and Your Adolescent* by Laurence Steinberg and Ann Levine. Copyright © 1990 by Laurence Steinberg and Ann Levine. Reprinted by permission of HarperCollins Publishers Inc. Copyright © 1990, 1997 by Laurence Steinberg and Anne Levine. Reprinted by permission of William Morris Agency, Inc. on behalf of the Author.

Page 69, Judith Rich Harris, "Smoking." Excerpt from pp. 281-283 of *The Nurture Assumption: Why Children Turn Out the Way They Do* by Judith Rich Harris. Published by The Free Press, August 1998. Simon & Schuster, Brockman. Reprinted with the permission of The Free Press, a Division of Simon & Schuster Adult Publishing Group. Copyright © 1998 by Judith Rich Harris.

Page 72, Donald Murray. From *Shoptalk: Learning to Write with Writers* (Boynton/Cook, 1990).

Page 73, John Updike. From Donald M. Murray, *Shoptalk: Learning to Write with Writers* (Boynton/Cook, 1990).

Page 76, Helen Nearing. Excerpt from *Loving and Living the Good Life* by Helen Nearing. Copyright 1992 by Helen Nearing. Used with permission of Chelsea Green Publishing, 205 Gases-Briggs Bldg, P.O. Box 428, White River Junction, VT 05001. www.chelseagreen.com.

Page 78, Edward Jones, "The First Day." Excerpt of approximately 200 words from *Lost In The City* by Edward P. Jones. Copyright © 1992 by Edward P. Jones. Reprinted by permission of HarperCollins Publishers, Inc. WILLIAM MORROW.

Page 81, Natalie Goldberg. From *Writing Down the Bones*, p. 68 (Boston: Shambhala Publications, 1986).

Page 83, Jamaica Kincaid, "A Walk to the Jetty." Extract from *Annie John* by Jamaica Kincaid. Copyright 1984, 1985 by Jamaica Kincaid. Published by Jonathan Cape. Used by permission of The Random House Group Limited.

Page 88, Judy Scales-Trent, "On Turning Fifty." From *Lifenotes: Personal Writings by Contemporary Black Women* by Patricia Bell-Scott, ed. W.W. Norton & Co, Inc. Copyright 1994 by Judy Scales-Trent. Reprinted by permission of the author.

Page 92, Carole Wade & Carol Tavris, "The Transitions of Life." From *Psychology* 6/E by Wade/Tavris. Copyright © Adapted by permission of Pearson Education, Inc., Upper Saddle River, NJ.

Page 99, lê thi diem thúy, "Pebbles." First published in *The Massachusetts Review*. Reprinted by permission of lê thi diem thúy and Aragi Inc.

Page 104, Kenneth Bruffee. From *A Short Course in Writing*, third edition (Little Brown, 1985).

Page 106, Fauziya Kassindja and Layli Miller Bashir, "Weddings." From *Do They Hear You When You Cry?* by Fauziya Kassindja and Layli Miller Bashir. Copyright © 1998 by Fauziya Kassindja. Used by permission of Dell Publishing, a division of Random House, Inc.

Page 113, Sandra Cisneros, "The First Job." From *The House on Mango Street* by Sandra Cisneros, pp. 51-52. Copyright © 1984 by Sandra Cisneros. Published by Vintage Books, a division of Random House, Inc., and in hardcover by Alfred A. Knopf in 1994. Reprinted by permission of Susan Bergholz Literary Services, New York. All rights reserved.

Page 111, Meredith Sue Willis. From *Deep Revision: A Guide for Teachers, Students, and Other Writers* (New York: Teachers & Writers Collaborative, 1993).

Page 116, Eric Schlosser, "Behind the Counter." Excerpt from *Fast Food Nation: The Dark Side of the All-American Meal* by Eric Schlosser. Excerpted and reprinted by permission of Houghton Mifflin Company and Penguin Books Ltd. All rights reserved. Excerpts from pp 67-83. Copyright © 2001 by Eric Schlosser.

Page 121, Marge Piercy, "To be of use." Copyright © 1973, 1982 by Marge Piercy and Middlemarsh, Inc. From *Circles On The Water*. Published by Alfred A. Knopf, 1982. First published in *Lunch*, October 1973.

Page 123, Ray Bradbury. From *Zen in the Art of Writing* (Consortium Books, 1994).

Page 124, Sarah Freeman, "The Model Medic." From *The Irish Echo*, December 18-24, 2002, p. 22, by Sarah Freeman. Reprinted by permission of the author.

Page 127, William Zinsser. From *On Writing Well*, Second Edition, p. 75 (New York: Harper & Row, 1980).

Page 128, Anne Lamott. From *Bird by Bird: Some Instructions on Writing and Life*, p. 145-146 (NY: Anchor Books/Doubleday, 1994).

Page 130, William Zinsser. From *On Writing Well*, Second Edition, p. 60 (New York: Harper & Row, 1980).

Page 132, Daniel Goleman, "Hope Emerges as Key to Success in Life." From *The New York Times*, December 24, 1991. Copyright © 1991, The New York Times. Reprinted by permission.

Page 137, Jane Brody, "It's OK to Cry." From *The New York Times*, February 22, 1984. Copyright © 1984, The New York Times. Reprinted by permission.

Page 141, Claire Braz-Valentine, "Going Through the House." From *Breaking Up is Hard to Do* ed. Amber Coverdale Sumrall. Published by the Crossing Press, Freedom, California 95091 (1994). 800-777-1048. Reprinted by permission of the author.

Page 143, Mary Oliver. From *Blue Pastures*, p. 89 (Orlando: A Harvest Original Harcourt Brace, 1995).

Page 144, Natalie Goldberg. From *Writing Down the Bones*, p. 87 (Boston: Shambhala Publications, 1986).

Page 146, Terry Tempest Williams, "Black Steer Canyon." Excerpted from *REFUGE: An Unnatural History of Family and Place* by Terry Tempest Williams. Published by Vintage Books. Copyright © 1991, 2002 by Terry Tempest Williams. Reprinted by permission of Brandt & Hochman Literary Agents, Inc. All rights reserved. Used with permission of Pantheon Books, a division of Random House.

Page 148, Larry Brown. From Susan Shaughnessy, *Walking on Alligators: A Book of Meditations for Writers* (San Francisco: Harper, 1993).

Page 152, John David Bartoe. From *Home Planet*, (p.86) conceived and edited by Kevin W. Kelley for the Association of Space Explorers. Published by Addison-Wesley Publishing Company, 1988. Copyright © 1988 by Kevin W. Kelley.

Page 154, Elizabeth Guillette, "Kids and Chemicals." Reprinted from *Yes! A Journal of Positive Futures*, PO Box 10918, Bainbridge Island, WA 98110. Subscriptions: 800/937-4451. Web: www.yesmagazine.org.

Page 157, Rick Weiss, "War on Disease." Excerpt from "Challenges for Humanity in 21st Century," in *National Geographic*, February 2000.

Page 157, Sophie Petit-Zerman, "No Laughing Matter." Reproduced with permission from *New Scientist Magazine* © RBI (2002) www.NewScientist.com. Reprinted with permission from *Utne magazine*, September-October 2000. To subscribe, call 800/736/UTNE or visit our Web site at www.utne.com.

Page 166, William Zinsser. From *On Writing Well*, Second Edition, p 71 (New York: Harper & Row, 1980).

Page 166, Toni Morrison. From Donald M. Murray, *Shoptalk: Learning to Write with Writers* (Boynton/Cook, 1990).

Page 167, Sharon Begley, "The Mercury's Rising." From *Newsweek*, December 4, 2000, p. 52, Newsweek, Inc. All rights reserved. Reprinted by permission.

Page 168, "Warming Seas Prompt Tuvalu Evacuation." Reprinted with permission from *Co-op America Quarterly*, No. 56.

Page 172, Bailey White, "Buzzard." From *Mama Makes up Her Mind and Other Dangers of Southern Living*. Copyright © 1993 by Bailey White. Reprinted by permission of Perseus Books Publishers, a member of Perseus Books, L.L.C.

Page 175, Rafe Martin, "The Brave Little Parrot." From *More Best-Loved Stories Told at the National Storytelling Festival*. Used with permission of Rafe Martin.

Page 180, Robert Cormier. From Donald M. Murray, *Shoptalk: Learning to Write with Writers* (Boynton/Cook, 1990).

Page 180, Alan Ziegler. Adapted from *The Writing Workshop Volume 1* (New York: Teachers & Writers Collaborative, 2000).

Page 181, Ernest Hemingway and George Plimpton. From Donald M. Murray, *Shoptalk: Learning to Write with Writers* (Boynton/Cook, 1990).

Page 182, "Chart." From *The State of World Population*, 1995. United Nations Population Fund. New York. 1995. Reprinted with permission.

Page 182, Elvia Alvarado, "Taming Macho Ways." Excerpt from *Don't Be Afraid Gringo: A Honduran Woman Speaks from the Heart*, the Story of Elvia Alvarado, pp. 50-56, translated by Medea Benjamin. Copyright © 1987. Reprinted with permission from Food First Books, 398 60th Street, Oakland, CA 94618. http://www.foodfirst.org.

Page 188, "Women and Work: Around the World, Women Earn Less." From *The Status of Women Around the World*. Published by Newsweek Education Program. Copyright © 2000 Newsweek, Inc. All rights reserved. Reprinted by permission.

Page 191, "Battling Chauvinism to Do a Man's Job." Reprinted with permission from InfoChange News & Features, www.infochangeindia.org.

Page 193, Patricia Kirkpatrick, "First Lullabye." Reprinted from *Minnesota Writes: Poetry*, Milkweed Editions/Nodin Press, Ed. Jim Moore and Cary Waterman, 1987. Permission from Patricia Kirkpatrick.

Page 198, Bill Duesing, "Kill Your Television." Excerpt from *Living on Earth* by Bill Duesing. Used with permission of Suzanne and Bill Duesing, Solar Education Farm, PO Box 135, Stevenson, CT 06491.

Page 202, Ian Ayres, "Lectures vs. Laptops." From Op-Ed, *The New York Times*, March 20, 2001. Copyright © 2001, The New York Times. Reprinted by permission.

Page 205, Natalie Goldberg. From *Writing Down the Bones*, p. 103 (Boston: Shambhala Publications, 1986).

Page 206, Jay Walljasper & Jon Spayde, "The 20th Century: What's Worth Saving?" Reprinted with permission from *Utne magazine*, May-June 1999, pp. 42-29. To subscribe, call 800/736/UTNE or visit our Web site at www.utne.com.

Page 210, Thich Nhat Hanh. "Entering the Twenty-first Century." From *Peace Is Every Step* by Thich Nhat Hahn, Copyright © 1991 by Thich Nhat Hanh. Used by permission of Bantam Books, a division of Random House, Inc.

Page 213, Kathryn Lance. From Donald M. Murray, *Shoptalk: Learning to Write with Writers* (Boynton/Cook, 1990).

Page 214, Barbara Kingsolver. From www.kingsolver.com/dialogue.

## ART CREDITS

Illustration credits: Cover, Unit Openers, and Reading Title Icons: © Iskra Johnson; page 42: Adam Hurwitz; page 155: © Elizabeth Guillette, courtesy of *Yes Magazine*

Photo credits: page 16: © Willie Maldonado/Getty Images; page 22: © Getty Images; page 92: © Kaz Chiba/Getty Images; page 102: © Barry Rosenthal/Getty Images; page 124: ©Corbis; page 145: © Richard Price/Getty Images; page 152: © Digital Vision; page 167: © Digital Vision; page 161: © James Muldowney/Getty Images; page 172: © Theo Allofs/Getty Images; page 172: all © Getty Images